FUNDAMENTALS OF JOURNALISM

FUNDAMENTALS OF JOURNALISM

Edited by

K.B. DATTA

AKANSHA PUBLISHING HOUSE
NEW DELHI - 110 002 (INDIA)

AKANSHA PUBLISHING HOUSE
R-37B, Vani Vihar, Uttam Nagar
New Delhi - 110 059
Email: ektabooks@yahoo.com

Showroom
4649/21B, Ansari Road,
Daryaganj, New Delhi-110 002
Phones: 23263193, 9811582579

Fundamentals of Journalism

First Edition 2007

ISBN 81-8370-074-8

PRINTED IN INDIA

Published by Akansha Publishing House, New Delhi and Printed at Aryan Enterprises Offset Press, Delhi.

Preface

Since journalism, like the subjects of all professions, is complex, this probing into the nature, functions, and general means of the work proceeds through many areas and levels. Thus, in addition to understanding journalism itself, the students must also strive to achieve an understanding of news, of interpretation, of evaluation, of advocacy. Regarding news, they need to examine the nature of news events and news reports. What do journalists attempt to achieve by these? By what potential means?

Fundamentals of Journalism is a comprehensive introduction to the field, covering how news is produced and delivered, how news organizations work, and how audiences react to and interact with the news media. For students preparing for a career in journalism, the text describes the range of job possibilities in the field and offers practical, basic instruction in the fundamental practices of journalism: reporting, writing, editing and presentation. Journalism helps students understand this exciting and important field and become more critical consumers of mass media. This book features up-to-date examples and discussions of current issues and controversies, allowing students to understand the principles of journalism in the context of issues that are familiar to them. It also focuses on the importance and challenge of maintaining accuracy and honesty in the media, encouraging students to think about ethics and values. It includes both practical and conceptual approaches to the study of journalism, giving students a full picture of the field.

—Editor

Contents

1

Introduction

WHAT IS JOURNALISM?

Journalism, be it working for newspapers, magazines, radio or television, is a 365-day, 24-hour operation going on just about everywhere in the world. Whether you are reading this in the middle of the day or night, journalists are hard at work preparing bulletins, writing features, producing documentaries, designing pages and editing tape ready for their next deadline. Stories can be totally unpredictable and crop up when you least expect them to. You don't stop being a journalist at 5pm. It is not just a job, it's a way of life and you are always on the look-out for a new idea.

When we turn on our television sets, tune in the radio or glance at today's front pages, we see names and faces which are almost as famous as the people in their stories. Indeed, journalism is a profession surrounded by mystique and glamour. But those most visible practitioners at the very top represent only a tiny fraction of journalists. There are literally hundreds of thousands of people working in the media in an enormous range of roles. This vast realm of journalism covers not only news but also documentaries, features, photojournalism, business and commerce and entertainment information.

The interesting thing is that while the media is now part of our everyday lives, we rarely see what goes on to produce articles and programmes or know who the key players are. This book is an attempt to describe the nature of the wide range of jobs in the media and to enable potential journalists to steer their way around the myriad of paths leading to a career.

Types of Media

While the scope of topics covered by journalists is unlimited, it is also the case that the range of media available to convey these stories is also expanding. This book will concentrate on the traditional media forms—newspapers, magazines, radio and television—with the addition of agencies, freelancing and public relations. But you will also read how the boundaries between all these media are blurring with the far-reaching developments in computer technology. More on that later.

Millions of newspapers are ready every day and they remain not only one of our primary sources of news and current affairs but are also a form of entertainment. Newspapers bring us detailed pen portraits of scenes and events taking place at home and abroad and, in their feature pages, give explanations and raise issues on topics of concern to the majority of readers. We also turn to newspapers for everyday information, from holiday sunspots to horoscopes, recipes to racing.

While newspapers have broad appeal, magazines come in many guises with mass readership or a clearly defined small market. Whoever you are or whatever you do, there is probably a periodical that will appeal to you as a reader. There are leisure and entertainment-oriented magazines, cinema and music publications and a periodical catering for just about every conceivable hobby. This book will also examine a massive sector of the magazine market, business and professional periodicals which serve the interests of those working in industry and commerce.

No household is without at least one radio because it can be listened to while you do other things. One of the strengths of radio as a journalistic medium is its portability which means radio is often the first source of information for people listening in their cars, on their personal stereos or just around the house. The popularity of radio is demonstrated by the rise of new stations catering not just for mass audiences but for specialist interests also.

With its ability to harness words, sound and pictures, television has immense impact for journalism. By appealing to many of our senses, major issues are beamed straight into our living rooms and seem more real and immediate than reading about them or listening to them.

As you will read, there are thousands of journalists working in each of these media. But there is also a growing number of journalists who choose to work one step removed from the mainstream organizations and instead provide a service to the media. These are people who work in news agencies and who operate independently as freelances who supply stories for publication and broadcast. In addition, there are those who not only want to report the news, they want to make the news. These people work in public relations, bringing to the media's attention issues and events for coverage.

But before any hopeful candidate starts enrolling for courses or applying for jobs in any of these media, they have to equip themselves with skills fundamental to all journalists whatever medium they are working in. That includes good judgment as to what issues or events make good stories, how to gather the facts and details essential to the topic being covered and how to structure stories in a way that makes them interesting, factual and unbiased. All these issues will be dealt with in this introduction along with a glimpse at some of the other characteristics and skills you can develop to help you on your career path.

It is advisable, therefore, to read this chapter before embarking on other sections as it will help you to understand the mechanics of specific media. In this chapter and throughout the rest of the book, you will find useful and unique advice from journalists working at the very top of their respective media, plus case studies to illustrate how stories are put together. First, let us examine that most fundamental of journalistic questions...

What Makes a Good Story?

Dictionary definition of news: report of recent happenings, tidings; interesting facts not previously known.

Ask any journalist how they would define 'news' and most would find it a very hard question to answer. The term 'newsworthiness' is used by journalists to describe any event or issue meriting coverage whether it be as a front-page headline on a daily newspaper or a half-hour radio documentary. Skilled journalists are often too intimately involved with their craft to be able to stand back dispassionately and analyse what they do. It is often a personal process and deciding what to cover relies on gut, human reaction. Journalists, academics, readers, viewers and listeners invariably clash over the invisible criteria used to determine why some events become stories while others go unreported. Journalists maintain they are responding to what the public wants, while theorists argue that news is managed and constructed to suit the needs of people in powerful positions, from politicians to advertisers. Regardless, anyone working in a newsroom or hoping to make a career out of journalism must have a clear understanding of newsworthiness even if, as is often the case with the most senior, experienced news people, they cannot articulate what news is.

Lord Reith, first General Manager and later Director General of the BBC, developed the principle that it was the duty of the new medium of broadcasting 'to inform, to educate and to entertain'. This is still the main objective of journalists today although to what degree they concentrate on one or more of these is debatable. No matter whether they are cookery writers for a women's magazine, war correspondents for a national news agency or bulletin editors on a local radio station, journalists are aiming to grab the readers' attention, stimulate and inform them. Most members of society have a natural interest and a healthy curiosity in those changes that affect their personal lives. At a national level, we will be affected by a new rate of income tax, a spell of severe weather or a strike by train drivers. There are other factors which people look to the media for as well as information-entertainment and leisure. So journalism may not only touch our physical lives but may also inspire, amuse or outrage us. It is a highly responsible and demanding task.

Perhaps the best place to start unravelling the definition of news stories is to consider the words themselves. *New(s),* those first three letters mean so much as it is often the closeness, or newness, of the event to the time of publication or broadcast that determines whether it will be mediated. Then there is *story*. All journalists are acting as story tellers, relating to the rest of us what has taken place and, possibly, why. It is that very selection, packaging and delivery that transforms something from being a happening to becoming a story.

Most journalists maintain there is no mystique in selecting a story topic from the countless mundane events that make up our everyday lives. A news producer for television network Sky News says:

> You don't think about it too deeply or intellectually, you just know as it's a very personal thing. You first decide an event's interest value. It's a very basic measure but if something makes me think 'oh really'

or 'blimey, did you see that' or 'how dare he' or 'isn't that awful', it is news. It's that kind of human emotion that you use and anybody you'll meet in a cafe or pub will tell you what is interesting, so it is not something special to the job of being a journalist.

Journalists might cover something very good-human achievement, medical breakthroughs, the latest box-office hit-or something very bad like murders, tragic accidents or factory closures. There are important reasons for this if you try to disentangle the tight web of factors that determine what is reported. These are some of the questions a journalist may ask of a story:

1. *Does it involve human beings?* You may have heard of the term human interest angle which is simply the way a journalist will introduce the event to their audience to evoke a response. If a new factory is opening, the story will lead on how many job opportunities are created rather than how efficient the machinery is, simply because the human implications are ones that we can sympathize or empathize with. Any story which is likely to evoke emotion, whether it is happiness or sadness, anger or delight, on the part of the reader is more likely to be included. Events involving injury or death are newsworthy because of the value we place on the sanctity of human life. That goes for vulnerable members of society, too, which is why we are more likely to see a story reported about a child or an elderly person than someone who is middle-aged.
2. *What is the scale of the event?* The more people are involved or implicated in an occurrence, the more chance it will attract an audience. That is why anything to do with the Government is reported because laws affect all of us. Disasters with major human costs will also hit the headlines because of

the numbers involved. Scale might also apply to money, particularly if someone has won-or stolen-a massive amount.

3. *Is it unexpected?* It goes without saying that if an event happens out-of-the-blue it is more likely to take us by surprise and get a reaction than if we had been expecting it. Unfortunately, a lot of what we might term bad news happens unpredictably, which is why so much of it is in the headlines. A proportion of major news, however, is predicted and can be prepared ahead with reporters knowing precisely where they will be going and what is expected of them, for instance a major trial, a council meeting or a news conference held by a big multinational organization.
4. *Is it relevant to the audience?* For a story to be newsworthy, it needs to mean something to its audience which can vary depending upon the medium. Relevance in journalism can rely on factors such as geography, gender, occupation, age and interests. The sheer range of journalistic material available should give you some idea of the diversity of the market. A local weekly newspaper in Scunthorpe is unlikely to report upon a supermarket robbery in Birmingham, unless, that is, the manager is a local person which would make the story of human interest to its readers. A business-to-business periodical aimed at engineers is unlikely to run as its front-page lead story a new medical breakthrough. On a very basic level, a national tabloid newspaper will opt for a more sensational story than a broadsheet simply because its proprietor and journalists know that that is what will attract its particular readership.

You will read in this book how every medium has a different agenda for different reasons. Television is largely led by pictures and therefore stations may raise the status of a story if there is some sensational footage to go with it. Radio, by virtue of its reliance on sound, is more flexible. Editors find it easier to break into programmes with news flashes and a lead story does not necessarily have to be anything more than a single voice telling listeners what has happened. Like television though less so, newspapers and magazines are visual so pictures can determine a story's placing. The time involved in the printing process, although short when compared with methods used only a few years ago, means that newspapers and periodicals will aim to tell the story behind the news or issue rather than always be first to break it, with the exception of a special exclusive story or investigation.

Similarly, if you are working for an international news agency, supplying the first reports to all media on a coup in a remote part of the globe, you view the world completely differently to the way you view it from, say, a local radio station for which a comparatively minor event occurring on their doorstep is likely to take priority. News worthiness and the work of a journalist therefore depends on what paper, magazine, programme or station he or she works for as much as the potential story itself. Journalists cannot assess the newsworthiness of a story in a vacuum; they must always consider who they are telling it to and how interested that audience will be. To illustrate this, here is an account by one journalist on how he determines what is covered. His account gives some insight as to how personal a decision it is.

Head of News, national network radio news agency

'The first rule of journalism is to know your audience otherwise you won't be in tune with them. Local radio stations and local newspaper offices tend to be closer to their audiences. Most journalists have very fond memories of their readers walking through the door of their office and telling them face-to-face what they thought of a story. At local level, you are very close to your audience but by the time you get to national level it is easy to forget exactly for whom you are writing. On the other hand, readers probably look at national papers with different expectations than those they have of their local papers.

'I would suggest that to be a good journalist, you have to have an innately inquisitive nature, a sense of wanting to know what's going on around you and caring about it. A lot of people have this sense but then you need to be able to develop this skill and learn how to adapt it. News is creating interesting stories about things going on in our lives and presenting those stories so that large numbers of people will be interested. You can have good news which is interesting. But the fact is that, by nature, human beings tend to see baddies as the anti-heroes and therefore as interesting people. If news was about the usual you'd be bored rigid. After years of experience it becomes second nature to a journalist to know what makes news, and I would recommend journalists not to analyse what they do because you are in danger of fudging what you are trying to do. I hate the word but you do need to decide on your 'priorities', and this is an ability people improve as they come into a national newsroom like this. You start off by thinking, would this story interest someone in Manchester as well as in Inverness? With experience, that thought process happens in about one-and-a-half seconds.'

Understanding what makes news is to some extent innate in all of us. As social beings we unknowingly categorize life into the usual and unusual and use our emotions to help us make sense of the world to ourselves and other people. But what makes people journalists is something extra. They need to know how to mediate that information to other people. This is something that involves a mixture of skills, training and experience, some of which will be described in this book.

The pleasures of working in journalism are not just about the people you interview or the stories you cover in the course of your day. Working in a busy editorial department is one of the most exciting and satisfying experiences you can have; for the interaction with colleagues as you work in an intense environment as much as the spontaneity of the issues you encounter.

The Working Environment

The working environment for a journalist is barely recognizable when compared with newspaper, magazine and broadcast offices as recently as 10 or 20 years ago. Films depicting shabby rooms, with raincoat-clad hacks hunched over old typewriters surrounded by overflowing wastebins is not too distanced from the reality of media establishments a decade or so ago. Now, in most cases the clattering of typewriters has been replaced by the much quieter clicking of computer keyboards, with barely a sheet of paper to be seen. But while the surroundings are much more modern (and many lament the loss of the atmospheric old newsrooms) the fundamentals of the job have changed very little over the decades. From the end of the First World War until the technological revolution of the 1970s and '80s, there was remarkable uniformity and continuity in journalism. A journalist beginning their career even as late as the early 1980s was schooled by older professionals who may have begun their working lives in the 1920s and '30s. And the skills they taught these junior reporters-such as note-taking and cultivating loyal contacts-are as relevant and fundamental to the work of journalists today as they ever were. It is higher up the production ladder where changes in working routines are most evident and this is mainly the result of new technology. In newspapers, whole departments have been wiped out as computers transform print production methods. In broadcasting, the razor-blade and chalk style of editing has been replaced by sophisticated digital machines.

The Jobs of a Journalist

Many would-be journalists are attracted to the media because they enjoy writing. Sadly the literary-minded are often disappointed when they discover they have around five minutes to compose a hefty story and are restricted to the simplest English. That is because unless you have the privilege of being a columnist or working in some other area of journalism that permits lengthy prose, most of the reporter's time is spent on the telephone or out in the field. But for the majority who choose to make a career out of journalism, that is the most exciting part. It sounds a cliché but being there when history is unfolding is a remarkable experience. The job of a journalist is a three-phase thing and not simply down to sitting at a keyboard all day and writing as so many mistakenly believe. It requires:

1. *Researching:* news is about knowing what information is required for the story and where to lay your hands on those facts quickly. You have to be informed about current affairs and know who are the key players in a variety of areas so that you can judge instantly the swiftest and most profitable research route.

2. *Judgment:* unless you can judge how to treat the material, you may be a good researcher or writer, but not a good journalist.

   Judgment involves knowing how important the story is to readers. What sort of information should be included? How should the story be structured-as a two-paragraph filler or a half-page feature, a headline or an 'and finally...'? Should it be accompanied by pictures or audio? Good judgment means being able, perhaps with only the first, limited information about a story, to visualize it in the context of a finished page or bulletin.

3. *Presentation:* following on from the last point, once you have the information you have to know how best to mediate it to your audience, a skill which will be determined by who you are working for as much as by your own command of the English language.

The practical application of these stages in every medium is the development of contacts, interviewing skills, application of the law and the ability to write.

Sources of News

Where information comes from is the aspect that dominates most journalists' working lives. If a journalist cannot get a story or the necessary information in to back it up, they cannot mediate the facts to the public. A contacts book is the journalist's most guarded and private possession because it contains the names, addresses and telephone numbers of everyone who can provide details or comment upon any issue or event they cover. Stories are gathered from information gleaned by journalists from members of the public, commercial companies, agencies such as local authorities, emergency services, charities, schools, hospitals, Government departments, industry, commerce, pressure groups, professional organizations, political parties, the list is endless. Contacts books come in various guises and rapidly grow in size as the journalist builds their career and encounters more helpful people. Some choose a small ring-bound folder so that they can insert extra pages as they make more contacts. Many journalists carry portable computers and will store their contacts' names and numbers on their VDU.

A great deal of time is spent by journalists finding stories by contacting organizations and individuals directly. The relationship between journalists and their contacts is double-edged: the journalist needs the story and the contact is likely to want publicity.

Interviewing Skills

All journalists have to know how to conduct successful interviews in person or on the telephone. Personal interviews conducted either face-to-face or over the telephone are the main way in which journalists get their information. Even when the story is obtained another way, such as from a letter, the journalist must still speak to individuals involved to check the facts and 'flesh out' details to make interesting copy. The art of interviewing is an essential skill for all journalists and it can be learned even by the shy or tongue-tied. Often, you have no choice but to interview someone at very short notice. With experience, this becomes second nature but for the beginner it is better to prepare for the interview in advance.

In an interview it is important for the journalist to direct the conversation so they gather the details they require quickly and fully and are not driven off the point by a forceful interviewee who may be trying to duck the issue. This is achieved through preparation. Likewise, by being prepared, you will appear more confident which may put a nervous interviewee at ease. The first thing a journalist must do after making the appointment is to find out as many background details about the subject as they can. Most media organizations keep a back catalogue of newspaper cuttings which are filed under subject titles for this purpose. The next step is to jot down a few essential questions to use as reference so you do not miss anything vital to the story. These questions are meant to be a guide as the path of the interview might change or the interviewee may answer them before they are asked. The main questions that need to be answered in all stories are *who, what, when, where, why* and *how?* These have to be tailored to suit the story. For example, who is raising the petition? Where exactly will the supermarket be built? When are you planning to release your next album? What exactly did you see? How did the child come to be playing in that road? Why didn't doctors spot this earlier? Most questions should be open-ended, which means they cannot be answered with a straight yes or no. The best stories contain sections where the interviewee is allowed to describe the situation in their own words.

When it comes to carrying out the interview itself, journalists must always be sure they are speaking to the right person as there might be two John Smiths living in the same road. They must also identify themselves clearly so the interviewee knows they are talking to a journalist and that their words will be reported. As long as your contact is clear they are talking to a journalist for publication or broadcast, whatever they say can be used and attributed to them. If however, they tell the journalist that what they are about to say is 'off the record', they mean that they do not want it written down or broadcast. For example, the interviewee might have some background information about a subject which, if divulged publicly, might jeopardize their job. The basis of a good interview is a friendly, positive manner on the part of the journalist. The golden rule is to remember you may have to speak to them again next week. The journalist must always be polite and calm and tailor their approach according to the circumstances. It is best to keep as much eye contact with the interviewee as possible. This is considered polite practice with the added factor that you might also catch facial expressions that would lead you to believe the interviewee is not telling you the whole truth. This is much easier for broadcast journalists who will use a microphone or camera to record the information. Print journalists are usually trained in Teeline shorthand which enables them to jot down details quickly, or they use a mini-cassette recorder. All journalists will inevitably encounter problem interviews. A typical case is where a hassled official replies 'I don't know' or 'no comment' to a probing question. Here, the reporter has to employ assertiveness skills to try to draw out the information. This may involve politely repeating a question or re-expressing it in a way that might elicit a response. At the end of the interview, the journalist might wish to go over the facts of the story with the interviewee again to check they have understood them correctly. They should also ensure they have several paragraphs or extracts of directly quoted speech before they begin to write their story. As a reminder:

1. make an appointment;
2. prepare by researching interviewee/subject;
3. write out a list of questions;
4. identify yourself and ensure you are interviewing the right person;
5. be friendly, positive and polite;
6. check facts.

Ability to Write

There is an art to writing copy that will attract an audience and keep them interested while remaining unbiased. Journalism involves one of the most disciplined forms of writing and is a skill that is mastered by reading or listening to others' work as often as possible and through dedicated practice. While they are known as stories, articles are not written in the same way as the stories you might read in a book. Whereas you might have to wait with baited breath until the very last page of a novel for the plot's climax, the most important information in an article should be contained in the first few paragraphs. That is why journalism is frequently described as a conversational form of writing: if you were verbally describing to a friend an incident you had seen on the way to the supermarket, you would be likely to mention the most attention-grabbing aspect first. It works exactly the same way with journalism because your aim is to grab the audience's attention. Before they start writing, journalists must consider three golden rules which are:

- accuracy,
- conciseness,
- clarity.

Accuracy is essential. If a journalist reports inaccurate information, they and their newspaper or station may be sued for libel or prosecuted under Contempt of Court laws. Even if a name is misspelled, it ruins the journalist's integrity with their contact as it appears that they are careless.

News, in particular, should always be written concisely because pressure of space and airtime means journalists must convey the maximum amount of information in the fewest words. This is also better for the audience as they are able to glean the information easily and quickly without having to plough through irrelevant detail. Paragraphs in journalistic writing are only a couple of sentences long and the language within them is simple and clear so that concepts will be mediated in as few words with as little punctuation as possible. For example, instead of writing 'Freda Smith, who works as the Director of Education in the city Bigtown, replied by commenting...' a journalist would put 'Bigtown Education Director Freda Smith said...'.

If language must be clear and concise in journalistic writing, it follows that the content of the story itself must be easily understood. The reader should not be in any doubt about the facts of the story; there should be no ambiguities.

The story should consist of relevant facts, the answers to the questions *who, what, where, when, why* and *how,* interspersed with directly quoted material, which is marked off as in quotation marks. These are the interviewees' owns words or recorded speech for broadcast. Quotes, as they are called, add credibility and authenticity to the piece as well as providing relief and interest. The most important paragraph in a story is the introduction because this must convey the main point of the piece, the angle. This is the narrative standpoint taken by the journalist on the strength of the news values upon which the story is based. Writers use their judgment to consider what aspect of the event or issue will be of most interest to their audience. Having written the introduction, the journalist unfolds the rest of the story, leaving the least important information until the last couple of paragraphs. This is a common practice in newspaper journalism where a ruthless sub-editor, who has the task of fitting the story into a page lay out, may simply cut off the last few sentences if short of space and time.

News journalists are required to endeavour to report objectively, which means they must not express an opinion or any bias in favour of any of the conflicting sides of a story. Their role is to convey facts and represent all sides in an argument fairly, and, ultimately, to allow the reader or listener to make an informed judgment on the basis of the facts presented. This is not an easy aim to achieve when you consider the range of stories a journalist might cover. Some issues are so emotive it is almost impossible not to convey your own anger or disbelief. Other types of journalists, such as those who write features or columns, are allowed to express their opinions because it is clear that their pieces are separate from the objective, factual news content of the day. It is important to stress that while newspapers and magazines have scope for expressing opinions, there are strict laws which prevent radio and television from bias in their news output. In writing their piece, the journalist will always be conscious of the laws affecting their work. As a reminder:

1. Be accurate, concise and clear;
2. Keep sentences and paragraphs short;
3. The introduction is the most important paragraph;
4. Stay objective.

So now that you have an insight into the fundamental questions asked by prospective journalists and the skills and attributes common to all those working in the profession regardless of the medium, we can start to examine newspapers, magazines, radio, television and other forms of journalism in more detail.

The media world resembles Spaghetti Junction. It is a big network with many crossovers and the roads all seem to lead somewhere new. To the aspiring journalist seeing the junction from overhead, it's a daunting prospect wondering which route to take into the profession. But where the roads all meet at the core of the system, common factors exist which are excellent foundations for building your career. Then you can enjoy a journey with many surprises and diversions in store.

DEFINITIONS OF JOURNALISM

In excitement and importance, few human enterprises surpass the making of a discovery. The excitement increases when we recognize that what we have found is, like a long-buried dinosaur bone, the old become new. The excitement is even greater when we realize that our discovery reopens and helps explain much of the world around us.

The aim of this book, therefore, is quite simple. It involves, first of all, blowing the dust off journalism and setting forth what exactly we now can find it to be. It will come as no surprise when we discover that it is a peculiarly human activity and one that touches and affects almost every other facet of personal and civic endeavor. Thus our next objective—a more difficult and lengthy one—will be to describe how journalism interacts with, affects, and is affected by the world around us. We should not be surprised if, along the way, and as many who engage in an expedition of discovery are wont to do, we come to new realizations as to how journalism and the world might better achieve a beneficent coexistence.

Who will be the fellow members of our expedition? They include, of course, all those who, when writing their biographies, can say, "I am a journalist." (We may be surprised at the large number who deserve that appellation, and perhaps, also, at some of those who do not.) Also included are those who are being educated to be journalists and those who are doing the educating. In addition, a much more numerous group includes all those who realize they are affected by journalism, who are not certain whether or why the effects are what they should be, who would like to do something (although they are not quite certain what) to make the world affected by journalism a better place than it is. To all such would-be discoverers: "Welcome aboard."

A few other questions should be addressed before we begin. How should we organize and then progress on our journey of discovery? What will we need to take along with us? If we have disagreements, what is the best way to resolve them? Where, most important of all, do we begin?

The Power of Words

We will begin, progress, and organize our expedition with the consideration of words and their meanings. If we have disagreements—and we may have many—they will probably focus on the meanings of words. In any serious venture, words are like numbers: they have to be employed with great care. The approximate word, like the approximate number, is often insufficient to get one very far. Granted, not every endeavor needs to be met with equal precision: for the archeologist, the dimension of the egg she had for breakfast need not be as precise as the breadth of the cranial bone she has just unearthed. The same is true for us when we discuss the nature and functions of journalism.

The greatest care, time, and attention should be devoted to whatever is most important. Anyone can easily stimulate an argument by claiming to know which are the truly significant words in the field of journalism. A news reporter might state that "objectivity" is a crucial term that any journalist must thoroughly understand. An editor might say the same about "verification." A broadcaster might add "actuality" to the list. For certain discussions in certain contexts, each one would be right.

Certain words are right for the context of this book. The words that will be given special attention possess no automatic claim for preference; they happen to be those most important for the discussion that we hope will clarify and enhance our journey of discovery. But why give these basic terms prolonged attention? One reason was set forth quite well by John Henry Newman. In the tenth of his *Fifteen Sermons Preached Before the University of Oxford*, he said:

> Half the controversies in the world are verbal ones; and could they be brought to a plain issue, they would be brought to a prompt termination. Parties engaged in them would then perceive, either that in substance they agreed together, or that their difference was one of first principles. This is the great object to be aimed at in the present age, though confessedly a very arduous one. We need not dispute, we need not prove—we need but define. . . . When men understand

> each other's meaning, they see, for the most part, that controversy is either superfluous or hopeless.

Much that we will discuss in these pages is likely to be subject to dispute. But dispute not preceded by mutual understanding is fruitless. It is like two combatants standing back to back and shooting arrows in opposite directions. Furthermore, mutual understanding requires that, to begin with, all parties attach the same meanings to the words that they employ. Even if the reader does not agree with the nature of the reality that the writer ascribes to this or that term, there is, nevertheless, some hope for a fruitful discussion if the reader knows what the writer means when he or she uses that term. This verbal understanding is not by itself our crowning achievement, yet it is an excellent start. Understanding will not always lead to agreement, but without understanding, agreement is only accidentally possible and thus almost never successful.

To illustrate this point, let us look, for a moment, at one of the classics in the literature of journalism, Walter Lippmann *Public Opinion*. No one who wishes to discuss the subject of public opinion dares ignore the work. Most scholars would agree with Curtis MacDougall assessment (1952, 39) that Lippmann was the "one outstanding journalist who has made a sizable contribution to the understanding of public opinion." Yet, on some points, it is exceedingly difficult to disagree with Lippmann, not because he is so convincingly correct but, rather, because one finds it enormously difficult to figure out what he means.

It would not be correct to say that Lippmann neglects to define. He does, in fact, define most of his key terms. But some of his definitions are adequate to achieve the mutual understanding that is the goal of communication and others fall short, primarily because they lack adequate discrimination, elaboration, and exemplification.

Defnitions given by Lippmann

For instance, in his introduction, Lippmann ventures definitions of three key terms in his analysis. Part of the context in which he does this and the definitions themselves are as follows:

> The world that we have to deal with politically is out of reach, out of sight, out of mind. It has to be explored, reported, and imagined. . . . [man] is learning to see with his mind vast portions of the world that he could never see, touch, smell, hear, or remember. Gradually he makes for himself a trustworthy picture inside his head of the world beyond his reach.

Those features of the world outside which have to do with the behavior of other human beings, in so far as that behavior crosses ours, is dependent upon us, or is interesting to us, we call roughly public affairs. The pictures inside the heads of these human beings, the pictures of themselves, of others, of their needs, purposes, and relationships, are their public opinions. Those pictures which are acted upon by groups of people, or by individuals acting in the name of groups, are Public Opinion with capital letters. (Lippmann 1946, 20)

Those last three sentences carry the burden of explaining to us, his readers, what Lippmann means by three terms of major significance in his book: public affairs, public opinion, and *Public Opinion.* True, he says many more things about each of them, but making a statement about public opinion, just to take one example, is often not an effective device to let us know what the term "public opinion" means. For instance, late in the same book he observes, "In real life no one acts on the theory that he can have a public opinion on every public question, though this fact is often concealed where a person thinks there is no public question because he has no public opinion" (300). This is an important insight, but it does not help explain the meaning of the term.

Even more problematic are the situations in which a later use of the term seems to add confusion to a previous definition. Only a few pages after giving the definition quoted above, for example, Lippmann discusses "the distance which often separates your public opinion from the event with which it deals". This latter statement suggests that public opinions are our mental pictures of events, but Lippmann's definition says they are pictures people have "of themselves, of others, of their needs, purposes, and relationships." We ourselves, others, their needs, purposes, or relationships are normally not thought of as events.

What is "Public Opinion"

Now if "public opinion" were like, for example, "telescope," the latter being a term that has few meanings and even those not subject to much dispute, we would have no major problem. But such is not the case. Almost every writer who has ever used the term "public opinion"—and there have been many of them—uses it, as Francis G. Wilson pointed out in his article "Concepts of Public Opinion" (1933, 371-91), in a different sense.

We might consider merely the first half of this compound term. What kind of an opinion is one which, as Lippmann is using the term, could be called a *public* opinion? Is it an opinion of a public, that is, of a mob, a group, a collectivity of some sort? Or is it an opinion that is *made* public, rather than, for instance, one that is kept to one's self, one that is kept secret? Or is it an opinion about something that is public, rather than about something personal or private? Lippmann doesn't really let us know. His sequence of sentences quoted earlier would lead one to believe that public opinions have something to do with public affairs, yet the latter are concerned with "the world outside" whereas public opinions, he says, can be pictures which human beings have "of themselves." Whether these opinions are held by "human beings" individually or collectively is left unsettled. And since each member of a group can act on his or her own individual opinion without otherwise reporting those opinions to others, we are not sure that even "Public Opinion with capital letters" has to be made public.

It may seem unfair to badger an author about the words he uses, especially one who is no longer able to reply. Yet if we cannot understand what an author is saying in his most major points, whatever wisdom the author had in mind is greatly diminished. When the writer is as great as Lippmann, a judgment we make about him, by the way, on the basis of those propositions (such as his perceptive views on stereotypes) that we can understand, the loss is most serious.

Definitions of Wilbur Schramm

This deficiency in definition, although it is not universal, also is not rare. We might consider, for instance, Wilbur Schramm, another giant among communications scholars. Like Lippmann, he strives to provide, in his *Responsibility in Mass Communication* (1957), a comprehensive view of journalism. But also like Lippmann, Schramm sometimes leaves us uncertain about what he means.

For instance, although he devotes considerable space to explaining the nature and functions of mass communication, the edges of the term are not precisely delineated. He mentions three types of communications: interpersonal, mass, and what he calls "individual," that is, the type done by "the ministers, teachers, writers, artists, and political orators of the society".

What he has to say about the first is not difficult to understand: "In interpersonal communication—in talking with our friends, for example—we can watch the face of the person we are talking to, or listen for his quick answers, and thus tell in a fraction of a second whether our message is being received, whether it is being understood, whether it is being accepted". Mass communications, he says, do not permit these. So far, so good.

Difficulties arise, however, when he attempts to explain the similarities and differences between mass and individual communications. The two, he says, have essentially the same public functions; they differ in that "Whereas the individual's decoding, interpretation, and encoding are carried on in the central nervous system, the central nervous system of mass communication is an organization of individual communicators who themselves make up a highly intricate communication network". In other words, in individual communications, all the work is done by the individual; in mass communications, the work is done by an organization of individuals.

One challenge to our understanding arises from his switching back and forth between discussions of communic*ations* and communic*ators*. All of those he names as individual communicators can and often do make use of what he identifies as mass communications to convey their messages. Ministers often use the religious press, radio, television, books, and magazines; teachers often use public television, public radio, magazines, books, or film.

Schramm casts a further shadow over our understanding by using such terms as "organization of individual communicators" and "highly intricate communication network." How many and how organized must the individual communicators be? How intricate the network?

The Boundaries Defined by Schramm

Is the politician who shouts out her message to a group of people from a platform at the Fourth of July picnic a mass communicator? Schramm would probably not think so, for, although the number of persons who receive her message greatly exceeds the number who respond in like manner, she does not "make up a highly intricate communication network." If we move the politician into a hall and have her use a public address system to reach her listeners, would Schramm now say she is a mass communicator? Probably not, for, although she now uses a machine (which he says is an essential aspect of mass communications), one politician plus one public address system hardly seems to be a "highly intricate communication network." If we add a speech writer, an elocution coach, and a sound technician, we become even less sure how Schramm would classify her activity. And what happens when the politician owns her own small radio station and delivers her political message over the airwaves? Now the answers become increasingly more uncertain. A "mom and pop" radio station is more complicated than a public address system, but even a 500-watt station with engineer, announcer, and ad salesman may seem somewhat less than a "highly intricate communication network." Or do we think so only when we contrast it with NBC or CBS?

Whatever we think, Schramm falls a little short of providing us with sufficient guidelines to resolve our doubts. And the doubts multiply if our politician surfaces as owner, editor, and operator of a small country weekly (more than 8,000 weeklies were being published at the time Schramm was writing his book), a magazine, or a newsletter. What are we to do, for instance, with the communicator who chooses to use the name "my" and who "started with a mimeograph, a list of friends, and a gloriously impractical Pay-What-It's-Worth Subscription Plan" and produced for thousands of readers his *Observations from the Treadmill* (my 1973, 4) or with I. F. Stone and his four-page newsletter, "without tiers of editors above him and an institutional consensus to smother him" (Hentoff 1973, viii)? Private presses, many of them employing only one or two persons, have existed from the days of Gutenberg to the present. Their owners have produced and often also have circulated the products of their work. The publications that issued forth from these small shops have had enormous influence, especially during the colonial period of American history. We cannot say that Schramm is either right or wrong for including or excluding these publications or shopping guides or underground radio stations from the category of mass communications, since his definitions are not sufficiently precise to enable us to determine what he would do. We cannot argue unless, first of all, we understand.

Philosophical Problems of Journalism

What are the reasons for this apparent lapse in journalism scholarship? Why do eminent journalists and journalism scholars leave inquisitive readers and anxious journalism students perplexed about the meanings of the most important words the writers are using? Perhaps no one can give a final answer to such a question, but Dennis J. Chase suggests some interesting reasons for the situation:

> The problems of journalism are, at base, philosophical problems. They involve questions of definition and function: What is news? What is truth? How can one know truth? What is the relationship between news and truth? These are the recurring and unstated issues behind most journalism disputes. Yet when it comes to this matter of philosophy, publishers, editors, broadcasters and journalism educators are virtually unanimous in their conviction that any theories about journalism should take second place to the hard reality of practice.

In other words, Chase first claims that definitions are a process favored by the philosophically inclined, and most journalists, he says, lack such an inclination. The idea tantalizes. Yet Lippmann, for example, certainly cannot be identified as a person who is disinterested in philosophy. One of his books is titled *The Public Philosophy*; one of his consultants was the philosopher Mortimer Adler; and his book includes a multitude of citations from Plato, Aristotle, Yves Simon, John Courtney Murray, John Stuart Mill, Etienne Gilson, Thomas Hobbes, John Locke, and numerous other philosophers.

Chase also writes that, since it is "impossible to escape philosophy because of the nature of things," the underlying problem is the philosophies that have "maintained a stranglehold on . . . journalists": pragmatism and subjectivism. Thus the problem may not lodge in a lack of interest in philosophy but, rather, in the type of philosophy in which writers are interested. Since pragmatism, however, is not intrinsically anti-definition, it would seem that, if Chase is correct, the reluctance to define is due to subjectivism. In fact, the principal bits of evidence provided by Chase for the charge of subjectivism are instances of the failure of journalists and journalism scholars to provide definitions or the inadequacy of the few definitions that are provided. This would be characteristic of subjectivists, many of whom adhere to the relativist view that the truth is nothing but each person's settled opinion. If, as they believe, there are no objective criteria of truth, they would deny the validity—or even the possibility-of defining anything that is outside of the individual person. But if this is a cause of the problem, it is probably only one of several causes.

Other Reasons for Denial of Definitions

Long before Chase wrote his essay, strong movements among journalism scholars attempted to assign to the field the characteristics of science. As Herbert Altschull points out (1984, 126), a widespread view in the 1930s held that "Man and his institutions could be understood only through the use of the scientific method, through dispassionate observation and the assembly of verifiable data." Scientific advances in the following decades gave further impetus to the movement. Soon, such terms as "precision journalism," "information science," and "communication science" became common, among both journalists and journalism researchers.

But as Mortimer Adler says (1958, Vol. 1, ch. 9, 69), science and philosophy live quite different lives and differ markedly in "the way in which [their] representatives agree, disagree, and deal with their differences." Scientists settle their differences by experiments or observation; philosophers by controversy and rational debate. The latter, he says, requires dialectical effort, and at the heart of this effort is definition. But the greater the journalistic concern with science, the greater the assumption that definition has already taken place.

If it were true that all the key terms have already been adequately defined, a writer might be excused for not redoing what has already been done. Not every writer need be his or her own lexicographer.

But this explanation is overly simple, and Mortimer Adler and Charles Van Doren (1972) remind us of some of the attending complexities. First, the obvious difficulty: most of the words in a dictionary have many meanings, and it is not always easy for the reader to know which one the writer has in mind. Part of the responsibility for determining meanings belongs, of course, to the reader; but the first responsibility, in particular concerning the key terms, belongs to the writer. Second, the Catch-22: if Chase is correct, many journalists give little attention to definitions because they are not philosophically inclined.

But Adler and Van Doren point out that the writers who are philosophers "are notorious for having private vocabularies." They coin new words or "take some word from common speech and make it a technical word." We can see some evidence of this in the earlier material quoted from Walter Lippmann, for both public opinion and Public Opinion (with capital letters) are combinations of common words that are given special meanings, meanings that need to be explained at greater length than he deigned to do for complete understanding by his readers.

If one turns to specialized dictionaries for elaborate explanations of the major terms used in journalism, one is again disappointed. For example, *The Longman Dictionary of Mass Media and Communication* (Connors 1982), with over 7,000 entries and described by its publisher as the most comprehensive single-volume dictionary of terms in the communication field, does not even attempt to define such terms as "communication," "journalism," or "news." Similarly, *A Dictionary of Communication and Media Studies* by James Watson and Anne Hill (1984) contains no definitions of "journalism," "news," or "objectivity." Howard Boone Jacobson *A Mass Communications Dictionary* (1961) lacks a definition of "journalism."

Moreover, some of these dictionaries devote only a few lines to the definitions they do give and make little effort to distinguish the words being defined from others with which they are sometimes confused. They are at their best when they introduce novices to the jargon of mass communications operations (telling them, for instance, that "nemo" means "a program originating outside of the station's studios") or trace historically the contexts in which special communications terms have been used.

Some Dangers of Definition

In addition, because of the nature of journalism, it seems that some efforts at definition may, in fact, pose real dangers. This is particularly true if the government does the defining. Some writers, for example, are wary of so-called shield laws, which protect journalists from being required to divulge to a court the confidential sources of their information. Those writers point out that such laws require a legislature to define who is and who is not a journalist, for only "journalists" (along, usually, with doctors, lawyers, and the clergy) are provided with such protection. But once a governmental body can define who is a journalist, that body has assumed the power to decide who belongs to this special class of persons and with what criteria those persons must comply in order to continue to belong to it. Licensing of reporters and journalists, the critics point out, is only a step or two away. Media law scholars Harold Nelson and Dwight Teeter (1982, 381) express the dilemma succinctly: "Who deserves the shield? and following that: Would not defining 'reporter' in effect be to license the newsman and thus bring him under state control?" But if we define "journalist" in sufficiently broad and encompassing terms—as will be done in this book—the danger of licensing would disappear.

Congressman Glenn English of Oklahoma, chairman of the Government Information, Justice, and Agriculture Subcommittee of the House Committee on Government Operations, was willing to opt for diversity of meanings if uniformity of meanings involved bureaucratic definitions of terms. In 1987, he strongly objected to the Office of Management and Budget guidelines, which defined some of the terms contained in the Freedom of Information Reform Act of 1986:

> Congress specifically declined to provide specific definitions for terms such as "news media" and "commercial use." These are admittedly difficult concepts, and the intent was to allow each agency to make a case-by-case determination. OMB's role was limited to the promulgation of a uniform schedule of

> fees and not to telling agencies how to interpret the substantive parts of the law. These definitional determinations were left to the agencies. (*Congressional Record* 1987, H2104)

Objections to Definitions

A seldom articulated but deeply felt belief holds that efforts toward definition, at least those that go beyond the contributions of the standard dictionaries, are pointless. Take, for example, the term "news." Steve Hannah, then managing editor of the *Milwaukee Journal*, told the reader-contact editor (1986, 7J) that "news is so broad that I can't even define it." Since one of our key terms, "news," means different things to different people, and we cannot get everyone to agree on a single meaning, why should we try to define it at all?

Many communications thinkers believe the problem of inadequate definition is not really serious, for we still know what most writers and speakers mean when they use the common language. In their discussion of objectivity, John C. Merrill and S. Jack Odell (1983, 174-75) set forth the position this way:

> One of the main problems with any discussion of objectivity is that there are so many ways of viewing it, so many definitions. . . . Just as a tree is something more than trunk, branches, and leaves, so also is objective reporting more than verifiable facts. There is something more: Just what this something is escapes precise description, but any thoughtful person recognizes its overriding and integrating character.

Finally, it would not be accurate to assume that the neglect of definitions is a universal phenomenon. In particular, when a word interests more than journalists, when it also attracts the interest of political scientists, sociologists, and social psychologists, for example, it is likely to receive extensive and sometimes massive attention. One such term has already been mentioned: "public opinion. That term even has, in a sense, its own journal, *Public Opinion Quarterly*.

A. Lawrence Lowell, a former president of Harvard University and a professor of the science of government at that school, is one of several writers who have presented an extended definition of public opinion as they have used the term. Likewise, Charles R. Wright begins his book *Mass Communications* (1959) with an elaborate explanation of what he understands the title words to mean. Similarly, Robert Park gives extended attention to the meaning of "news" in his article News as a Form of Knowledge (Park 1967, 32-52).

Where then, if anywhere, is the problem? A diligent search might well reveal that all the key terms in the field of journalism already have been defined. Even if one were to believe that many of the definitions do not adequately reveal the nature and boundaries of the realities designated by the terms being defined, writers such as those mentioned might reasonably point out that such dissatisfaction is merely a personal problem. They have done what good communicators should do: they have made clear what *they* mean by the most important words they are using. What more can we ask of them as communicators? We might disagree with what they have to say, but that is vastly different from claiming that they have not revealed what it is that they are writing about. Is there really anything more that needs to be discovered? Yes, there is much, much more.

A Seeming Digression

Instead of beginning by looking at words, let us start by observing the world in and around us. What do we perceive? Objects, actions, feelings, persons, thoughts, and so on. Some of these actually exist; some are products of our imagination. But, for the sake of convenience, let's refer to all of these as "realities," that is, entities that we know or can come to know.

Those who want to talk about these realities most often use those things we commonly refer to as words. But, for the moment, let's try to forget about the words and keep our attention focused on the realities.

These realities do not exist in total isolation. Some are causes of others. Some are effects. Some precede but do not cause another. Some follow but are not effects. Some are next to one another. Some are parts of another. Some are varieties of one major reality. And so on through a multitude of relationships.

Thus, if we were to start by focusing our attention on one of these realities—let's take one that is a process by which one person shares his or her knowledge with one or more other persons through the medium of signs—we could quickly see that other realities are related to that first one. For instance, we have the reality in which those who first have the knowledge are one or a small number of persons, those who receive it are relatively many, and those many receivers obtain the knowledge more or less simultaneously. This second reality is related to the first by being a variation of it, a type of the first. And we can think of other variations and relations, some depending, for example, on the type of knowledge that is conveyed (that which is simply worth knowing for its own sake and that which is worth knowing because it can be put to use), or on the medium used for conveying the knowledge, such as visual or aural signs.

When we give names to these realities, we quickly discover an arbitrariness in the naming process. Thus, although we call the first reality mentioned "communication," we could, if we wanted and if we could get others to agree, give it quite a different name, "foosies," for example. On the other hand, the name we have given the reality is also used to name other realities: "communication" sometimes is the name given, not to a process but rather to the material, such as a letter, by which the process is accomplished, as when we say, "Henry sent Hilda a communication"; sometimes the word names a passageway, as when we say, "The house has no communication between the kitchen and the dining room."

Words are arbitrary, *but the realities they name are not arbitrary*. A given reality actually is or is not related to another reality and, if so, in some determined, nonarbitrary way. Some particular thing, for instance, really is or is not a species of a more general thing, and if it is, that's it: we cannot change the reality. We may not know the reality as it actually is, of course, but mistakes in our knowledge do not change the nature of the reality.

If we were concerned merely with the major words used in the practice and discussion of journalism, were bothered simply by the fact that many writers and speakers do not make clear what they mean by the words they use, and were to attempt to solve this problem by giving elaborate, developed definitions of these words, anyone who reads these pages could reasonably and correctly say, "Good. Now I know what *you* mean by some of the words you use. But that's all. You certainly cannot pretend to tell others what they mean by the words they use, much less what they ought to mean."

But the aim of this book is not merely to propose definitions for important words. Rather, the objective is to go beyond mere definitions of words and attempt to discover the realities named by those words. In addition, when a number of words are frequently used together, we assume they belong together and are related. Each word is part of a context, and, in fact, we often determine which of several meanings a word should be given by the context in which it is used: "hit" in a baseball context means something quite different from "hit" in a theatrical context. What is true of a number of words can also be true of the realities named by those words. The realities are related to one another to form a set, a structure, an architectonic plan, an integrated theory. When words are used in conjunction with one another, those words ought to be defined in such a way as to reveal the interrelationships of the realities they name. It is true that some definitions are better than other definitions. Why? Because some reveal these interrelationships and others do not. Unfortunately, even those writers who have provided elaborate definitions of some of the major words used in the field of journalism have neglected to place them in the contexts that would justify their definitions.

This voyage of discovery, therefore, will attempt to locate the coherence of many meanings. Beneath words, we want to locate an integrated philosophy of journalism.

Philosophy as "Ordinary Human Talk"

It may seem presumptuous, even a little intimidating, to refer to anything as a "philosophy." Perhaps we can avoid these pitfalls by indicating what "philosophy" means in the context of this volume. A suitable explanation can be borrowed from that delightful publication *The Underground Grammarian* (1987, Vol. ii, No. 4). The anonymous writer of *TUG* distinguishes between philosophy as a subject, "a very hard subject indeed, and full of spiffy terms," and philosophy as a way of life, as it was lived by Plato and as it will be employed here:

> In Plato, we see and hear people sitting around and talking. And, while their way of talking is not the

> same as that in which we reminisce and gossip, it was not all that special either. It was ordinary human talk called to order from time to time, and frequently sent off on long but essential detours so that a term might be thoughtfully defined, and a proposition tested. And it is, therefore, especially for those who imagine that efficiency is the same as effectiveness, long and slow.

True, a book is hardly a convenient place in which to sit around and talk, for readers do not have the opportunity to object or add or remonstrate to anything the author says, at least not immediately. But readers can be and will be treated here as active companions on a voyage of discovery.

Near the end of *Philosophy and Journalism*, the authors write that "one of the main purposes of the entire book has been to raise questions for speculation by the serious reader" (Merrill and Odell 1983, 179). One of the main purposes of this book is to suggest answers to the basic questions that Merrill and Odell asked.

But as *TUG* says, we will have long but essential pauses to define a term or test a proposition, especially the former. Definition, indeed, is the principal method of this book.

Conclusion

Having come only this far, we already find it apparent that we are about to traverse a large and dangerous minefield. It is easy to note imperfections in the writings of others; it is enormously difficult to avoid them in one's own writings. Thus the challenge is quite clear: we must attempt to make clear the meaning or meanings of what many have said are some of the key terms in the field of journalism. Those meanings should not be eccentric or merely personal; they must reflect what actually exists in the world outside our minds. The words name realities that relate to one another. Thus we must try to show the nature and the interconnectedness of those realities, a coherent pattern, a construct that, to the extent it is accurate, will help improve the theory, study, and practices of journalism.

2

Dynamics of Journalism

To explain the journalism we might consider that common usage suggests it is something that people *do*. Just as doctors practice medicine and architects work at architecture, so journalists perform journalism.

But does saying that really accomplish more than pushing us around in a circle? After all, if journalism is what is done by journalists, we can then swing around to the question: And who are journalists? They, of course, are people who do journalism. Whatever that is. We seem to have chased the question to the point where its mouth bites its tail.

But that is not quite true. First of all, we will later see that many streams flow from this source: Journalism is an *activity*. For now, however, let's focus on the other point. The statement that journalism is what is done by *journalists*, although it seems to dance us in a loop, may be just the means by which we break out of the circle and actually discover what journalism is.

Some twenty-three centuries ago, Plato faced a problem similar to ours. In the *Meno*, Socrates and Meno are attempting to answer the question: What is virtue? Any attempt to find the answer seems either unnecessary or impossible. That is, if one can talk about virtue, one must already know what it is; or, if one doesn't already know what it is, one cannot talk about it in order to explain what it is.

Mortimer Adler, who was also struggling with a definitional problem in his book *The Idea of Freedom* (1958-61, 19, n. 2), restated the Platonic paradox this way:

> How can men look for a definition of virtue if they have no definition of it to start with, for without a definition how can they identify the subject of their inquiry? On the other hand, if they can begin by identifying the subject of their inquiry, they appear to define it also, and so they have no need to look further for a definition.

Breaking out of the Circle

The solution to the problem, Adler suggested, lies in making a careful distinction between an identification and a definition. An identification points at and is a relatively vague designation of the subject under discussion; a definition, on the other hand, provides precise knowledge of that subject. One way to make an identification is to give examples of what one wishes to define. For instance, Adler says, one could identify "democracy" by indicating that it is represented by the present governments of the United States, Great Britain, Switzerland, France, and the Scandinavian countries. With this start, one can then examine the governmental form in the examples, see what they have in common, and proceed to structure a definition.

Why not use the same process in our endeavor to determine what journalism is? Let's identify some journalists, see what they do in common, and, proceeding from there, begin to bring journalism forth for further examination. Which persons exemplify journalism?

Horace Greeley seems to be a safe person to head our list. This nineteenth-century founder and editor of the *New*

York Tribune was described by Willard G. Bleyer as the person whose influence "has never been exceeded by that of any other American journalist" (Bleyer 1927, 238).

We can next add Frederick Douglass. This contemporary of Greeley wrote for many papers, but is probably best known for his antislavery publication *The North Star*, a weekly with circulation in Europe and the West Indies as well as in the United States (Emery and Emery 1978, 157-58).

The journalistic muckraker Ida Tarbell deserves mention, especially for her exposé of the Standard Oil Company in a nineteen-part series for *McClure's* magazine that helped strengthen antimonopoly laws in the first decade of this century (Hiebert, Ungurait, and Bohn 1974, 210).

Finally, let's include Edward R. Murrow, whose World War II broadcasts from London were a key factor in establishing CBS leadership in the radio news field and who later brought the news documentary to television with his See It Now series (Barnouw 1970, 3:47-48).

Thousands of additional names could be added to this list. Although the four we mentioned may not be entirely typical, we can have little doubt that all of them would be identified as journalists; all are likely to be mentioned in any contemporary history-of-journalism book. They also remind us that journalists are not limited by sex, race, or the type of medium for which they work. But what, if anything, do they have in common?

Journalists and Communication

One identifying mark of journalists is that they are participants in the process of human communication. Since at least two parties always play a part in the process of human communication—one who transmits stimuli and another in whom a response to that stimuli is evoked (Cherry 1966, 3), often referred to as senders and receivers or, even more simply, as writers and readers or speakers and listeners—it is important to note which of these parties the journalists most characteristically are.

Journalists do an enormous amount of reading and listening. That work as receivers of communication is, in fact, along with observation, among the chief means by which they gather the knowledge that they formulate into messages. But those who *only* do this are not recognized as journalists. Greeley, Douglass, Tarbell, Murrow, and all the others we identify as journalists are most noted for originating the messages that are part of the communication process.

Journalists are those who are responsible for the *content* of what is sent out, transmitted, and conveyed to others. Greeley began his career as a typesetter and printer, but that was not the work of a journalist, for he was not then responsible for selecting or creating the messages that he set into type and then duplicated.

Pressmen, studio technicians, laboratory workers, delivery people, and many others may greatly assist the process of journalism, but their work is not the work of journalism. Journalists have control over what is said; the others may be responsible for the reproduction or circulation of what the journalists produce.

The signs that journalists use to convey their messages are most often verbal and probably more often written than oral. Graphic signs such as pictures, graphs, and drawings also play a part in both the print and oral media. Most of the messages that we will consider will be those that are expressed by written words, but unless stated otherwise, the comments will refer also to the other means of communication.

Other Communicators

Journalists, however, are not the only ones who create messages. Poets, novelists, playwrights, and others are also responsible for the content of pieces of communication. How do they differ from journalists?

Journalists send out messages that purport to be literally and at least preponderantly true or factual. Such words as "true" and "factual," of course, almost cry out for definition and explication, and in later chapters will be given their due. For now, it will suffice to restate this characteristic in negative terms.

Journalistic messages, let us say, do not purport to be false, erroneous, made up, invented, imagined, or fictional. They may, of course, actually be false or invented, but the journalists do not introduce them that way. Journalists are responsible for messages about things that they claim have really happened, are really happening, or are really intended, planned, or likely to happen.

The media in which pieces of journalism appear, it is true, are rarely occupied only by journalistic communications. Commercial television gives most of its time to pieces of fiction. Some may be *based* on fact, a circumstance that, as will be explained in a later chapter, can cause serious confusion, but usually the viewers are provided with sufficient clues to enable them to distinguish the journalistic fact from the fiction. Radio devotes much of its time to music, a nonverbal form of communication. The periodical media that rely heavily on the written word are the forms most strongly devoted to journalism, but they also are likely to contain at least some material that is not to be read as though it were literally true. Historically, newspapers are the media most frequently associated with journalism, but newspaper work and the work of journalism are not identical. Not all newspapermen or -women are journalists. In general, therefore, journalism is a function that should not be identified with any of the media, although it does rely on some of them.

Differences of Communicators

Journalists, however, are not alone as originators of what they purport to be nonfiction communications. Philosophers, economists, sociologists, physicists, and many others also devise messages that they intend their readers to accept as literally true. Among them, the group that seems most akin to journalists are the historians. Journalism, in fact, is sometimes referred to as contemporary or current history. But a careful examination of the differences between historians (as well as philosophers, economists, and similar communicators) and journalists will reveal a crucial characteristic of journalism.

Does the difference consist of this: historians write about the past whereas journalists write about the present? Not at all. Although historians commonly say such things as "the task of the historian" is "to order and interpret the events of the past" (Carr 1961, 161), the time factor is not critical. What is the present? It is but a moving edge between the past and the future. Most journalistic messages, just like historical writings, deal with what has happened, not with what is happening or will happen. The historian's past is often more remote than that in which the journalist is interested, but that is only a matter of degree, not of essence.

What, then, is the essence of history? That is a difficult question and historians themselves disagree on the answer. Erich Kahler (1964, 16-17) insists that "history is to be understood as the happening itself, not the description or investigation of this happening." Edward H. Carr (1961, 35) does not think so. History, he says, "is a continuous process of interaction between the historian and his facts, an unending dialogue between the present and the past."

R. G. Collingwood (1956, 9) says, "Every historian would agree, I think, that history is a kind of research or inquiry . . . generically it belongs to what we call the sciences: that is, the forms of thought whereby we ask questions and try to answer them." Collingwood has surely overstated the degree of agreement, yet his does seem to be the preponderant view. Arnold Toynbee (1972, 477), for instance, has a similar opinion: "I do not think that history . . . is a succession of facts, nor history-writing the narration of these facts. Historians, like all human observers, have to make reality comprehensible, and this involves them in continuous judgments about what is true and what is significant."

History and Journalism

Even if one accepts the dominant view about the nature of history, what, if anything, does it say that will help us distinguish history from journalism?

First, we must be careful not to be misled by one obvious but not unimportant difference. Journalism is a type of communication. History is not that. If one accepts Kahler, it is what has been going on. If one accepts Collingwood and most other historians, it is knowledge, organized knowledge, of what has been going on. Thus the parallel with journalism is not history itself but rather the *communication* of history.

But this is not the crucial point. Both journalism and history deal with knowledge. Journalism is the communication of a type of knowledge that has been acquired. History is the acquisition of a type of knowledge that will be communicated. Both are concerned with the communication of knowledge. But the important factor is not *when* the knowledge is acquired nor *when* it is communicated. Rather, what requires our attention is the *type* of knowledge that is acquired and communicated.

Traditionally, two broad categories of knowledge have been recognized. One is knowledge that is acquired for the sake of knowledge. It is knowledge for its own sake. It is knowledge for the sheer pleasure of knowing. This is called theoretical knowledge. The other is acquired to procure by some kind of activity the good of, people. It is knowledge that is put to use. This is called practical knowledge (Maritain n.d., 149). In *How to Read a Book*, Mortimer Adler and Charles Van Doren (1972, 66) explain the difference this way:

> Some books and some teachers are interested only in the knowledge itself that they have to communicate. This does not mean that they deny its utility, or that they insist that knowledge is good *only* for its own sake. They simply limit themselves to one kind of communication or teaching, and leave the other kind to other men. These others have an interest beyond knowledge for its own sake. They are concerned with the problems of human life that knowledge can help to solve. They communicate knowledge, too, but always with a view to and an emphasis upon its application.

Historians are interested in this first kind of knowledge. If one asks why historians do what they do, Toynbee answers that there can be several reasons; "the strongest and most estimable of these" is simply to satisfy curiosity. "In the field of human affairs," he says (1972, 46), "curiosity prompts us to seek a panoramic view in order to gain a vision of reality that will make it as intelligible as possible for a human mind." When historians communicate their historical knowledge they do so, dominantly and most properly, simply to help people understand what has happened.

But journalists, to the extent that they are practicing journalism, have a practical goal in mind. They acquire and communicate knowledge for the sake of providing people with what they need to know to make good decisions about what should be done or what should be avoided concerning the issues currently facing them.

If one wants to distinguish historians from journalists, one can say that the former are concerned not only with the past but with the past primarily as merely something to be known. In one sense, this type of knowledge might be viewed as useful, but it is useful for increasing understanding, not for determining future actions. Journalists, on the other hand, are ultimately concerned with helping people decide what would be good things to do or to avoid doing.

As events discussed by historians creep closer to the present, a temptation tags along to apply historical knowledge to the solution of contemporary problems. If historians give way to this temptation, however, they edge into the domain of the journalists. But journalists also face their own temptation. They may fall short of the practical goal that is their reason for being.

Perceiving, achieving, and maintaining the distinction between the theoretical and the practical are enormously difficult, for they require the concurrence of message senders and message receivers. History and journalism both can be misdirected and misused.

For example, a historian examining the letters of Thomas Jefferson finds they set forth some radical changes in his attitudes toward newspapers. Before he became president, Jefferson esteemed the press highly, writing that, if he had to make a choice, he would prefer newspapers without government rather than government without newspapers. But after he was president, Jefferson criticized the press mightily, claiming it was so filled with lies that a man who never reads a newspaper is better informed than one who does (Padover 1953, 93, 97).

Now the historian's proper task is to discover what, in many contexts, Jefferson's letters mean and to find, if he can, the reasons for the changing attitudes reflected in them. But instead of communicating to us this knowledge, he might discard the historian's garb and, using these letters as evidence, try to convince us that we should not trust the campaign words of presidential candidates when they laud the press, for even the best of them is bound to have a change of mind once elected.

Sometimes we can spot what pseudo-historians are doing, especially if they are blatant in their misuse of documents or relics of the past. We might even charge that, no longer historians, they have become propagandists. By that we probably mean that they are trying to mislead us, trying to incline us toward what we believe to be some inappropriate course of action. We are less likely to spot the sacrifice of history if the writers are proposing something with which we agree. Yet whether we agree or not, propaganda is not good history.

Even when a piece of writing *is* historical writing, some readers might misuse it by attempting to turn it to some practical purpose. Just as Pablo Picasso's great painting *Guernica* might be cut in half and hung sideways merely to cover a long crack in the wall, so one might try to turn Thucydides' *History of the Peloponnesian War* into a guidebook for fighting a twentieth-century battle. In a more recent example, General Albert Wedemeyer book *Wedemeyer Reports!* (1958) was intended to help us understand the major battles of World War II, but it could have been misused as a handbook for conducting the war in Vietnam.

Journalism, too, can be misdirected or misused, as will be seen in some of the chapters that follow. But for now and throughout the succeeding pages, we must keep in mind one dominant characteristic of journalism: properly done, it deals with useful, practical knowledge. If we lose touch with this core, the effort to discover journalism will fail.

Practical Knowledge

Journalists, however, are not the only ones who communicate useful knowledge. Parents, profiting from their own experience, advise their children on how to make the first car purchase or diaper the first grandchild. A dietician informs a heart patient of the foods that will lower fat and cholesterol. A psychiatrist tells an overworked employer how to reduce stress. All of these tend to work on a one-to-one, face-to-face basis. Perhaps more instructive for our purposes would be the comparison between journalists and trial lawyers, since lawyers, in addition to their one-on-one dialogues with judges and witnesses, often have a group of people—a jury—with whom to communicate.

In addition to their mutual interest in the recent past, trial lawyers, like journalists, have practical goals in mind. Their ultimate goal in criminal trials is ostensibly to help assure that the guilty are punished and the innocent set free and exonerated. Both journalists and lawyers engage in communications to help others determine what ought to be done or avoided. But how do they differ?

Once again, some of the most obvious differences may not be the most important. Whereas journalists communicate about a wide range of topics, lawyers travel within the relatively narrower compass of the law. More significant, however, is the extent of the communications, and the number and type of persons reached by the communicators.

Lawyers who communicate in the process of a jury trial attempt to reach several people, thus exceeding the one-to-one communications previously mentioned, but they are not engaged in what is usually called "mass communications." Journalists, however, whenever they are functioning as journalists, are always participants in mass communications. But how does communicating with several or even many persons differ from communicating with a mass of people?

The Mass Communications

The term "mass communications" means different things to different writers and speakers. Chapter 1 showed some of the difficulties one encounters in attempting to determine what the thoughtful scholar Wilbur Schramm meant by the term. Another excellent scholar, Charles R. Wright, a contemporary of Schramm, presented (1959) a somewhat clearer explanation—clear enough, at least, to show what modifications must be made if we are to see the relationship between journalism and mass communications.

Wright makes quite clear that he is writing about "modern mass communications", but he does not identify or describe any mass communications before the modern period. At least he does not do so explicitly. One can look at what he has to say about modern mass communications, subtract the modern and qualify a few other items, and then set forth the characteristics of basic mass communications. But why go to all this trouble? Why not simply accept Wright's formulation as he expressed it?

Well, even if one extends the modern period back to the middle of the last century, limiting mass communications to that time forces a dilemma: either journalism did not exist before approximately 1850 or journalism, if it did exist before that time, must not be a type of mass communications. The first choice would ignore the hundreds of books on the history of journalism that set earlier dates for those working in this field, including one of our prototype journalists, Horace Greeley, who was already an experienced journalist when he founded his *New York Tribune* in 1841. The second removes an effective means by which we can distinguish journalism from other practical communications, such as law.

Another, perhaps stronger, reason for removing the "modern" qualification is that the notion of "modern mass communications" is no longer apt.

Wright (1959, 15) distinguishes modern mass communications from earlier individual communications in this way:

> Mass communications is organized communication. Unlike the lone artist or writer, the "communicator" in mass media works through a complex organization embodying an extensive division of labor and an accompanying degree of expense.

To be sure, in the 1950s when Wright was preparing his book, mass communications seemed to be moving in the direction of complexity, expensiveness, and a division of labor that resulted in more workers per communication enterprise but fewer and fewer independently controlled media institutions. What Morris L. Ernst had ironically called the "sweep of progress" (1946, 53) had continued, seemingly unabated, a decade later. The tide apparently was moving toward bigger but fewer media institutions. Both print and broadcast outlets were getting larger, but their number, and the competition between the members, was decreasing. This movement, especially among daily newspapers, had flowed along steadily since the second decade of this century. A new type of mass communications, therefore, seemed to be acquiring characteristics that were the inevitable flooding from the past. Thus it could have seemed quite reasonable to Wright to ignore the fact that the communications operations of a century or two earlier were *not* complex and expensive, for the flow of history seemed to show that those days were gone forever.

But technology outwitted the course of history. The machines that had been growing larger, requiring more people to operate and vastly more money to acquire, suddenly began to move in the opposite direction. Computers that had occupied enormous air-cooled rooms shrank until they fit on the lap of a businessman jetting from Chicago to Los Angeles. Minicams plus public access channels brought the possibility of television journalism within the financial range of even the lower middle class. Desktop publishing moved the production of periodicals into small offices, even into homes. Computer bulletin boards opened a vast range of new ways of distributing messages. In other words, technology opened doors back into the mass media environment that had existed at the beginning of the nineteenth century: once again, a single person with only a modest investment could convey messages to large numbers of persons in a very short period of time.

If those processes that possess the characteristics of mass communications, except that they involve simple and inexpensive production, are not included in the category of mass communications, then we would have to create another category to accommodate them. But what are we to call the broadsheets introduced by the missionaries in Nigeria a century before that country's independence (Altschull 1984, 155)? They were examples of mass communications, but they were not produced through complex or expensive facilities. The handwritten newsletters circulated among the refusniks in the USSR; the wall posters that appeared in China during the Cultural Revolution; the mimeographed sheets of church agencies, universities, and justice and peace groups in South and Central America; the *Drudge Report* that appears on the web pages of the Internet: these and many other relatively contemporary communication activities have all the characteristics of early nineteenth-century mass communications. It seems unnecessary to invent another name for the category that merely lacks the complex organization, the division of labor, and the great expense mentioned by Wright.

The Range of Mass Communication

Many others of Wright's points about mass communications, however, help clarify this confusing term. He says, for instance, that the audience of mass communications is relatively large and that so many people are exposed to the message in a short period of time and are of such numbers "that the communicator could not interact with its members on a face-to-face basis". He also says that the audience is anonymous so that its members "generally remain personally unknown to the communicator". Moreover, mass communications are public; because the messages "are addressed to no one in particular, their content is open for public surveillance." Also, "They are rapid because the messages are meant to reach large audiences within a relatively short time, or even simultaneously." And, "They are transient because they are usually intended to be consumed immediately".

Even so brief an account tells us enough to help us distinguish journalistic communications from lawyer-courtroom communications. When lawyers address juries, they are addressing several people, but not so many that the lawyers are unable to be aware of them as individuals. Jurors cannot normally respond verbally to the words of the lawyers, but they have available many nonverbal means of communicating. If one jury member's facial expression indicates skepticism at what the lawyer is saying, the latter can modify his or her communication to take that into consideration. If another juror shows surprise, the lawyer may realize that an opportunity for pressing a point now exists. If still another juror is falling asleep, that may tell the lawyer it is time to request a recess.

Thus interpersonal communication can exist even when a number of people are involved. How large can that number be? There is no magic figure. Normally, the limit is the number of people to whom the communicator can react as *individuals* when they provide verbal or nonverbal responses to what the communicator is saying. Consider, for example, the politician who is addressing a thousand people at a political rally. They may cheer or they may boo at what the politician has to say. The speaker may modify what he had intended to say as a result, but the reaction is to the audience as a collectivity, not to them as individuals. The speaker is engaging in mass communications. But let's say that one person leaps up and begins to engage the speaker in a debate. If the speaker responds, what had been only mass communications then becomes a mixture of mass and interpersonal communications.

When a young couple sends out a thousand wedding invitations to friends and relatives, the process is interpersonal communications in spite of the large number of persons to whom the message is sent. Each person to whom that message is sent can—and is probably expected to—respond individually. Some will attend. Some will send regrets. A few might ask whether they may bring a friend. But when the commander of a thousand troops orders them to attack at dawn, no individual responses are expected and none is likely to take place.

Then the process is solely mass communications. Thus, although in mass communications one or a relatively few people send a message to relatively many people, the exact size of that receiving group is not important.

More important is what Wright refers to as the anonymity of the audience. The audience may be known as a certain *category* of persons, as when the army commander knows he is addressing infantrymen rather than pilots or when the publisher of a religious newspaper knows the readers are Lutherans rather than Methodists. But these people are not individually spoken to or even precisely thought of as individuals. Likewise, when a magazine publisher goes to a list broker to buy a thousand names and addresses of people who the publisher hopes will become subscribers, the subscription offers will go out to individually named persons, but they are persons unknown to the publisher. They are as anonymous as "occupant."

The last example reveals a slight modification of Wright's statement that mass communications messages "are addressed to no one in particular" and that the messages are "open for public surveillance." What Wright says is very often true, especially when broadcast mass communications are involved. But it is less true when the mass communications medium is a periodical sent to a list of subscribers. Large circulation magazines are usually open for public scrutiny at newsstands and libraries, of course, but there are many hundreds of highly practical and specialized publications—for example, trade journals such as *Implement and Tractor, China Glass and Tableware,* and *Western Outfitter*-that are not. They are rarely available for inspection by anyone other than subscribers.

Wright's point concerning the transience of mass communications also needs qualification. Mass produced novels, poems, and other works of fiction may endure for centuries, and so also may theoretical nonfiction works such as books of philosophy or natural science. Such works as Charles Dickens *A Tale of Two Cities* and Albert Einstein *The Meaning of Relativity* possess all the qualities Wright attributes to mass communications except transience. Interestingly, however, the mass communications that are transient are likely to be the journalistic ones, for once they have served their practical purpose, once the decisions have been made from the knowledge that journalism supplies, then the messages cease to be useful, cease to be journalism, and become, like treaties, diaries, and other artifacts, the raw materials of history.

Roots of Mass Communications

Thus there is a type of mass communications that not only exists in the modern period but also has existed for many earlier centuries. In this basic mass communications, one person or a relatively few people (relatively few in comparison to the number of people who receive the message) convey one or more messages to a relatively large number of persons. Often the receivers perceive the messages simultaneously; if not simultaneously, at least they perceive them more quickly than they would if the message had to be originated for each individual. Even if the messages are individually addressed, the receivers are not thought of as individuals; they are thought of as groups or types or masses of people; for all practical purposes, the receivers are anonymous. Each of those who receive the message does not prepare and deliver an equivalent response to those who send the message. They may, however, respond as a group (as when Pontius Pilate asked the people what he should do with Jesus and they all replied [Matt. 27:23], "Let Him be crucified!"). Sometimes the group reply will be through action rather than through words (as when soldiers, in response to the commander's order "Charge!" go dashing into the field of battle). Thus, although mass communications seem to be one-way, they are not totally so; the sender may well get a response, but not an equivalent response, from each one who receives the message.

A few situations require special attention. Although not *all* the receivers will give an equivalent response, *some* of them might do so. For example, a newspaper reader might respond to an editorial with an equivalent letter to the editor. If this letter is delivered to the editorial writer, that person may or may not provide a personal reply. If the editorial writer does so, then there has been a transition from a mass communication to an interpersonal communication between the letter writer and the editorial writer. Or the editor may decide to publish the letter in the newspaper; if so, a new phase of mass communications takes place, one in which the letter writer is the sender and the other readers of the paper are the receivers.

Quite clearly, not everyone who is involved in a mass communication process is a mass communicator. That name is reserved for those who have control over the content of messages and intend to deliver their messages to masses of people. The readers of newspapers, although participants in the mass communications process, are not normally mass communicators. Nor are the printers, delivery people, newsstand salespersons, and others who lack the authority to originate or modify the content of the messages. Writers, speakers, editors, photographers, cartoonists, and the like, however, can be mass communicators, *if* they intend their messages to go out to the masses.

To clarify this latter point, let us consider for a moment the call-in programs often heard on radio, often late at night. The subjects discussed are sometimes quite personal: the sex life or economic problems of the callers, for example. The host of the show is clearly a mass communicator. He or she wants the program's messages to be heard by as many people as possible. The host's popularity and income depend upon a wide, anonymous, unrestricted audience.

The host, in other words, is not communicating only with the person who calls in; the host would like to think that he or she is communicating with "the world." But what about the person who calls in? That person is also involved in a mass communications process and originates a portion of the messages that are sent out. But is that person also, like the host, a mass communicator?

Perhaps not. Although the caller participates voluntarily in a mass communications process, he or she does not, in many instances, really desire to do so. To obtain free advice, the caller tolerates one type of communication, mass communication, but would probably prefer another type, interpersonal communication. If the caller happens to be an exhibitionist or propagandist, however, then the caller does become, like the host, a mass communicator.

But because we cannot always establish the truth of intentions, it will sometimes be difficult or impossible to know whether or not a certain person is a mass communicator. Yet in most instances, the evidence and circumstances are so clear that we have no doubts. To those who participate in the mass communications process regularly and for a living, it is particularly easy to grant the title of mass communicator.

Two additional glosses on Wright's mention of anonymity as a characteristic of mass communications are relevant. First, not only do mass communicators not know the recipients of their communications as individuals, but those recipients usually do not know one another as individuals. They often think of themselves as existing in isolation. Second, partly because of the anonymity of the audience, mass communicators must guess at the level of background knowledge, literacy, and sophistication of the message recipients. The messages are often directed at a level somewhat below the median, to the distress of those who exist at the extremes.

Journalists and Lawyers

With all this in mind, we can perhaps better understand how journalists differ from lawyers, even when both groups employ the communication of literally true, practical knowledge. The former are mass communicators; the latter are not. Courtroom lawyers may direct their messages to a number of people—the judge, jurors, witnesses, the other lawyers—but they are people with whom it is possible for the lawyers to interact as individuals. Although there are prominent exceptions, most lawyers in the courtroom are not interested in addressing the nebulous, anonymous public at large.

The lawyers defending civil-rights activists in the 1960s and 1970s may have been extending their remarks to an audience far outside the courtroom. They may have wanted their words to be political statements to the entire nation about racial injustice. If so, to that extent they were assuming the role of mass communicators. But, usually, trial lawyers direct their messages to the limited group of persons at hand in the courtroom. Their aim, like that of journalists, is a practical one, but their audience is the relatively few people who are able to determine the outcome of legal proceedings. In most instances, lawyers control their messages so that they impact on that select group.

In addition, this is an immediate group, one whom lawyers, simply by a turn of the head, can address face-to-face. Any overt reactions by members of this group can be readily known and dealt with by the lawyers. Thus, not only in their private relations with clients in their offices but also in the public arena of the courtroom, lawyers are normally interpersonal communicators. Journalists, on the other hand, are mass communicators.

The Generic Meaning of Journalism

We have reached the point where we are ready to set forth the basic definition of journalism. Many refinements will be added in the succeeding pages, but the following seems to sum up the comments we have made so far.Journalism is a type of mass communications

1. That provides useful and practical (rather than theoretical) knowledge;
2. That actually is or at least purports to be literally true, rather than invented or fictional;
3. That is provided by persons who have at least some control over the content of the messages that are communicated;
4. And that aids the recipients of the knowledge in making decisions on issues presently facing them.

Journalism is the type of activity that has all of the attributes just described. Journalists are the persons who engage in that type of activity.

Journalism does not exist aside from the persons who practice it. It is not like a tree or a frying pan or a light bulb; it cannot grow by itself, nor, once made, can it exist by itself. The *products* of journalism—news stories, editorials, video tapes, photographs—can have an independent existence, but journalism itself cannot.

Journalists, however, do exist independently of their journalism. A sleeping Horace Greeley, Frederick Douglass, Ida Tarbell, or Edward R. Murrow would have been identified as a journalist even though, while sleeping, he or she was not practicing journalism. All of this seems quite clear. What may not be so clear is the correlative point: just as those readily identified as journalists often continue to be called journalists even when they are not practicing journalism, so also those who are not ordinarily identified as journalists ought to be called journalists as soon as they begin to practice journalism.

Journalism is not a custom-made dress or suit available to only a few select people. It is a cloak which almost anybody can throw on. Journalism is an activity that can be employed by everyone except those who have not yet acquired or who have lost their communicative faculties. Whenever plumbers or clerks or architects or musicians become participants in the activities identified earlier, *they become journalists.*

This point, sometimes ignored, becomes especially important when questions concerning the legal protection of journalists arise. Such protection belongs to all of us. It is also important when we consider our national educational system, for it means that all citizens should be prepared to practice the arts of journalism, should they ever desire to do so. Thus one of the dangers of attempting to define journalism, as mentioned in the previous chapter, now becomes less worrisome. There is no need to license journalists as a restricted class of people when nearly everyone is or legitimately can be a journalist.

Recognition of Journalism

Some people would grant the title of "journalist" only to those for whom the work is a full-time job. But such a viewpoint not only carries with it some of the dangers already mentioned but would be analogous to denying T. S. Eliot the title of poet because he made his living working at Lloyd's Bank or saying William Carlos Williams should not be called a poet because all his life he was a practicing physician.

Thus it seems much better to recognize that, although for some their regular, full-time job is doing the work of journalism, there are many more who practice journalism only occasionally. *New York Tribune* editor Horace Greeley belongs to the first group; Robert Dale Owen, a Democratic congressman from Indiana, who wrote a letter published in the *Tribune* on October 23, 1862, appealing for a Proclamation of Emancipation, belongs to the second. The first are often called professional journalists in the sense that the principal source of their livelihood is the practice of journalism. For the second, we have no well-accepted designation. Perhaps it is adequate simply to call them amateur or occasional journalists. Although professional journalists are sometimes given privileges not available to occasional journalists, access to a press box at a baseball game, for example, or access to the press gallery in the U. S. Senate chambers, the legal rights of both the amateurs and the professionals are the same, and whenever they are doing the work described earlier they deserve to be called journalists.

Another set of species is quite obvious, for it is based on the medium employed by journalists to convey their messages to the public. Thus there are newspaper, magazine, radio, television, film, book, and other types of journalists, even though no journalist is inextricably tied to a single medium. Many, in fact, move from one to another, as did William L. Shirer, who switched from the *Chicago Tribune* to radio, television, and books. Others use several media at the same time, as did David Gergen, who was an editor of *U.S. News and World Report* at the same time that he was a news analyst on public television. But most professional journalists are usually identified with the medium to which they devote most of their time and from which they derive the greater part of their income.

Journalism: Public Affairs and Personal Affairs

One of the most important, yet also one of the most ignored, divisions of journalism is that into public affairs journalism and personal affairs journalism. It is easy to understand why it receives so little attention: although both journalists and the public have a quiet awareness that the distinction exists, they seldom discuss it explicitly. But it is so essential to an understanding of journalism that explicit discussion is essential, briefly here and more extensively later on.

The brief description of the generic meaning of journalism is that it provides useful, practical knowledge. But useful for what purpose? Useful to help those who are consumers of journalism decide what should be done or what should be avoided concerning the issues currently facing them. Journalism exists to help all of us decide what is good to do and what is good not to do.

The concept of good, of course, has a multitude of meanings. Here we think of it in relation to those for whom something can be considered good. We can say that something is good for me or we can say that something is good for us. That is, we can make a choice in order to improve, profit, delight, enhance, benefit our individual selves or to do one or all of these things for the improvement and benefit of the community, group, organization, or society of which we individuals are members.

For example, let's consider a fictitious Hiram. Hiram never married and is now retired from his job as a clothing salesman. He lives in a small apartment, is in good health, likes spectator sports, has a satisfactory income from Social Security and a few investments, pays taxes, and is, in general, a rather average person. Every day, Hiram has to make thousands of decisions. Some are so personal—shall I sleep another five minutes or should I get out of bed right now?—that no other person can be of much help to him in deciding what is the good thing to do. But hundreds of his decisions can be more or less well made depending on the knowledge that is communicated to him from the outside world.

He likes to watch the local baseball team. Is the team playing today? Is the weather likely to be good for baseball? Are the normal means of transportation in operation? Is the admission price the same as last time he went to a game? What time of the day will the game be played? Will it also be shown on television? How well has the team been doing? Has any starter been injured and thus is unavailable to play? He can probably find the answers to these and to numerous other questions affecting his personal welfare by consulting his daily newspaper or listening to the news reports on radio or television. The knowledge he receives will help him decide whether or not it would be good for him to attend the baseball game.

Learning that the game will be shown on television, Hiram may decide to watch it at home rather than go out to the ballpark. Many others, receiving the same information, may decide just the opposite. Hiram's decision is a personal decision in the sense that he decides what is good for himself. Other baseball fans can make similar or different personal decisions. It is not necessary that there be just one decision.

Now let's say that while reading the newspaper Hiram learns that next Tuesday the city will hold a referendum to determine whether or not money will be borrowed to build a new high school. In this situation, the decision to be made is not what is good for Hiram but rather what is good for the city, not "for me" but "for us." Whatever the decision is, it will be one decision. It will be assumed that even those who might have preferred a different decision will go along with the one that is made.

If the voters decide to approve of the borrowing, that decision will be against Hiram's personal welfare: his taxes will probably increase, and he has no children who will benefit from the new school. But if the new school is truly needed, the public welfare might well require that money be borrowed to build it. In fact, Hiram himself, recognizing the dominant character of the public welfare, of the common good, might put aside consideration of his own personal good to vote in favor of the referendum.

What, then, is the difference between personal affairs journalism and public affairs journalism? The first type provides the knowledge people can use to make good decisions about their personal, current welfare. Each person decides what is good for him or her, independent of the decisions being made by others. Much of the journalism dealing with sports, business, and entertainment (just to name a few possibilities) is of that type. The second type of journalism provides the knowledge people need for decisions concerning the current welfare of some community, group, organization, or society of which they are a part. Here a decision will be made (perhaps by all the members, perhaps by one or a few) concerning what will be good for that community or group. It will be a decision concerning the welfare of the whole collectivity, and the members will be expected to go along with it even if they would have preferred some other decision. Most of the activities of federal, state, and local governments are the business of public affairs journalism, but the latter can also extend to private groups: fraternities or businesses, for instance. The welfare of these, too, requires decisions concerning the good of the whole, and public affairs journalism contributes to the goodness of those decisions. If one company is considering a merger with another, this decision concerns the welfare of both companies and is a decision in which the managements, stockholders, and employees have a stake. All need knowledge so that the decision can be well made, and most of the knowledge that is needed comes through the work of public affairs journalism.

One might ask: Why should members of a public pay attention to issues-such as a proposal to raise tax rates—

which seem beyond the public's powers of determination? Some answers will be found in our later discussions of public opinion and electoral processes. For now, it may be sufficient to recollect that mass communications always extend messages to more people than have a direct need for them.

The Place of Public Relations and Advertising

Can we also say that the communications tasks associated with public relations and with advertising ought to be viewed as additional types or species of journalism? That question has been the source of many heated disagreements.

One of the most vigorous of these disagreements took place in the 1950s when Sigma Delta Chi, the Society of Professional Journalists (SPJ), debated the problem of membership eligibility. Having already excluded advertising people from the organization, the members now decided that, in the future, public relations practitioners would also be excluded because neither group was composed of true journalists (Bostrom 1984).

Some public relations practitioners do spend their time analyzing situations and providing interpersonal consultation to their clients. Similarly, some advertising people spend time in market and media research and in similar interpersonal communications. Thus, to the extent they are not engaged in mass communications, they would not fit the definition of journalists. But the activities of most people in both fields culminate in their preparing messages for the mass media. To the extent that those messages convey useful knowledge that at least purports to be true, the work they do fits the concept of journalism.

Why, then, did SPJ claim they were *not* journalists? For years, the society had differentiated between those acceptable persons who prepared and disseminated information in the "public interest" and those nonacceptable persons who did so in what the members called the "private interest." They concluded that all advertising people were in the latter category; but in 1952, they admitted, at least for a few years, that this was not true of all public relations practitioners. Those who wrote for civic organizations, social agencies, benevolent foundations, educational institutions, and governmental departments (with the interesting exception of the military) and who had an "acceptable background of experience in news work for newspapers, magazines or in broadcasting" could be considered to be working in the public interest and thus be eligible for membership (Bostrom 1984, 21). But in the summer of 1958, a select panel had second thoughts about even these exceptions and submitted a report proposing, among other things, that there be no initiation of public relations men in the future. A heated and extensive debate ensued, much of it carried out in the pages of *Quill*, the society's journal, concluding with a vote at the 1958 national convention that endorsed the report.

One of the more interesting contributions to the debate came from a group of distinguished public relations persons themselves. Although they were grandfathered into the society, they said they recognized differences between their work and that of many other members:

We accept your tighter definition of journalism. Although we prepare and disseminate news stories, we admit we do so, at least in part, in the interest of our clients and employers. Newsmen, on the other hand, generally work without obligation to any special interest. Both activities may well be in the public interest, but there is a fundamental difference which is important to Sigma Delta Chi. (Bostrom 1984, 24)

Several years later, David Berkman seemed to express a similar thought. In discussing whether public relations courses have a place within journalism programs, he wrote, "If we accept—and how can we not do so?—that the purpose of the journalist is to discover and report truth, while that of those in public relations is to serve the interests of their clients or employers, then the answer is clearly 'no'" (Berkman 1992, 32). Even though public relations practitioners serve the interests of clients or employers, it does not necessarily follow that such a type of service precludes the discovering and reporting of truth. Journalists, no matter whether they are newswriters, public relations practitioners, or advertising personnel, can have a variety of motives when they do their work. They can be working for their own welfare, for the welfare of a cause in which they are interested, for the welfare of their employers, for the welfare of the public, or for many other possible objectives. To say that only one of these goals is good and all the rest are suspect is to assume an arbitrary and unreasonable moral standard. Any or all of them can be good, and no one of them need necessarily exclude the others. Any moralistic approach to the definition of journalism depends in part on the precarious possibility of detecting the intentions of message senders.

Although some journalists are morally good and some morally deficient, it is not the case that all newspeople are in the first category and all public relations and advertising people in the second. It did not seem, for instance, that former *Wall Street Journal* reporter R. Foster Winans had been acting as a very ethical journalist when he was convicted in 1985 of using his "Heard on the Street" stock market column to further an insider trading scheme that netted him $31,000. Unfortunately, deceptions on various levels have not been infrequent among newspeople during the history of journalism. During the first months of 1998, Stephen Glass of the *New Republic*, Patricia Smith of the *Boston Globe*, and April Oliver of CNN lost their jobs for concocting material that turned out not to be factual. But they certainly are not typical of all reporters, columnists, and television producers. Likewise, some advertising and public relations practitioners lack the integrity we ought to expect of people who work in those fields even though most of them adhere to the goals of their professions. The Public Relations Society of America *Code of Professional Standards* says, "A member shall conduct his or her professional life in accord with the public interest." Also, advertising personnel aim at stimulating business competition, resulting in improved products and more economical ways to produce and distribute them; thus in the end "the consumer benefits by the availability of new and better products" (Backman 1967, 2; also see Galbraith 1968, 209-10; Wells 1972, 150). To increase the likelihood of such good performance is one reason for incorporating advertising and public relations instruction in journalism programs.

The journalism/advertising identification is further complicated because some advertising, like newspaper, magazine, and broadcast editorials, argues for or against public issues. The Mobil Oil Company produces this type of editorial advertising frequently. The American Federation of Teachers buys space in the *New York Times* on the first Sunday of each month so that its president can discuss matters of public policy.

Similarly, political public relations contributes to the public discussion of public affairs. The public relations writer, of course, advances the position of the person or party who is paying the bill, but print and broadcast editorial writers also advance the positions of the editors, publishers, or station managers who employ them.

Ideological, ethnic, religious, and other special interest newspapers, magazines, and cable systems are as much devoted to advancing private agendas as are public relations and advertising practitioners. And at least since the period of the penny press in the 1830s, a strong feeling has existed that some members of the information media function more to sell copies and enrich their owners than to serve the public (Altschull 1984). The contemporary members of this trend might be the tabloids conveniently placed along the supermarket checkout lanes.

Thus it seems that as long as advertising and public relations people use the mass media to convey purportedly true knowledge that can help people make good decisions about what to do and what to avoid in regard to issues currently facing them, advertising and public relations people ought to be considered journalists as much as anyone else who does that type of work. They are, in particular, much like print and broadcast editorial writers, columnists, and commentators. Like them, advertising and public relations practitioners are persuaders. It is true that they advance products or causes in which they or their employers are interested, but so also did Greeley, Douglass, Tarbell, and Murrow—and nearly all of those whom we are proud to identify as journalists.

It is also true that, unlike some other journalists, advertising journalists buy space or time in media that they do not own. This makes them different from those who own or those who are employed by those who own their media. But every type of journalist is different from other types: photojournalists differ from word journalists, broadcast journalists from print journalists, public affairs journalists from personal affairs journalists. The fact that a person is this type of journalist rather than another *type* of journalist need not deprive that person of identification as *a journalist*.

Many public relations practitioners produce their own media: newsletters, company newspapers, brochures, slide presentations, annual reports, and video-tapes Many of the others supply, at no cost, informational, analytical, and persuasive material to the general mass media. Some studies indicate that more than half of the nonwire, nonsyndicated editorial content of newspapers comes from releases or memos generated by public relations sources (Clark and Blankenburg 1973, 183). Some press agents have misused their abilities, it is true, but the same can be said of those in any field of endeavor. Nothing in the nature of the work they do requires either the lying or fictionizing that would exclude them from journalism.

The News and Journalism

As we continue to examine the nature and functions of journalism in greater detail, we see immediately that another term is so closely associated with journalists that it is sometimes used as a synonym. During the prolonged Society of Professional Journalists-Sigma Delta Chi debate on the meaning of journalism, for example, Edward Lindsay, editor of the Lindsay-Schaub newspapers in Decatur, Illinois, sometimes substituted "fraternity of newsmen" for "society of professional journalists" (Bostrom 1984, 25). Indeed, in the mind of many persons, news reporters and newswriters seem to occupy the centermost chambers in the house of journalism. Therefore, although journalism consists of much more than the acquisition and presentation of news, it is appropriate that we now turn our attention to that important but highly ambiguous term.

3

Making Journalists for the Future

As mentioned earlier, some people make their living by doing the work of journalism and others practice journalism only now and then. Let's look, first of all, at the former, the professional journalists, and examine the type of education most appropriate for them.

At the very core of any professional education lies the consideration of what one is doing. As is true of medicine, law, and dentistry, journalists also have to understand the basic nature of the work they are setting out to perform. What is it? What is it intended to accomplish? Through what means can those purposes be achieved?

Since journalism, like the subjects of all professions, is complex, this probing into the nature, functions, and general means of the work proceeds through many areas and levels. Thus, in addition to understanding journalism itself, the students must also strive to achieve an understanding of news, of interpretation, of evaluation, of advocacy. Regarding news, they need to examine the nature of news events and news reports. What do journalists attempt to achieve by these? By what potential means?

And the questions continue: in what situations and under what conditions can the goals of news presentation best be accomplished through verbal means, when through nonverbal means? If the former, when through spoken, when through written words? If through nonverbal means, when through graphics and when through pictures? And, if through pictures, when through still and when through moving pictures?

But the journalism student must also step back from the specifics to the megaview, asking, for example, how the presentations of news, interpretations, evaluations, and persuasions relate to one another and to the nature of journalism.

Since journalism is not merely a subject to be studied but primarily a work to be done, the education appropriate for professional journalists must also involve a great amount of directed doing.

Arts of Journalism

Like good woodworkers, automobile designers, and architects, journalists are constantly producing useful products that are unique. In that sense, they are artists—not fine artists, like poets and landscape painters—but artists nevertheless.

Artists develop their abilities not merely through discussion but primarily through practice. Thus student journalists acquire the arts necessary to produce good news stories by practicing the writing of news stories. And, like other developing artists, they work with and under the careful tutelage of master artists.

Art is much more than mere skill or technique. Skill enables one to manipulate tools that are useful for the artist, as reporters, for instance, need to possess the skill of word processor operation. And, since technique is the ease, speed, and accuracy with which one can use a skill, good reporters can enter a story into a word processor with seemingly little effort, quickly, and without mistakes.

Art, however, transcends all this. It is the power to determine what needs to be done to create an object that has never previously existed. If it is to be truly useful, the news story written today must differ in important respects from any other news story; mere repetition has value only for those who did not receive the original. Skill and technique may be important in accomplishing this, but they are still only the servants of the art.

Not all journalistic works, of course, require the same degree of artistic ability. For example, the journalist who prepares the agate material for stock tables or box scores needs very little. But most others, especially those who strive to satisfy the people's needs for knowledge about public affairs, must be true masters of their profession.

In addition, the distinctions among news gathering, news itself, and news reporting reminds us that journalists must possess a double set of arts. The news report requires the arts governing the presentation of useful knowledge, but preceding those are the arts that enable the journalist to possess the knowledge itself, the news that is to be communicated. Those master artists who are journalism teachers, therefore, must also instruct the student journalists—and require them to practice—the arts of observation, reading, listening, interviewing, and organizing that are needed to acquire and fashion the useful knowledge we call news.

Some of the tasks of journalism are given distinctive names even though they are basically only combinations of the arts already mentioned. The very important work of editing, for instance, is at heart a combination of reading, organizing, and writing—and, in some instances, graphic design. Instructional time may be needed, of course, to wed these combinations, but more important are the decisions that must be made regarding selection and placement. These latter judgments are enlightened by the knowledge that is provided by the liberal arts. Before turning to them, however, we need to give thought to what Host refers to as the "external demands" upon and within the work of journalism itself (Host 1973, 12).

The Context of Journalism

Journalism does not exist in a vacuum; it is practiced in a real world and is affected by that world. Thus potential journalists need to know those outside factors that influence, limit, or direct the arts of journalism.

One of these is the history of the field the journalism students are about to enter: of all that is possible in journalism, what has been attempted? What has worked? What has not worked and why? What has never been attempted? What did success require? Questions such as these are the fires in which the theories of journalism can be tested.

When prospective journalists see the present as just one point in a long sequence of happenings, they can begin to understand why practicing journalists today do so many of the things they do and, to a great extent, why they think as they do.

What Arthur Schlesinger, Jr., said about the relation of history to the individual and the nation applies equally well to the relation of journalism history to the journalist:

> For history is to the nation [to journalism] rather as memory is to the individual. As an individual deprived of memory becomes disoriented and lost, not knowing where he has been or where he is going, so a nation [journalist] denied a conception of its past will be disabled in dealing with its present and its future. (Schlesinger 1992, 45-46)

History tells us repeatedly that things change, and because things have changed in the past, it reminds us, we might be due for other changes today. History may even suggest that a practice that formerly failed may, if attempted again today, fall on more welcome soil.

For example, the conventional news story today attempts to answer, in the first paragraph or two, six basic questions: Who? What? Why? Where? When? How? Has it always been such? If not, when and why did the practice begin? Do the reasons for its beginning still exist today? Even if they do, does the present environment still support the dominance of those reasons? Was anything else done in the past that might better suit the conditions under which we live today?

The proper study of the history of journalism can raise questions such as these. Just as travel opens the mind to other worlds, so history opens the mind to other times. The journalist who is locked in the present is the captive of a very small world.

Journalism: Law and Ethics

Journalists, like all other doers and makers, are subject to the external requirements of law and ethics. Sometimes one or the other or both will prevent a journalist from doing what he or she might otherwise have done. Sometimes one or the other or both free a journalist to do what he or she might otherwise not have done.

Consider the photojournalist who is sent to a public park along a riverbank. Three boys have just drowned in the river. The mother stands weeping, a baby, her only remaining child, in her arms. To get a good picture of the two of them, the photographer must move close to her. She does not want to be photographed, certainly not at this tragic moment. But since this tragedy is being acted out in a public park, the photographer is legally free—but not morally free—to infringe upon her privacy. Ethics alone restrains the photographer from taking the picture (Hodges and others 1981, 31). Ethics, of course, also gives direction to the picture editors who give assignments to the photographers.

In another situation, a radio journalist might want to broadcast a federal court trial, but might be prevented from doing so even though such a broadcast is not morally wrong. The obstacle would be a provision adopted by the Judicial Conference of the United States. The force of law steps in to stop the journalist (Franklin and Trager 1981, 459).

Frequently, of course, as when libel or slander of private persons would be based on falsehoods, both law and ethics ought to prevent journalists from acting.

Sometimes, however, journalists who lack knowledge of law or ethics might be inappropriately restrained from informing the public. Reporters who are ignorant of the Freedom of Information Act, for example, would be unlikely to use that law as a means of obtaining documents showing illegal Central Intelligence Agency surveillance of domestic political groups, disclosing unsanitary conditions in food processing plants, revealing the presence of poisonous wastes in drinking water, and in similar situations (Middleton and Chamberlin 1988, 478). An understanding of ethics will also help the journalist make the proper distinctions between what is merely distasteful and what is immoral, preventing him from mistakenly forgoing news or illustrations that might be of great public significance (Bovée 1991).

All journalists need to be educated in the moral principles that govern their work. It would probably be best that nearly all of them—including those who have ready access to professional lawyers—be at least generally knowledgeable about media law, if for no other reason than that a minimum knowledge is needed to enable the journalist to know when to consult a lawyer.

Information and Journalism

In addition, other exterior demands will importantly affect the work of some journalists but not of others. Graphic artists, for example, need to know that even with the compression of type made possible by computers, there is still a limit to the number of characters that can be crowded into a certain line length and still result in a readable text. Even with high-speed presses, there is still a limit to the number of pages that can be printed within a certain time. On the other hand, the electronics revolution has now made possible operations—such as the almost instantaneous transfer of both pictures and text from remote locations to centralized printing plants—that were only dreams a few decades ago.

But most journalists need only be *informed* about these limitations and possibilities. The provision of mere information is not the main task of education. Information may be a prerequisite to education, and it accompanies education, but the well-informed person is not necessarily an educated person.

The word "information" is used here as the synonym for data, facts, and materials that only need be memorized in order to be possessed. A person aiming at the intellectual qualities of a journalist seeks more than possession of a mind crowded with information. As Cardinal Newman put it:

> There are men who embrace in their minds a vast multitude of ideas, but with little sensibility about their real relations towards each other. These may

> be antiquarians, annalists, naturalists; they may be learned in the law; they may be versed in statistics; they are most useful in their own place; I should shrink from speaking disrespectfully of them; still, there is nothing in such attainments to guarantee the absence of narrowness of mind. If they are nothing more than well-read men, *or men of information*, they have not what specially deserves the name of culture of mind, or fulfills the type of Liberal Education. (Newman 1941, 154, italics added)

Literate persons need not attend educational institutions in order to acquire information. Facts can be obtained from almanacs, workbooks, encyclopedias, and guidebooks; from newsletters and professional periodicals; from the electronic media and personal inquiries. Journalists pick up an enormous amount of information every day on the job. Some of it is highly useful, necessary for those who want to know and keep up with whatever is going on in their field. But, except perhaps as it is needed for true education, the acquisition of information itself does not require interaction with a teacher. And even in the exceptional circumstance in which an instructor is needed (as in learning a foreign language), the teacher is often required only to guide students to the best sources and to enforce the disciplines of acquisition and memorization.

Sometimes what seems to be the same subject matter can be either acquired as mere information or learned as a proper object for the development of intellectual excellence. Media law is a good example of this. Journalists can obtain a small handbook that will set forth the basic caveats concerning libel, slander, invasion of privacy, and violation of copyright and that will provide guidelines for use of the Freedom of Information Act. This would appear to satisfy the needs of most news reporters. Even if one were to specialize in coverage of the courts, a somewhat larger handbook, such as Lyle Denniston *The Reporter and the Law*, would seem more than adequate. Such persons might be passably well informed.

But they would not be truly educated in media law. If mere information were all they had, they would not understand the reasons for the provisions; they would not see relationships; they would not judge what was important and what not; they would not be able to weigh likely consequences; they would not be able to generalize. They would lack those attributes that Newman ascribes to a true enlargement of the mind: "the power of viewing many things at once as one whole, of referring them severally to their true place in the universal system, of understanding their respective values, and determining their mutual dependence" (Newman 1941, 155).

Strictly speaking, information is situation specific. For each new situation, one needs new information. And since journalists—except those who handle the most routine agate material—are always dealing with new situations, their information is always a step behind what they really need. It is true, of course, that anyone likely to be employed as a professional journalist would be able to stretch beyond the mere information stage; such persons are always to some extent truly educated. It is not the facts alone, however, that make them so.

Of the many consequences that flow from this distinction between information and understanding, two seem to be especially pertinent.

Education and Journalism

Let us consider, first of all, the many editors and publishers who, over the years, have denigrated formal journalism education. "Send me broadly educated persons," they might say, "and in a year those beginners can pick up all they need to know about journalism while they are on the job." Hundreds of competent and highly respected journalists have never devoted an hour of college classwork to the subject by which they make their living.

Does this mean that college courses devoted to journalism are a waste of time? In his 1904 article, Joseph Pulitzer considered this question. As in medicine and law, he said, we once thought that on-the-job training was all that was needed in journalism. But work on the job, he pointed out, "is not intentional, but only incidental training . . . in which every participant is supposed [already] to know his business." At present, he said, newspaper offices are like hospitals, except that journalism students come to them "knowing nothing of principles or theories." Like a hospital, a journalism job "furnishes the patients for its young men to practice on, puts dissecting-knives into the hands of beginners . . . and pays them for the blunders by which they gradually teach themselves their profession" (Pulitzer 1904, 647-48).

Journalism Education

This leads to the second consequence. What passes for journalism education in many colleges is sometimes not true education at all. Instead, especially when the teachers themselves are not truly educated in the principles of journalism, they merely shower students with facts. Sad to say, this seems most likely to happen when the teachers are those who have enjoyed a long professional career. During those years, they picked up an enormous amount of information; now, in the classroom, they can, often proudly and enthusiastically, transfer that information to their students: "This is what happened. This is what I did. It worked out successfully. Now you go out and do likewise." Facts can be interesting. Enthusiasm can be contagious. Thus, many of these young people do go out and do likewise. And the result may be another revolution in the gyre: another generation of journalists enter the field, acquire experience, and then return to classrooms to fill more students with even more facts. To the extent that only this happens, true journalism education never takes place.

Liberal Education

Several times, mention has been made of the broader education—often called Liberal Education—that journalism students need along with their journalism education. Yet it has also been stressed that they need to be liberally educated *in journalism itself*. Why is not the latter sufficient? Why is it necessary that, beyond being liberally educated in journalism, journalists should also be liberally educated—period?

We take it for granted that journalists ought to understand the appropriate subject matter of their particular tasks and ought to possess the arts relevant to those tasks. A reporter whose beat is the state legislature, for example, ought to understand—not merely possess facts about—the history, workings, personnel, organization, objectives, and relationships of *that* political body; such a reporter ought to possess the arts by which knowledge of the situations and events of *that* body can be clearly, easily, quickly, and accurately acquired, organized, and conveyed to the readers or listeners or viewers to whom he or she is reporting.

But this reporter and all other professional journalists ought also to understand the nature, objectives, general means, and demands of journalism itself and how one's particular task relates to that broader subject. This latter knowledge is needed not only to know one's place on a table of organization: to whom do I report and who reports to me? It is also needed in order to understand how one's particular task relates to the other workings involved in what is usually a complex, cooperative, sequential, and intellectually hierarchical operation. Reporters, editors, photographers, designers, editorialists, copywriters, and the many others who call themselves professional journalists ought to know not only their own job but also the journalism to which they are all contributors.

Isn't that, however, enough? Is it not sufficient that they receive the education that helps them acquire the understanding and arts necessary not only to do their own job but also to understand the broad field in which they work?

No. Just as reporters or other journalists ought to understand, in addition to their own particular tasks, the broad field of journalism, so also ought journalists to understand the still broader cosmos in which journalism itself plays a relatively small but important role. In fact, just as an understanding of the whole of journalism itself helps particular journalists do their own special tasks better, so also does understanding of the wider orbit—even when it says nothing specifically about journalism—help journalists understand journalism and their own tasks better.

Let us consider, for instance, those highly typical professional journalists, the news reporters. And let's say that these reporters are covering the candidates entered in the presidential primaries. Clearly, they must know a great deal about each primary: dates, places, times, eligibility requirements, persons entered, and the like. They must know or come to know much about each candidate. Some of these facts—age, present position, previous experience—are obvious and easy to obtain. But, as was pointed out in Chapter 5, it is much more important that the voters be informed of those matters that will reveal the character of each candidate. No one can foresee the problems and opportunities that may exist during the days after the election. Thus the public must judge which candidates seem to possess the knowledge and good sense, the moral qualities, and the dedication to the public welfare that good leadership requires. The people must know whom they can trust to lead them and the country into an unknown future.

Whence comes the understanding that these are the types of matters about which the electorate needs knowledge? In some universities, journalism students may acquire such understanding from courses within their own department. A perusal of college course listings, however, indicates that this is unlikely. But, even if it did take place, it is clear that journalism would be borrowing from another discipline, from political science.

This would not be the only instance in which the understanding and work of journalism are dependent upon the knowledge and arts within the broad area of liberal studies. What journalism students learn about media ethics, for example, must depend on their understanding of general ethics as taught in philosophy departments. John C. Merrill and S. Jack Odell make this quite explicit in their book (1983, ix). They set the general ethical basis for considering media ethics, and they point out that their aim is to provide "a philosophical context for the consideration of [many] journalistic matters."

Similarly, the context and methodology of journalism history are derived from general history courses; publication layout and advertising design are based on fine arts courses; even the news-writing and other more advanced writing courses are dependent upon basic composition arts usually taught in English departments.

Also in more subtle ways, it is essential that properly educated journalists be educated in the liberal arts. If we return again to political reporters, we notice that they do not endeavor to know everything that could be known about each primary and each candidate. They would not attempt to find out, for example, what each precinct captain plans to eat for lunch on primary election day. They would not attempt to find out whether each candidate attended a nursery school before beginning kindergarten. Moreover, of all that they do come to know, the reporters do not attempt to convey to readers, listeners, or viewers every snippet of that knowledge. They may notice, for instance, that one of the candidates wears brown shoes or parts his or her hair on the right side, yet they leave these facts out of their stories.

For the political reporters (and other journalists), the work is a constant series of *judgments*: what to seek, what to ignore, what to include, what to place first, what to place at what position on the page, which pictures to select, and on and on. Even the most objective of journalists must make some judgments. Even when almost all the choices are predetermined, they still must repeatedly make at least this one decision: Shall I tell the truth or shall I make something up?

The liberal arts help us develop what can be truly described as knowledge, as judgment. No doubt, that knowledge *can be* useful. But that is not its primary purpose. "This is how it comes to be an end in itself," Newman writes, "this is why it admits of being called Liberal. Not to know the relative disposition of things is the state of slaves or children; to have mapped out the Universe is the boast, or at least the ambition, of Philosophy," that is, of true knowledge (Newman 1941, 130).

What a liberal education aims at providing, Newman said, is an understanding of human nature and of the universe in which people exist: "That only is true enlargement of mind which is the power of viewing many things at once as one whole, of referring them severally to their true place in the universal system, of understanding their respective values, and determining their mutual dependence" (Ibid., 155). That is good in itself; it needs no additional justification. But in addition to being good in itself, it is also useful. For journalists, it is useful primarily in the powers of judgment that it provides.

That, however, is not the only way in which a liberal education is useful. Paul Dressel, for instance, describes three values: it provides "a broad knowledge of the various major areas of learning"; it enables one "to cultivate those skills and habits of reasoning which constitute intellectual competence, the capacity to think logically and clearly, the ability to organize one's thoughts on the varied subjects with which the citizen today must unavoidably concern himself"; and it aids one in the possession of "at least a provisionally formed and examined philosophy of life, a *Weltanschauung*, a religion around which he organizes the varied purposes and activities of his existence" (Dressel 1960, 8-12). The second point, "the ability to organize one's thoughts," is particularly important, for it fills the gap between the journalistic arts of knowledge acquisition and knowledge communication.

What subjects should university students study in order to acquire a liberal education? No knowledge comes amiss. All of it is good, a contribution to the perfection of that faculty that distinguishes us from the other species of creation. That is one reason why those who are truly liberally educated do not put a period to their education once they earn their baccalaureate degree. They continue to travel, to read, to study, to converse—not merely to acquire more information, for information is at best only the doorstep to true understanding; nor to deepen one's self in his or her specialty, for specialization sometimes narrows one instead of providing the wide sweep of liberal studies. No, they continue their liberal education to move closer to the unachievable aim: the complete broadening of the intellect.

Nevertheless, within the few years of university life it is not possible for the embryonic professional journalists to study everything. They must make choices. They seek knowledge for its own sake, yet they also realize that the broad understanding provided by a liberal education can be useful to them. Since their work is so basically a human activity and human service, the humanities tend to make first claim upon their attention. Theology, philosophy, history, literature, and the social sciences quite properly dominate their schedules. Introductory courses in mathematics, the natural sciences, and the fine arts are added as time permits. None of these courses should be merely the first course of a major—the Chemistry I, for example, that is intended for those who want to be chemists. They should be introductory in the proper sense of that word: the type of courses that emphasize the nature, principles, basic facts, standards, objectives, and methodologies of a field to the extent that people can continue their studies in that field on their own after their graduation from college.

College Level Education

The studies that take place within the walls of academic institutions constitute only a small portion of the total education required for and obtained by professional journalists. As was indicated earlier, not only is a good amount of information picked up on the job, but also, at least for those who have grasped what Newman called "the imperatives of True Knowledge," the journalists continue to do the relating, synthesizing, ranking, and unifying that characterize the liberally educated.

Since, therefore, not all of the education required by journalists takes place within the halls of academe, they do not need to attempt to achieve it all at that single location. Nevertheless, a college is a convenient place in which future journalists can acquire the basic professional and liberal arts education that they will need. For this to happen, however, those who design and those who monitor these programs must have a clear idea of what type of education is needed.

Unfortunately, the Accrediting Council on Education in Journalism and Mass Communications (ACEJMC), the organization chiefly responsible for evaluating and accrediting schools and departments of journalism, has had great difficulty in specifying what would be the proper education for persons who want to work as journalists. For many years, for instance, the ACEJMC required that, to gain accreditation, a program must limit to 25 percent the number of courses students devote to journalism, with the other 75 percent being non-journalism courses, ideally in the liberal arts. But this so-called 75/25 rule proved to be an ineffective means to assure that students would be both professionally and liberally educated.

First of all, the ACEJMC soon became aware that a good number of students were taking many non-journalism courses in subjects normally not thought of as liberal studies. Students interested in advertising and public relations journalism, for instance, were enrolling in multiple courses in marketing, management, finance, and entrepreneurship—not journalism courses, but also not standard liberal arts courses. Students interested in medical reporting were taking courses in clinical radiology, clinical procedures, and laboratory instrumentation. Students interested in sports reporting were enrolling in classes in coaching and officiating.

At the same time, the ACEJMC began to recognize that the content of many courses bearing the journalism label were actually comparable to courses normally taught in the liberal arts programs. Journalism history, properly taught, is no less liberal than the military history, diplomatic history, or black history taught in the schools of liberal arts. Journalism ethics need not be any less liberal than the medical ethics course often taught in a philosophy department.

In 1985, therefore, the Accrediting Council substituted a 90/65 rule for the previous 75/25. The new rule provided that in institutions requiring at least 120 semester hours for graduation, no fewer than 90 semester hours should be in nonmedia courses and no fewer than 65 of those 90 hours should be in the liberal arts and sciences. This helped meet the criticism that many nonmedia courses were also nonliberal arts courses: of the total nonmedia courses required for graduation, at least 65 of them would have to be in recognized liberal arts and sciences subjects. Concerning the objection that many journalism courses are as "liberal "—using the term in the way Newman explained it—as the standard liberal arts courses, however, the Accrediting Council budged only slightly. In 1992 and 1993 changes, the council said some media courses that schools claimed were equivalent to liberal arts courses could be counted toward the 90 "outside" hours, but not toward the 65-hour liberal arts requirement (Task Force Report 1996, 102-19).

The rule systems just described are actually a simplification of the accrediting provisions currently in force. Obviously, the Accrediting Council has had to set forth additional requirements for the many schools that require 124 or 125 or 128 or more credit hours for graduation. It is easy to understand why the emphasis should be on numbers of courses, numbers of credit hours: numbers are easy to measure. Efforts to consider and evaluate the essences of studies would be much more difficult.

For example, for the several types of journalism, it seems reasonable that there should be several different types of journalism education. A Curriculum Task Force of the Association for Education in Journalism and Mass Communications accepts at least this general point, for they specify five different objectives for media education (Task Force Report 1996, 102). But their listings could be improved. For instance, the first objective they list—"to provide students the competencies they need for successful careers in media-related professions"-ignores the difference between public affairs and personal affairs journalism.

That crucial difference suggests that different types of education ought to be required for each. Both, it is true, rest on common bases, bases that should be required of all journalism students and could be adequately established through ten or twelve journalism courses.

Professional Journalism: Basic Courses

A core curriculum for those who intend to be professional journalists would include five courses devoted to the arts of journalism. Two of these would each combine the arts of information gathering, stressing observation, listening, reading, interviewing, computer searching, and public document retrieval; and of information presentation, with emphasis on selection and organization of details and clarity and accuracy of expression. One other course would deal with explanatory writing, with attention to definition, description, narration, comparison, contrast, exemplification, and causal analysis. Because evaluation and persuasion are often combined in journalistic communications, they can be covered in one more course, including the criteria for and the selection of grounds for criticism, as well as evincing the good character of the journalist, emotional appeals, construction of probable arguments, and development of an appropriate style for persuasion. One additional course would deal with the arts of editing, the perfecting and titling of the writing of another person, and graphic design.

Four courses would be given over to journalistic knowledge: one on the general theory of journalism and others on journalism history, law, and ethics.

In addition, courses in audio and visual communications could be made available for those students who wish to make a career in broadcast journalism.

Personal Affairs Journalism

But what about education for those who intend to become advertising journalists or public relations journalists? Don't they also need some special journalism courses? Indeed, advertising and public relations are both types of journalism. But both of them, with rare exceptions, are concerned with personal, rather than with public affairs. That does not make them any less journalism or second-class journalism. But it does make them a *different* type of journalism, and thus deserving of a different type of educational preparation. Like those in other areas of personal affairs journalism—sports journalism, personal finance journalism, entertainment journalism, health journalism, fashion journalism, home improvement journalism, and the like—advertising and public relations journalists do need the liberal arts core curriculum described previously. Do they also need more?

Yes, they surely do. But future personal affairs journalists need not turn to journalism departments to obtain the additional knowledge they need. Future sports journalists can acquire the special knowledge they need from athletic departments, sports clinics, or by work with talented coaches. Personal finance journalists can study finance in a business school or in an economics department. Entertainment journalists can take courses in art, dance, music, or similar areas. Health journalists can enroll in public health programs. Some courses (history of music, economic theory) may belong to the liberal arts and others (practice of physical therapy, sports refereeing) may belong to professional programs. Both types may be suitable, even highly appropriate, for the education of personal affairs journalists.

Similarly, future advertising journalists can obtain the special education they need in marketing, economics, and computer programs taught outside the journalism department. Future public relations journalists can obtain needed knowledge in psychology and business departments, also outside the journalism department.

But again, we must emphasize that true liberal arts studies, no matter in which department they are taught, provide knowledge for its own sake. Professional courses, no matter where they are taught, provide knowledge useful for the work of professionals. And programs that provide mere information, while useful, are neither professional nor liberal arts studies.

No doubt in large journalism programs it may be convenient to have special courses in these nonjournalism areas especially designed for and limited to journalism students. Some of them may be taught by journalism faculty who have special competence in these areas. But such a trend has its dangers: it runs the risk of a great proliferation of courses that are not in themselves truly journalism courses and that may distract the students from that core program that really is instruction in journalism.

Failure to recognize the special character of personal affairs journalism may also pose problems for the colleges or universities of which the journalism program is a part. Since the personal goods that can be served by personal affairs journalism are almost beyond number, the additional education or information needed to provide the totality of the required knowledge is also exceedingly extensive. So extensive, in fact, and much of it on an informational level, that does not require the resources of a university, that it would be neither possible nor desirable for any one school to attempt to satisfy all the needs.

Most universities have avoided the temptation to serve the full profusion of personal affairs. Instead, some offer, in addition to a core journalism program, several other strong specialties, such as the music school at the University of Indiana. Or some journalism programs are themselves narrowly specialized, as is the Department of Agricultural Journalism at the University of Wisconsin. Sometimes, students must acquire each type of education at a different school, as when a medical doctor looking to become a writer enrolls in a journalism program, or when a student completes a college journalism program and then attends a vocational school to acquire the specialized knowledge he or she requires.

Students who have both a sound liberal arts education and a basic journalism education can acquire much of the additional knowledge they need on their own, without the need for any additional institution other than, perhaps, a good library.

Public Affairs Journalism

Is there anything more than a liberal arts education and a core professional journalism education that students intending to become public affairs journalists will need? The answer is both no and yes.

No more should be needed for the majority of future journalists who will work in the vital field that provides society with what the people need to know in order to live well in communities. Those graduates who understand the interior and exterior demands of the work of journalism and who continue to develop the arts of journalism through guided practice should grow in competence and satisfy the basic goals of the profession.

But, yes, there is also a great need for journalists who can transcend society's basic needs for useful knowledge. The profession also needs some number of persons who can be leaders in and spokespersons for the ideas and realities of public affairs journalism itself. In fact, society itself needs such persons.

To achieve this, a new level of education is needed. Just as law, medicine, dentistry, and other professions found it necessary to develop professional education on the graduate level, so also must journalism. This was the goal that Joseph Pulitzer said, nearly a hundred years ago, ought to be achieved by the end of this century. Although there are a number of universities that already offer graduate *professional* (as distinguished from scholarly or Ph.D.) programs, including Columbia University, none has yet established an independent professional college that offers, as law, medicine and other professions do, a professional doctoral degree, a Doctor of Journalism degree that would be on a par with a Doctor of Law, Doctor of Medicine, or Doctor of Dental Surgery degree.

Graduates of such a professional journalism school could more easily move to the top of their profession and achieve the prestige now held by medical doctors, lawyers, and dentists. They would probably merit better salaries than most journalists are now paid, thus leveraging upward the pay of all the other journalists, pay now so low—at least on the starting level—that many talented young people are deterred from entering the field.

But they could also, if these new schools were to provide them with the proper education, achieve more benevolent and public-spirited goals. The graduates could forcefully remind both the public and other professional journalists of the vital need for media freedom and media responsibility. Just as the words of lawyers or medical doctors receive more attention than the words of paralegals or physician's assistants—even though all of them are doing important and honorable work—so the statements of these doctors of journalism could have an influence transcending that of present professional journalists. And, most important, they would be as well educated in journalism as our knowledge and facilities now make possible.

Without attempting to set forth a detailed curriculum for this new graduate program, we can mention a few of the characteristics it might possess.

First, all the students admitted to this program would already have earned an undergraduate degree in the liberal arts. Their pre-journalism program would include no courses in journalism itself, thus providing time for additional courses in the social and natural sciences; in theology, philosophy, history, and literature; and in such "tool " courses as foreign languages, both modern and ancient.

The graduate program would cover the communication arts that were previously described as suitable for a core undergraduate program, but with greater intensity and higher expectations. A six-month internship would be required of each student, somewhat similar to the residency required of medical doctors in that it would be closely directed by top professionals already in the field. Among the courses added to the core curriculum would be two of special importance.

One would be a careful analysis of freedom of speech and the press: of the nature and purposes, the history, the obstacles, the constitutional bases, the extent and limitations of the concept that sustains the very work of public affairs journalism. Such a study would reveal, among many other things, that this freedom extends to *all* citizens, not merely to professional journalists. In other words, it would make these future professional journalists recognize that that freedom also applies to those who were described in Chapter 2 as amateur (or part-time) journalists. And since this freedom extends to the citizenry generally, these future professional journalists will have some obligation to assist all these others in exercising it. To the extent that the graduates of this program gain positions of authority, they ought to find ways to increase public involvement in the discussion of public affairs, to promote a vigorous consultative assembly.

Just as that course would focus on the freedom of the press, another course would focus on the social responsibilities of the press. It would attempt to determine the grounds for media responsibility in the political society, to examine the past and current successes and failures of the media in meeting those responsibilities, to analyze means—both those already attempted and those yet untested —by which the media could do a better job of meeting those responsibilities. Again, to the extent that the graduates achieve a special status in the area of public affairs reporting, they will be able to exercise leadership in achieving the improvements that are needed and possible. They will be better prepared, at least intellectually, to resist the temptations of mere financial or popular success.

This new level of professional journalism education, although somewhat like that provided in law and medicine, should not lead to any type of licensing. The freedom of the press course should make quite clear that the practice of journalism cannot be limited to only a few specially qualified persons. It is open to all of us. In fact, everyone who can think and can communicate *ought* to be a journalist, at least an amateur one.

Journalism Scholarship

Basically, the second general type of journalism education, the education needed by those who intend to examine closely and then write *about* journalism-as distinguished from that for those who intend to *be* journalists—is not different from that education required for any field of scholarship. Journalism scholars, like other scholars, must acquire a broad understanding (but not necessarily a facility in the relevant arts) of their field. They must also develop an understanding of the nature, functions, assumptions, and procedures of the special research skills required for intense study in the field.

All researchers in any field of scholarship have and follow without further thought an underlying set of assumptions and operating principles. Scholars use this model, this paradigm, to make practical decisions concerning the ways questions will be asked, the methods that will be used, the criteria that will be accepted, and the standards that will be employed in evaluating the validity of the knowledge claims (Porter, Cooper, and Dupagne 1993). Increasingly, journalism scholars have been adopting the social science paradigm and, like the neighboring disciplines of sociology, psychology, and political science, have been relying on quantitative data as evidence in their research studies (Ibid.).

Nearly all of these journalism scholars are either college and university faculty members or graduate students who hope to attain that status. Since evidence of scholarship is required, first to obtain a teaching position and, later, to achieve the rank of associate professor and that level of faculty security known as tenure, faculty members have powerful incentives to produce and publish vast amounts of journalism research. That challenge has been met with almost overwhelming success.

This great outpouring of scholarly research has greatly enhanced the field of journalism. But the very emphasis on scholarship (the Ph.D. degree—a research, not a professional degree—is widely viewed by schools and departments of journalism as a minimum requirement in hiring new tenure-track faculty) has sometimes had unfortunate results.

The time required to earn the Ph.D. degree often makes it difficult for the prospective teacher in professional programs also to develop the *arts* of journalism sufficiently well to be a master teacher. Consequently, positions for teaching these arts are frequently filled by part-time faculty who are, or recently have been, working as professional journalists. Some of these teachers can do little more than attempt to replicate their own practical experience. But even the good number of professional part-time faculty who are excellent teachers of the arts of journalism lack—if they do not also have the Ph.D. degree—the academic prestige of those who are the scholars. As a consequence, the full-time faculty—and, increasingly, the senior faculty—tend to be those who are more interested in the scholarship *about* journalism than in the practice *of* journalism. Senior faculty, of course, set the tone, the hierarchy of interests, of the journalism departments. This, in turn, may mean that those who teach the arts of journalism are viewed as second-class faculty.

In addition, since journalism scholars are heavily devoted to the social science approach in their graduate studies, some of the faculty with this background are strongly tempted to cast journalism programs in the mold with which they are most knowledgeable and comfortable. Those who give in to this temptation try to make journalism education a species of the social sciences. Through this approach, the concept of journalism as a profession—which identifies journalism as primarily practical work rather than as an object of study—suffers a fatal blow. At the time of this writing, these situations only endanger—fortunately, they have not yet destroyed—the proper education of professional journalists.

Journalism and Other Education

When the Curriculum Task Force of the Association for Education in Journalism and Mass Communications said that the second objective of journalism education should be "to educate non-majors about the role of the media in society," they had in mind the education that could be provided to the non-journalism students at colleges and universities. But if it is true that our form of government presumes that all literate citizens will contribute their thoughts to the discussions of at least public affairs, then it seems that the education necessary to promote that aim needs to be provided to many more people before they are of college age. Even today, more than half our population never attend a college or university.

The ideal time for this education would be when students are in high school. High school education is mandatory for most young people, and during those years they ought to be taught at least (a) what knowledge they need to be good citizens and how much of that knowledge they have a right to expect from the mass media, and (b) sufficient skills in the communication arts so that they can contribute their own knowledge and opinions to the discussion of public affairs. By their senior year, most high school students have reached, or are close to reaching, voting age. By then, their education should have prepared them to be capable of achieving the understanding and the facility in communication that would qualify them for participation in the public forum.

Are high schools doing the job that needs to be done? It is hard to tell for several reasons.

Educators do not agree on what high school students need to know, on what they ought to be able to do, or on what it takes to be an active and productive citizen in the several areas of public affairs.

Good citizens confront the media in two ways: as sources from which they can obtain the knowledge they need to participate in the civic processes and as places that will accept the people's contributions to the public forum.

If the media are not providing the knowledge we need, whose fault is it? Well, it is often said that we the people get the media that we deserve. If the media are inadequate, then it is our fault for not requiring more of them. But this assumes that we know what we really need. Such knowledge does not arise spontaneously. Rather, it is the product of education.

In addition, an effective contribution to the public forum is not merely a howl in the night or an explosion of incoherent verbiage. A real contribution adds something worth attending to. Although we cannot expect the amateur or part-time journalists to have all the verbal skills of the professional, nevertheless all must achieve a level of presentation that deserves attention and respect. This artistic achievement also does not arise spontaneously. It, too, is the product of education.

One would expect that these two needs would be met in, respectively, the social studies and English composition components of secondary school education. Although anecdotal evidence indicates this is not being accomplished, there are no comprehensive and convincing studies that will either verify or refute that impression. Since education is primarily a state rather than a federal responsibility, such studies would need to examine fifty different sets of curricular guidelines. Further research would be required to determine to what extent the curricular guidelines are being followed in each school system (there are more than 14,000 public school districts in the United States), in each high school (in addition to public high schools, there are also 2,500 private secondary schools), in each appropriate classroom. It is not surprising that, in so vast and disparate a field, no unified research has as yet been achieved.

Even the national organizations that attempt to develop some consensus on educational programs have not been successful in focusing on these needs. The National Council for the Social Sciences (NCSS), for instance, includes, among the ten thematic strands that form the basis of the social studies standards, one devoted to "Civic Ideals & Practices." This contains many admirable comments and recommendations. The council notes, for example, that "an understanding of civic ideals and practices of citizenship is critical to full participation in society and is a central purpose of the social studies," and it proposes that there be, among the questions that ought to be examined, one asking, "What is the role of the citizen in the community and nation, and as a member of the world community?" But neither this nor any of the other thematic strands makes any explicit reference to the relation of the citizen to journalism and to the journalistic media (NCSS 1994, 365-68).

The other seemingly appropriate organization, the National Council of Teachers of English, recognizes an obligation to give attention to the mass media in English courses, but the organization has difficulty determining what that attention should encompass. Some proposals are directed toward developing a critical attitude toward the media; others aim at providing some basic training for the few students who show interest in working on school publications. And those who attempt to develop in students the ability to evaluate the quality of the media often direct attention to the mass media as a whole rather than concentrating on the journalistic media. As a result, some members of the organization recommend that much class time be devoted to a study of the comics, recordings, entertainment television, and the like. No attention is given to teaching students how to write persuasively about public affairs (Boutwell 1962).

If students are not being adequately provided an understanding of journalism and its many roles in society and are not being adequately taught how to use the journalistic media, then the root of the problem may be this: we have not yet succeeded in searching beneath the language we use and thus discovering and explicating the realities of journalism.

4

Journalism and News

An initial problem is the tendency of many journalists and other communicators to use the word "news" to refer sometimes to an event or situation and, at other times, to the material that is written or otherwise communicated *about* an event or situation. In other words, it is quite common for these professionals to refer to certain types of events as "news" and to refer to certain portions of publications or broadcasts as "the news."

Even so careful a scholar as Robert E. Park had a difficult time avoiding this temptation. He quite correctly pointed out that news is generically a form of knowledge, yet he sometimes made such statements as "An event ceases to be news . . ." and "the event under discussion soon ceases to be news" (Park 1940, 669-86).

Nearly a decade later, Wilbur Schramm firmly reiterated Park's fundamental point. He began his article "The Nature of News" by insisting, "News exists in the minds of men. It is not an event; it is something perceived after the event" (Schramm 1949, 259).

But even this forceful statement failed to nail down securely the fact that news exists in the mind, in the world between that which is known and the report of that knowledge. Thus, by 1962, Frank Luther Mott admitted that "the event itself is not news." But then, unfortunately, he proceeded to insist that "News is always a report" (Newman 1989, 47).

Beyond the fact that we already have an adequate vocabulary to talk about certain happenings—we can call them "news events" or "news situations "—and about certain types of reports—we can call them "news stories" or "news photos" or "news film"—is there really any problem here? After all, our knowledge has to be knowledge of *something*, and our knowledge is not going to be known to others unless we communicate it through some type of *message*. Thus it seems quite reasonable to focus on those realities that we can perceive through our senses rather than on the reality that exists only in the mind.

Yet the happenings and the reports are quite different things, and to refer to both by the same word is often confusing. Furthermore, not all happenings are news events and not all reports are news stories. For example, many schoolchildren are told of an event—the fall of an apple—that first put the notion of gravitation into Isaac Newton's mind; yet we do not consider that event to be a news event, at least not today. And libraries contain long shelves of books containing reports of events that we do not consider to be news reports. An encyclopedia, for instance, provides us with the reports of many events, yet it is not our custom to say that the encyclopedia provides us with news stories.

But there is a more important reason for emphasizing that news is essentially a type of knowledge. Doing so enables us to make our understanding of news compatible with our understanding of journalism, as the latter was discussed in the preceding chapter. There we considered journalism as the branch of mass communications that provides people with a certain type of knowledge, a practical knowledge that will aid publics in making good decisions about what should be done or what should be avoided concerning issues presently facing them. Once we see how journalism and news are related to one another, we begin to understand better what each is individually.

If we do not blend the concept of news into the concept of journalism, we may find ourselves bothered by questions that could have been avoided, such questions as: How recent must an event be to deserve the designation of "news event"? How new must a person's knowledge be to categorize it as "news"? How new to a public must a report of a person's knowledge be to permit us to say that it is a "news report"?

As to the first question, we know that in early periods of journalism the lag between the time an event happened and the time it was reported to some newspaper readers often stretched from days to weeks to months. In the 1820s, for example, the time gap between an event and the report of that event in newspapers of the Lower South averaged twenty-nine days (Emery and Emery 1978, 138). The October 31, 1765, issue of the *Pennsylvania Journal and Weekly Advertiser* reported events that had taken place in Rome on July 24, more than three months earlier (Bleyer 1927, 78). Much more recently, beginning in February of 1987, newspapers throughout the world were reporting the birth of a supernova. As the *New York Times* pointed out on March 8, 1987, "The supernova actually occurred 160,000 years ago, but its light is reaching Earth only now." It seems clear, therefore, that an event need not be a recent event to be a news event.

Events and News

Not all the news that is reported is knowledge of a single or isolated event. Often, the news story is the report of someone's knowledge of a series or accumulation of connected events. For example, to know whether our planet has become free of international wars, we must know the status of armed conflict in a great number of countries. To determine whether graffiti is a citywide problem, we must become acquainted with a large number of events occurring throughout the municipality. Before we can report on the spread of AIDS in the United States, we must accumulate many medical reports.

Sometimes the news is knowledge that an event is *going to* take place, as when it is announced that the United Nations Security Council will meet next Tuesday. At other times, news is knowledge of the *absence* of an event. Knowledge that not a single homicide has occurred in a town during the past year may be news. Or knowledge that a community has not seen a single case of scarlet fever in two years. Or knowledge that a tornado did not touch down in spite of warnings.

In all these instances, but particularly when no event has occurred or when an event is yet to take place, the knowledge has been revealed by an announcement or press release, but it is the knowledge contained in the announcement or release, rather than of the mere event of announcing or releasing, that is the news.

For the sake of convenience, let us refer to all of these instances of knowledge of multiple events, nonevents, or impending events as knowledge of *situations*, thus distinguishing them from knowledge of *events*. But whether we are speaking of events or situations, we have still not answered the question: How recent must they be so that knowledge of them can be called news?

Avoiding Questions

Is it possible that the connection between journalism and at least some news may help us avoid that question and perhaps even others?

If one accepts the statements that news is a kind of knowledge and that journalism provides people with a certain type of knowledge, then recalling the type of knowledge journalism provides ought to help us understand something about news.

In the preceding chapter, we saw that journalism provides useful, practical knowledge, the type of knowledge that helps people make good decisions about what should be done or not done. The type of news that belongs to journalism, therefore, should perform that function. (As we will discuss later, not all news is journalistic news.) Journalistic news ought to provide people with the knowledge of events or situations that will help them make good decisions. If one follows this line of reasoning, then it becomes clear that usefulness, not recency, is the concept upon which we must focus our attention.

In general, it would seem that, for knowledge to be useful in the making of practical judgments, it must be knowledge that is made known before the practical judgment is made and it must be knowledge that is not already known. For example, let's say that George and Marian are the only two candidates for a seat in the U.S. Senate from your state and that the election is next Tuesday. And let's say that, as part of his campaign, George has been advocating strong federal laws against divorced or separated fathers who do not fulfill their child-support obligations. A journalist discovered yesterday that, four years ago, George divorced his wife in another state and, for two years, refused to make any contribution to the support of their two young children. Up to now, this information has not been communicated to the voters of your state. Does the journalist have some news?

Yes. Although the events are old, they were not previously known by the voters and they have relevance to the decision the voters have to make next Tuesday. The knowledge will help the voters decide what they should do, for whom they should cast their ballot.

But what if the knowledge became known a day after the election? Would it still be journalistic news?

The answer, now, is not nearly so easy. Many additional factors need to be taken into consideration. For example, it depends on who won the election; on whether George, if he lost, will seek election to some public office again; on whether he already has been or is likely to be appointed to an office of trust, and similar possibilities. In other words, it is possible that the knowledge will still help some voters decide what should or should not be done; it is also possible that it will be of use to no one and thus not be journalistic news at all. Even if it is of use to no group of people, it is still quite likely that it would be of interest to many people. But, as we will see later, interest and usefulness do not always coincide.

If we recognize that news is useful knowledge and that journalistic news is knowledge that will be useful to, and is intended to be communicated to, a public, we can see that questions concerning the recency of the events or situations that are known are irrelevant. An event may have happened months or years ago, but if knowledge of it is not already known (if it is already known, it is redundant and thus not useful) and is also otherwise useful to a public, it can be journalistic news.

The Roots of News

If news is a kind of practical knowledge, it can exist only where knowledge itself can exist: in the minds of human beings. News never exists in events or in situations. We may refer to some events or situations as news events or news situations, but not as news.

If news does exist in human minds, in whose minds does it exist: in the minds of those who report the knowledge or in the minds of those who receive the reports?

News exists in both places. And news can travel from mind to mind, from reporters to recipients of reports, and then on to still other recipients. Thus, when a broadcaster begins a newscast by telling his or her listeners, "I have news for you tonight," we normally assume two things: one, that the broadcaster knows something that will be useful for others to know and, two, that most of the broadcaster's listeners—at least so the broadcaster believes—do not already possess this knowledge. And the listeners know that, once they receive that knowledge, they will be able to pass it on to others, assuming that the listeners possess the powers of communication and that there are others who do not already possess the knowledge.

It is not always possible, of course, to determine whether any or how many of the intended recipients of messages already possess the knowledge that someone intends to communicate. In interpersonal situations, we can say something such as "Stop me if you've already heard this" in order to preserve the integrity of news. In mass communications situations, the knowledge is sometimes so important that it is conveyed even though it may be news to only a small portion of the audience. The bare facts of the *Challenger* space flight disaster, for example, were news to only a small portion of the people who tuned in to the late evening television reports on January 28, 1986. Nearly everyone else had heard, seen, or read about the tragedy earlier in the day.

Journalistic News

By now it is probably becoming clear that the acquisition of news and the communication of news are not practices limited to the field of journalism. On the contrary, they pervade the daily activities of virtually all communicating persons. Even though everyone knows a few talkative souls who insist on repeating what they have already said a dozen times before and what everyone to whom they speak has already heard a dozen times, most individuals devote a large portion of their conversations to the exchange of new useful knowledge. Friends, acquaintances, even strangers transmit this type of interpersonal news. ("That section of sidewalk is very slippery today," the stranger said, and thus saved a man from falling.)

The process is carried out on a face-to-face basis or by means of letters, the telephone, telegraph, cable, e-mail, and other means, some yet to be invented. All of these are means employed in interpersonal communications.

But journalism is, as we also saw previously, a species of mass communications. Thus only when we have mass communications involved in the process of transferring new useful knowledge from the mind of one or a few persons to the minds of many persons do we have journalistic news.

Both the interpersonal and the journalistic uses of the word "news" are legitimate uses of that word. When, on a fall morning, a man leans over his backyard fence and tells his neighbor that he has discovered mowing leaves with a mulcher mower gets rid of them much more quickly than raking them, he will be, if his neighbor does not already possess this knowledge, communicating news. (We can reserve the word "gossip" for the type of interpersonally communicated knowledge that is not useful knowledge.)

For purposes of convenience, the word "news" will be used from now on to refer to journalistic news. But it is still important to recognize that journalistic news is not the only type of news. It is also necessary to realize that one type is not always more important and more deserving of communication than the other. For instance, the knowledge, gained by means of a personal remark from a stranger, that there is a slippery spot on the sidewalk, may be the most important news the hearer will receive that day.

Fit to Print News

In each issue of the *New York Times* published since 1896, the famous words "All the News That's Fit to Print" appear in the upper left-hand corner of the front page. The statement is an important reminder that even within the realm of journalistic news a greater amount is available than deserves to be published.

Elmer Davis's history of the *Times* points out that when Adolph S. Ochs became majority stockholder and when the motto was adopted, the new owner wanted "a paper whose first object was to get the news promptly and publish it with due attention to its relative value—a paper so conducted that nobody need be ashamed to be seen reading it, but containing all the solid content which intelligent readers want" (Davis 1969, 197). In contrast with Charles A. Dana's assertion that "Whatever Divine Providence permits to occur I am not too proud to report," Davis observes that "no newspaper is large enough to publish accounts of all happenings even if anybody would read them. In every newspaper office every day there must be a selection of the most interesting or important happenings, as many of them as can be crowded into the paper" (Ibid., 198). *Times* editors believed there are two broad categories of news that are unfit for publication: news that is false, obscene, grossly distasteful; and news that is insignificant, unimportant, worthless. To the extent that space permitted, therefore, the paper would attempt to publish that which was morally acceptable and had public value.

Although one might argue with some of the terminology Davis has employed, it is much more important to recognize the great amount of truth in his comments. He rightly emphasizes that much more news (practical knowledge) is available to mass media communicators than those persons are able to or choose to communicate further. This implies that news is not news because it is published or broadcast by a mass medium but rather because it is knowledge that is *available* for publication or broadcast by a mass medium. Just as news is not an event, so also it is not a story. Journalistic news is knowledge in the mind of a person capable of communicating it through a mass medium. The mere fact that it is not published or broadcast does not remove it from the category of news.

The explanation provided by Davis also reminds us that not all news is "good" news. Some of the practical knowledge *available* for communication through the mass media may be the type that is so dangerous—how to make a bomb—or distasteful—descriptions of torture victims—that people would prefer not to receive it. It may be the type that could lead to the performance of lawless acts, or it may be false knowledge. But considered in itself, news is morally indifferent; the moral qualities are derived from the means by which the knowledge is obtained or by the uses recipients make of it. As C. S. Lewis has said, "We must be careful never to adopt prematurely a moral or evaluating attitude. . . . [we are] more eager to praise and dispraise than to describe and define" (Lewis 1960, 27). Since not all news can be or deserves to be communicated, journalists must make selections from among the vast array of news. On what bases should those selections be made?

Classification of News

If we can distinguish two types of journalism, public affairs journalism and personal affairs journalism, then it seems reasonable to say that we can specify two types of news, public affairs news and personal affairs news. The latter would be the knowledge of events or situations that helps individuals make good decisions about the issues they personally are facing. The former would be the same type of knowledge except that it helps members of a community, organization, institution, or the like, make good decisions about the issues facing that social group.

Although we often associate public affairs journalism and public affairs news with governmental organizations—with the welfare of town, city, state, national, and international political societies—it is important to remember that public affairs is not limited to political affairs. Rather, it is better to think of "public" as a noun instead of as an adjective. Thus a public affair is an affair of a public. And publics include all pluralities in which the people are organized for the achievement of the welfare of that group. Thus publics include businesses, hospitals, universities, tennis clubs, Sigma Delta Chi, the National Rifle Association, the Museum of Modern Art, and many thousands of other organizations. All have in common this much: they are structured to achieve the welfare of that organization—to achieve a *common* welfare, a *common* good—and in each one, the means that are chosen to achieve that good must be accepted by all members of the organization, whether or not the members happen to agree with the choice that is actually made.

Thus, if a business decides that, for the welfare of the company, the price of its gizmo should be raised by 5 percent, everyone who is a member of the business must accept the decision. The sales people, the bookkeepers, the advertising people, the production staff, the packaging designers, the company treasurer, and all others who are members of the business must accept the price increase and go along with the choice, whether or not they agree that it is a good choice. They can, of course, sometimes continue to argue against the decision. But until the choice is changed, all within the business must accept it. The alternative is to cease to be a member of that business.

Although the final decisions are made by one or more persons, the choices are often attributed to the entire organization, to a public. An announcement might state, for example, "Podunk University has decided to build a new dormitory," or "The Happy Day Bridge Club will accept four additional members next fall," or "General Motors will spend all its advertising funds exclusively on television commercials this coming year."

Much that is true about nonpolitical organizations also applies to political societies: both can be designated as "public." This means, in turn, that many similarities will exist in the criteria employed to select from among all the available public affairs news that ought to be considered "fit to print." But the journalistic needs of political societies are so extensive that they will be discussed in separate chapters. In addition, such a discussion will be more clear after the types of journalistic knowledge that extend beyond mere news have been described.

PERSONAL AFFAIRS NEWS

For now, let's turn our attention to personal affairs news. What are the criteria one can employ in the necessary task of selecting the news that is "fit to print"? Personal affairs news is knowledge of events or situations that helps people make good decisions about what they should or should not do for their own personal welfare. News is a kind of practical or useful knowledge. That being so, it seems reasonable to conclude that the news most worthy of communication to people would be the news, the knowledge, that is most useful to them. What characteristics would such a type of knowledge possess?

Vital Knowledge

The Declaration of Independence asserts that the paramount rights of people are life, liberty, and the pursuit of happiness. Knowledge that would help people to achieve or preserve these rights would, therefore, rank high in importance. For example, knowledge of impending natural disasters such as tornadoes and hurricanes, of life-threatening poisons in the water or air, of impending dangers of war, rebellion, or widespread criminal activities would help us preserve our lives. Some of these plus knowledge of laws, ordinances, regulations, and the like, would help us preserve our liberties. Knowledge of new opportunities to lead fulfilling lives—knowledge of the establishment of a new library, a ballet company, a hospital, or a golf course; or the arrival in town of a circus, a rock group, a theater company, a business seeking to hire new employees-could add to our personal well-being or happiness. Because all these types of knowledge contribute to preserving or improving our lives, let's designate them as vital news factors.

Number of Persons for Whom the Knowledge is Useful

Since journalism is a type of mass communications, purveyors of personalaffairs journalistic news also need to take into consideration the number of persons to whom this knowledge would be useful. All other factors being equal, the larger this number the more the news deserves media attention. Thus the development by Dr. Jonas Salk of a vaccine against polio, a disease that at the time was directly affecting tens of thousands of persons, seemed more important news than the development of the biosynthetic human growth hormone, which aids only the relatively few children who have dwarfism.

It is important to stress that the figures we are talking about here pertain to the number of persons who can *do* something once they have the knowledge that personal affairs news provides. It is also important to emphasize that the persons we are referring to are those who are reached by the individual mass medium whose editor is attempting to ascertain the value of the knowledge. Thus the number of persons who are involved in an event may not be highly significant, even when that number is quite large.

For example, six million Ethiopians were victims of the famine that struck that country in 1984. Despite the enormous number of people, the number that the editor of a midwestern newspaper in the United States needs to focus on is the number of readers of that paper who can do something about the famine. If relief activities have been organized and if many of the newspaper readers are able to contribute to the relief efforts, that number may be large. If, however, the readers themselves are having a hard time making ends meet, there may be few of them who would find the famine information useful. (Of course, the federal government may be able to provide emergency help to the Ethiopians, and the newspaper readers can act to influence governmental action, but that moves into the area of public affairs news, to be discussed later.)

Implicit in the statement that the value of news increases as the number who can make use of that knowledge increases are two other values. Let's attempt to make those implied values explicit.

Immediacy and Directness

Knowledge of an event increases in value for a number of people when that event has taken place or is taking place or is about to take place at a location that is geographically close to those people, for that closeness enhances their actual ability to affect that event, to do something about it. Conversely, the more distant the event or situation, the more difficult it is for people to do anything about it; thus, the practical usefulness of knowledge of it tends to decrease. Let's call this news value "immediacy."

Closely allied to this is the recognition that the more directly people can affect an event, the greater the importance of their knowing about it. When effective actions have to move through intermediaries, there is a risk that what actually happens may not be what was intended. Our control of the effect we choose increases to the extent that we are independent of the involvement of others. Let's call this news value "directness."

For example, if the people being reached by a medium of mass communication live in Boston, then, all other things being equal, knowledge that a new supermarket has been constructed in Boston is more useful than knowledge that a new supermarket has been constructed in Dallas. The knowledge has greater immediacy.

Similarly, knowledge that a new drug is available over the counter has greater news value than knowledge that the same drug is available only by prescription, for the former knowledge can be acted upon directly by those who wish to obtain it rather than indirectly through their physicians.

Often, the number of persons who can make practical use of knowledge of events and situations, and the directness and immediacy with which they can use that news, come together and help explain the general importance of local news. These factors also justify the advice editors often give their reporters to "localize the news"—that is, when distant events are under consideration, to find the aspects that will increase the immediate and direct value for a large number of the actual readers or listeners of a medium of mass communication.

Urgency

Quite obviously, the importance of personal affairs news increases as the urgency with which the decisions based on this knowledge increases. A brush fire in the hills above Santa Barbara, California, requires great attention in the local media because, for one reason, people with homes in the area must act immediately to protect their property and their lives. On the other hand, if the event about which persons need to make decisions for their own welfare lacks this urgency, it falls lower on the scale of importance. Sometimes, in fact, the knowledge may not even be journalistic news. For instance, knowledge that a large wedding is going to take place in two months might be satisfactorily conveyed through interpersonal communications: personal invitations, telephone calls, word of mouth, and the like.

Uniqueness

Finally, when people can acquire useful knowledge about the events and situations that affect them only through one medium of communication, that knowledge, all other things being equal, has a unique value for that medium. Frequently, for instance, only one publication or broadcast station in a community will have a specialist in medicine, science, and similar topics, who is capable of understanding and communicating to the public new developments in those specialties. Or the medium may have on staff the only person who has sources for reliable information about race relations, business developments, and the like. The knowledge that those persons can convey to the people to help them make practical decisions thus becomes uniquely "fit to print" in the medium that employs them.

Sometimes this factor is not limited to a single medium but, rather, may apply to several. For instance, in any given community, much knowledge of local events or situations will be known to the staffs of the local media but not to journalists elsewhere. For those media, therefore, local news is particularly fit to be printed or broadcast. Clearly, the people in those communities cannot depend on media in other localities or upon national media to supply them with the practical, hometown information they need to make good decisions about their personal welfare.

Other Things

In discussing these news values, the expression "all other things being equal" has been used repeatedly. In the real world, of course, all other things are never exactly equal. If they were, we might be able to devise a formula by which we could measure the value, the degree of claim to publication space or broadcast time of any specific piece of news. But no such formula exists. Even if it were possible to devise one, the mystery inherent in the very nature of mass communications would continue: prior to conveying the message, the mass communicator never knows exactly who will receive it, or who will actually be able to make good use of the knowledge.

Journalism is not a science. It is an art, or, as will be explained in greater detail later, a complex of arts. But for the arts of journalism, just as for all the other arts, we can find general principles that guide the heart and hands of the artist. They are not adequate for specifying precisely what the journalist must do in any individual situation, but they do give a general direction to the work and, negatively, warn of temptations that may lead to disaster. For example, the person who selects journalistic news on the basis of the number of recipients who can *do* something with the knowledge will make choices quite different from the person who bases selection solely on the number of persons involved in the event that is known.

Consider, for instance, an event that took place in 1985. By October 28 of that year, a tropical storm in the Gulf of Mexico increased in intensity and became Hurricane Juan. Since the direction in which hurricanes will move is often difficult to predict, knowledge of this storm was news of great importance for daily newspapers and broadcast media along the entire Gulf Coast. All of the news factors discussed here were present. Life and property were threatened; people had to make vital decisions. The number of people who could make good use of knowledge about the storm was more than a million and included virtually the entire audiences and readerships of many of the media in the area. Since the storm could move ashore at any moment, decisions (Should I move farther inland? Should I try to move my valuable possessions to a safer place? Should I buy more food and candles? Should I tape and shutter the windows?) had to be made urgently. For the people along the Gulf Coast, the event was in the immediate vicinity and provoked decisions that could be made directly, without going through intermediaries. Although no single publication or broadcast station was in a unique position to convey the news to those who had to make decisions, most of the media along the coast had to consider themselves in such a position because of the extensiveness and seriousness of the event; they could not assume that their readers or listeners would be reached by another medium in time to be helped.

But what about the media in such states as Washington, North Dakota, or Maine? *If* the media managers in those locations were to employ the news judgment factors described here, their choices would have been quite different. For them, that same event would have had much less weight as news. A few readers of the *Seattle Times*, for instance, might have been intending to travel to New Orleans or Houston, but it is unlikely that any airline would fly into the area of a hurricane, so any decision about going or staying home was taken out of the hands of those few affected persons. As for other decisions (What shall I do when the storm is passed? Should I continue doing business along the coast?), they did not have to be made urgently. For the vast majority of newspaper readers in the North or East, the news lacked immediacy, and the most likely decisions to be made (Should I contribute to the Red Cross for disaster relief?) would affect the stricken people only through intermediaries.

Of course, some knowledge of events is both personal-affairs and public-affairs news. Hurricane Juan might have warranted calling out the National Guard, providing federal disaster relief, and making other governmental decisions. But, as we shall see later, even as public-affairs news, this knowledge would not rank very high on the scale that media managers should employ in deciding what news is most "fit to print."

Factors Involved to Select News

These news factors may seem quite similar to those listed in almost every college textbook devoted to news-writing and employed as guidelines by most media managers as they make decisions on what to print or air. Indeed, there are some similarities. More important, however, is the fact that the differences are often greater than the similarities.

For example, one popular textbook contains a list of fifteen "factors [that] make for news": timeliness, conflict, closeness to home, prominence, numbers, curiosity, cuteness, information, self-help, entertainment, ritual, symbolism, educational significance, interesting trivia, and celebrities (Ward 1985, 14-17). There is some redundancy and ambiguity in the explanations of each of these items, but what the author calls timeliness, closeness to home, numbers, and self-help might be interpreted to be parallels to the factors I have described. Most of the others, on the other hand—especially conflict, curiosity, cuteness, entertainment, and interesting trivia—quite clearly would not provide knowledge that contributes, except accidentally, to the practical decisions people must make in their personal and public affairs.

If most of these are not news factors, then what are they? They can best be labeled *interest factors*. That is, they are characteristics of knowledge that often attract and hold people's attention. That, as will be explained on later pages, can be a good thing. If people pay no attention to the media, the media cannot survive. If people pay no attention to the content of the media, that content will do them no good.

But that to which the people give their attention ought to deserve that attention. Often it is possible to heap up the attention factors without adding one snip to the worth, the practical usefulness of the knowledge. For example, news about a taxicab standing near the intersection of 50th Street and Park Avenue in Manhattan in which the driver and passenger are arguing (conflict) in Swedish (curiosity) because a kitten (cuteness) is riding in the front seat with the driver and because the driver has been talking to the kitten and telling it cat jokes (entertainment) and pointing out to the passenger that although almost everyone knows that adult male cats are called tomcats many fewer people know that adult female cats are called queens (interesting trivia)—such news might have high interest quality yet not be news that is most "fit to print." Why? Because the knowledge lacks the prime ingredients of useful value: the qualities that help people make good decisions about the pending issues in their personal or public lives.

Attractive News Media

This does not mean that the publications and programs that wear the badge of useful news are necessarily doomed to dullness. Interest need not be anathema to the news media.

One reason: not every inch of space, not every second of time possessed by the news media has to be devoted to qualitatively important news. True, the real needs of the people for the knowledge crucial to their personal and public well-being must be satisfied, but normally that can be done without exhausting the space and time available to the media. If we look at the flip side of the factor of uniqueness, we realize that the obligation to inform the people properly does not fall totally on any one medium of mass communication. For instance, although a small-town newspaper may have to devote a great amount of space to local news, its readers may not need from it news about international affairs. That latter news may be adequately available from national broadcast and magazine media. The national media, in turn, cannot be expected to satisfy the local news needs in every city and town. If each medium manager focuses on taking care of the needs that are unique to his or her own particular medium, time and space may well be available for material primarily intended for attracting and holding the attention of its public.

The second reason is even more important: a good portion of the news that is most fit to print or air is news that is also inherently high in interest value. This is almost self-evident when we look at personal-affairs news. Why would any public be uninterested in knowing from a medium uniquely available to them about an event that would have a vital effect upon nearly all members of that public and about which they must make urgent decisions that will have a direct and evident effect? Knowledge that the dam just upstream from the town has burst is not only important news; it is also news of great interest to the members of that community. They would not complain if the local broadcast station interrupted a soap opera to let them know that news. Regarding public affairs, however (and unfortunately), the connection between high news value and high interest value exists less frequently. Many members of the public apparently do not consider, for example, that the decisions they can make in elections are vital. And they recognize that their influence on executive judicial, and even legislative decisions is usually, at best, only indirect. This, however, leads us to a third point.

Although some knowledge is not immediately interesting to many people, that knowledge can often be presented in a manner that attracts and holds the public's interest. Interest can be created. Often called the art of popularization, this art has had many successes outside the realm of journalism: Jim Bishop recreating history in *The Day Lincoln Was Shot*; C. S. Lewis writing theology in *The Screwtape Letters*; Lincoln Barnett presenting physics in *The Universe and Dr. Einstein*; Launcelot Hogben explaining mathematics in *Mathematics for the Million*. Nothing inherent in journalism prevents its application of this art. In fact, journalism is replete with successful efforts to attract and hold public attention, to popularize the products of journalism. The consequences of these successes, however, are so many and so diverse that this subject is another that deserves a chapter of its own.

Presentation of News and Journalism

The presentation of news of all types has been long and widely recognized as a basic activity of journalism. Sometimes such expressions as "news-writer," "news reporter," "newsman," or, less frequently, "newswoman" have been used interchangeably with the word "journalist," as though the sole job of journalists is news presentation. Even the media that convey the various works of journalism focus on the one type of content; so we have "newspapers" and "newsmagazines" and "newscasts."

Important as it is, however, news is not the only type of knowledge acquired by journalistic personnel, nor is it the only type of knowledge that deserves a place in the contents of the journalistic media. If we accept the proposition that the function of journalism is to provide people, individually and as members of communities, with the knowledge that will help them make good, timely decisions about what should or should not be done, then it is not difficult to recognize that knowledge of what has happened, is happening, or is about to happen may not always be sufficient. Sometimes much more may be needed. Let's now give attention to what that is.

5

Journalism and News Coverage

News stories, in other words, are often much more complex than novices first assume when they begin the study of journalism. Nevertheless, to the extent that the story is simply the presentation of news, it conveys knowledge of witnessed or verifiable events or situations. Moreover, to the extent that the story is a news story, it carries the assumption that each fact will be understood by the readers for whom the piece is written. In addition, in many instances, the communication of news is all that is needed to satisfy the primary function of journalism: to provide people with the knowledge they need to make good, timely decisions.

EXPLAINING THE NEWS

The basic function of interpretation is to explain whatever in the simple news story might not be readily understood by the intended readers, listeners, or viewers. Whereas the writer of the simple news story uses narration and description, the interpretive writer uses, primarily, exposition, although sometimes additional narration or description may be enough. (In the Getlin example, for instance, the narration of background information was adequate for explaining the reference to "cronyism.") Sometimes interpretive reporting is added to and made a part of the simple news story; at other times, an entirely separate story—or even several stories—may be primarily interpretive reporting. In all instances a separate or separable basic news story does exist. The interpretive material is always "something more," something added to the basic news story.

The ultimate goal of interpretive material is the same as that of the basic news material: to provide the people of a community with the knowledge they need to make good, timely decisions. Thus interpretive material is not added to the news primarily to make the public more erudite or to entertain them. It is included as a contribution to their practical decision-making knowledge.

NEED FOR EXPLAINING THE NEWS

Many techniques of interpretation, in addition to providing background information, are employed to help people understand the news. Some of the more widely used are the following:

Definition or Translation of a Term

Sometimes the explanation requires only a word or two, as when the media first pointed out that Soviet General Secretary Mikhail Gorbachev's new policy of glasnost means "openness." Other times, the explanation cannot be handled so briefly. For instance, in a *Los Angeles Times* report stating that some scientists fear a computer virus is spreading, the key term was defined this way:

> A computer virus is nothing more than a program—the instructions that tell a computer which functions to perform. But a computer virus differs from ordinary programs in one key aspect: It can reproduce itself.
>
> In this way the computer virus is aptly named. By copying itself and attaching to innocent-looking programs, it can rapidly spread from one set of

software or a floppy disk to another, usually through an electronic network. In malicious hands, it can do enormous damage long before it is detected. (Finke 1988, 6: 1)

Causes

Often, the causes of an event are so definite and generally acceptable that they are merely the answers in the early paragraphs of most news stories to such basic questions as *who* (caused the event), *what* (caused the event), or *why* (did the event take place). Thus, in a simple news story about a house fire, the fire chief might be quoted as saying that children (who) caused the blaze because they set newspapers on fire (how) because they wanted more heat in the house (why).

When the causes are disputed, complex, or otherwise puzzling, however, the interpretive writer must search out those causes for the readers or viewers. What caused a legislator to vote for a bill she had previously opposed? What caused the financial crisis in Brazil in 1998? Or consider the explanations provided by Linda Feldmann of the *Christian Science Monitor*. She reported that, although Americans had contributed generously to famine relief for Ethiopia in 1984, they were not doing so in 1987-88. Why the difference? She suggested many causes: The "I thought we fixed it last time" attitude, rebel sabotage of aid, bad publicity during the earlier famine, less media attention to an event similar to one that was already widely covered, the feeling of Americans that they should take care of the hungry in their own country, the stock market plunge in October 1987, and the new tax laws that reduced incentives for giving (Feldmann 1988, 3-4).

Examples

To cover the great variety of persons and circumstances that might fall under them, most laws, codes, and regulations have to be expressed in general terms. Because the public often find generalities difficult to understand, the media often explain general events by giving specific instances. The 1987 changes in the U.S. Tax Code provided an extensive opportunity for the use of this device. Thus *Newsweek* (1988) explained one of the modifications this way:

> *There's now a larger marriage tax for working couples with similar incomes.* Congress repealed the five-year-old tax credit for working couples, along with many special-interest write-offs. This hurts if your earnings are roughly equal, because joint returns thrust you into a higher bracket. For example, take two people, each with taxable incomes of $25,000. As singles, they might pay a combined federal tax of $9,488. As a couple, however, the tax on their joint income comes to $11,052. Adding insult to injury, their income is now too high for them to take a tax deduction on contributions to an IRA.
>
> The story is different if one spouse earns a lot more than the other. Joint returns assume that each of you earned one-half of the money, which can drop a high income into a lower bracket. An example would be two people showing taxable income of $5,000 and $45,000. If they file as singles, the total tax comes to $12,282. If they file jointly, it falls to $11,052.

Consequences

Sometimes causes and effects are so closely and clearly linked that they all become part of the basic news story report of what happened. For instance, when a truck loaded with scrap overturns on a freeway, five cars, attempting to avoid the debris, crash into one another. At other times, however, the effects of an event, although probable, have not yet taken place. In such situations the media can help the public understand the event by indicating some of the consequences that are likely to flow from it. For instance, soon after the Public Service Company of New Hampshire, unable to obtain a license to put the Seabrook nuclear power plant in operation, filed for bankruptcy, Timothy Aeppel of the *Christian Science Monitor* explained some of the likely results. Because one utility has, in fact, been forced into bankruptcy, he said, the efforts of other utilities to recoup investments in nuclear power plants may be strengthened. "Utilities often argue that if they are pressed to absorb too many losses, they might be forced into bankruptcy. The implicit threat has been that brown-outs and higher utility rates could follow" (Aeppel 1988). The possibility may seem more likely now that utility bankruptcy has actually taken place. Another possible consequence of this one utility bankruptcy, Aeppel says, is that "public utility commissions across the country might become less demanding of utilities" (Ibid.).

This cause-and-effect device helps the readers or listeners understand the significance, the impact of an event. The simple news report that a man in Florida was sent to prison for rape as a result of a deoxyribonucleic acid (DNA) test finding was made more meaningful by the *U.S. News & World Report* (1988) explanation that, even more accurately than through the use of literal fingerprinting, this "genetic fingerprinting" could convict criminals without eyewitness testimony and soon would be able to do so without having the defendant at hand.

Next Steps

This device is similar to consequences but indicates a more highly formalized process. For example, the day after Lieut. Col. Oliver North, Rear Adm. John Poindexter, and two others were indicted for conspiring to defraud the United States by illegally providing the Nicaraguan rebels with profits from the sale of American weapons to Iran, the *New York Times* described the many steps yet to be taken in what was expected to be a long, drawn-out legal battle (Taylor 1988). Likewise, news stories about committee votes in legislative bodies will often include explanatory material indicating the many steps still to come before the bill will become a law, and stories about the early stages of athletic tournaments will outline the games still to be played before a team is crowned as champion.

Comparisons and Contrasts

Normally, readers or listeners can be led to a greater understanding of one thing through a comparison or contrast with something with which they are already familiar. Thus, in a news story concerning recent experiments in nuclear fusion reaction, the writer mentioned that the nation's most energetic microfusion laser has 100,000 joules of energy, and then he clarified what a joule is: "A joule is roughly the energy of a flashlight switched on for one second" (Broad 1988). At greater length, by comparing and contrasting television 3-D with motion picture 3-D, Michael Rogers (1988) explained how a segment of the television program "Moonlighting" would be able to achieve a three-dimensional effect:

> Most 3-D movie-makers mimic nature by using two cameras, spaced slightly apart, to produce left and right images. When the movie is shown, both images are projected at the same time—producing double vision if the viewer isn't wearing special glasses to sort out the pictures. The "Moonlighting" 3-D segment will rely on a different trick: the illusion of 3-D can also be created with a single image if the film speed is increased and one eye sees a dimmer image than the other. Therefore the "Moonlighting" episode will be taped at a slightly faster pace, and one of the lenses in the cardboard glasses will be tinted darker. The advantage of using a single image for network television is that people who don't get the special

> glasses won't think their television sets have suddenly gone awry.

In some instances, however, both of the elements being compared and contrasted are generally unknown to many members of the public. For instance, when Richard Gibson (1988) explained a new supercomputer (model Y-MP) introduced by Cray Research by comparing and contrasting it with an older model (X-MP), only the readers well versed in computer technology would have fully appreciated the comparison, but they, of course, may have been the very persons for whom the story was intended.

Although the devices mentioned earlier may not include all the means used by communicators to help readers understand and grasp the significance of events, they do include those that are used most frequently. They are the same means (although perhaps with different names) that are used to explain theoretical knowledge, such as science and philosophy. In journalism, they are simply put to a different purpose. Often, of course, they are used in combination and at a greater length than the examples illustrate. If the event is exceedingly difficult to explain, the interpretation may be as long as—and thus published in—a book and, as a consequence, may follow the event by several months. Although normally employed to explain an event that has taken place, interpretations may also be used to explain an event that has not happened but that might happen if the people and their leaders do not make the right choices. Jonathan Schell *The Fate of the Earth* (1982)—especially the first long section, "A Republic of Insects and Grass," which tries to help us understand what a nuclear holocaust would be—is an arresting example. And, although the examples given here are from written verbal sources, interpretation is not restricted to words nor to the print media; visual and aural materials are often used in the media with great effectiveness. No matter what the variations, however, journalistic interpretive material retains the basic characteristic of all journalism: it exists to help people make good, timely practical decisions.

Events and Situations: An Evaluation

The third journalistic genre—often called evaluation or critical writing—retains this same general objective. Ideally, it is employed in situations in which simple news-writing and interpretive writing do not convey adequate knowledge to the readers to enable them to make good practical decisions. Even after people are well informed about an event and are helped to understand that event, they still may be in doubt about whether the event is good or bad, whether it is something they should tend toward, support, take advantage of, or something they should stay away from, oppose, or try to ward off. It is the task of the journalists who write criticism to judge events and situations and to offer the public the critics' evaluations and their reasons for them.

Most people immediately associate the term "critical writing" with the arts: with criticism of books, motion pictures, music, dance, and other creative efforts. And certainly the best of such criticisms are classic examples of this art. For example, when the former New Yorker critic Pauline Kael reviewed the movie Tootsie (1982) she presented the relevant basic information about the film: the title; the acting, directing, and production credits; a partial plot outline, and the like. She also did a superb job of interpreting the film. She explained some background issues that could often compromise the quality of a motion picture, especially that many writers had had a hand in producing the script: "When the screenplay had to be submitted to the Writers Guild for arbitration over the issue of who should get the screen credit, three large cardboard boxes were needed to transport the more than twenty scripts." She placed the film in the context of a half-dozen other of "the best screwball comedies." She helped the readers understand star Dustin Hoffman's acting by comparing and contrasting the ways he handled three different roles in the film.

Then, finally, she made clear her own judgment on the quality of the film, evaluating each of the major actors and, although she was not entirely happy with the climactic scene—it "needs reverberations or an aftermath—it's just shucked off"—concluded that, on the whole, "The picture is marvelous fun." Moreover, the evidence she supplied to support her judgments was more than adequate. Readers who might have been seeking an evening of pleasant enjoyment were aided in their personal decision making by the knowledge Kael gave them.

In spite of its strong association with the arts, however, criticism is not limited to that area or even to personal affairs. Public persons and their acts and proposals, public regulations, bills, court decisions, and similar matters often possess an ambiguity that must be resolved before people can decide to support or oppose them. Which of the nominees for United States Supreme Court justice deserve public support? Which of the candidates for president, for senator, representative, governor, mayor, city council? Which bills before the Congress, the legislature, the council are best for the country, state, or town? Does the latest report about the ozone layer, the trade deficit, or the Supreme Court's decision concerning the First Amendment rights of high school students indicate that things are going well or ill?

Some people, after receiving the basic news facts and explanations, are able to judge those persons and events for themselves and by themselves, and they are able to do so quickly and wisely. But most people find it helpful to know what others are saying and to examine the reasoning that leads them to their conclusions. The critical material in the mass media provides this assistance.

Persuasive Writing

The need for persuasive writing is based on the recognition that even when people are well informed about what is happening, when they understand what is happening and are able to determine whether it is good or bad or best or worst, even then they may not be able to decide what should be done about what is happening. It is the task of persuasive writing to provide knowledge about what should be done and even, on occasion, to motivate people to do what should be done.

On April 1, 1988, for example, the Labor Department reported that, although the national unemployment rate had dipped to 5.6 percent, the lowest level since May 1979, the jobless rate for blacks had increased from 12.6 to 12.8 percent (Cohen 1988). Most readers probably had no difficulty determining that the increase in black unemployment is a bad thing, not only for blacks but also for the entire country. But what should be done about it? Should minimum wages be lowered, with the hope that increased hiring would result? Should embargoes be slapped on imports, with the expectation that domestic production and employment would increase? Should public works programs be initiated? Should job training programs be expanded? The possibilities are numerous, but what specifically should be done? Decisions have to be made. Even the decision not to do anything is a decision. Although, in this case, the general public can do little directly, they can rally behind one or more courses of governmental action. That mysterious force called public opinion, which will be discussed in greater detail in a later chapter, can have a powerful effect, but only if it is aroused and directed. To achieve such an intellectual movement is one of the tasks of the journalistic persuasive writer.

On some public matters—especially the election of persons to fill executive, legislative, and judicial positions—

the decisions of the people do have direct effects. Media endorsements, at least when they are well argued, help the public make these choices. When Sig Gissler was editor of the *Milwaukee Journal*, he said (1988):

> We simply recommend, or state a preference, for two main reasons. One is to stimulate thought and discussion. The other is to provide some guidance, not in the know-it-all sense but rather as a sharing of judgments based on research. Most readers don't make public affairs a full-time job. Our editorial conference does, investing much time and effort in sorting out issues. Consequently, our election suggestions can play a useful role.

What Gissler said about the members of his editorial conference applies also to most full-time journalists who are persuaders: columnists, broadcast commentators, editorial cartoonists, and the others. All earn their living by thinking and communicating about public affairs. When they do their jobs well, those persuaders perform an important public service by helping the people make both personal and public decisions.

If we recognize that persuasive communication primarily attempts to determine what should be done about some person, event, or situation, we can see that the answer sometimes involves decisions on a great number of possibilities. For example, faced with large and increasing deficits, Congress, in 1985, passed Public Law 99-177, better known as the Gramm-Rudman-Hollings Act. Two years later, partly to avoid constitutional challenges, the law was revised; the Balanced Budget Reaffirmation Act of 1987 established new targets and extended the date for achieving a balanced budget until 1993. But what should be done to reduce the deficit, which the Congressional Budget Office (CBO) projected would be $183 billion for fiscal year 1988? The CBO, required by the Congressional Budget Act of

1974 to submit an annual report on budgetary options, listed some alternatives. In fact, without making any recommendations—it is prohibited by statute from doing so—it set forth in some detail 26 possible cuts in national defense spending, 26 in entitlements, 7 in agricultural programs, 38 in non-defense discretionary spending, and 8 in federal work force costs. In addition, it described 25 means of revenue enhancement (CBO 1988). Thus, on this one issue of deficit reduction, this one source alone presented 130 options for the consideration and decision of Congress and, supposedly, public opinion. In 1988, numerous persuasive journalists were attempting to provide additional guidance on decisions about budget surpluses.

The Real Journalist

Who is the journalist when a reporter quotes another person, especially a news source who offers explanations, utters criticisms, or proposes courses of action?

This happens with great frequency. For example, when Los Angeles County Assessor John J. Lynch sent a letter warning that he might strip churches of their tax-exempt status if they provide shelter to undocumented refugees, reporters Glenn Bunting and Paul Feldman (1988) turned to the Reverend Philip Zwerling of the First Unitarian Church and obtained this evaluation: "Mr. Lynch is acting in a very un-American manner and his strategy is better suited to the state in Poland than to that in California." When *Christian Science Monitor* reporter Barbara Bradley (1988) asked Georgetown University law professor Paul Rothenstein to comment on the news that President Reagan's former political director Lyn Nofziger was guilty of illegal lobbying, she obtained this reply: "Because of Mr. Nofziger's high political profile, this will have a great preventive effect." A *Chicago Tribune* reporter obtained this evaluation of the U. S. Supreme Court decision denying damages to evangelist Jerry Falwell for a parody in *Hustler* magazine: "Richard Schmidt, legal counsel for the American Society of Newspaper Editors, hailed the ruling as 'a great victory for free speech'" (Elsasser 1988).

Are the reporters or are the persons quoted by the reporters the real journalists? Both are; both have important control over the useful knowledge that is communicated to a public. The former are full-time journalists; the latter are occasional journalists. But all are journalists.

Journalists are not only those who own or are employed by the media of mass communications. All those who provide journalistic knowledge—including some free lance writers, public relations practitioners, advertisers, participants in call-in shows, writers of letters to the editor—belong in that category. To ignore this is to misunderstand the true nature of journalism.

Danger of Journalism

But the fact that interpretation, criticism, and advocacy can be incorporated into news reports does give the media owners and operators a great and potentially dangerous power. If those in control of a journalistic medium wished to do so, they could influence the people's attitude toward public affairs by including only material that agreed with the view of the medium's managers. Paradoxically, the policy of many American media—again, newspapers in particular-to maintain an evident distinction between news and "opinion" material may increase the power and the danger. People tend to read news stories less carefully and critically than they read obvious critiques and editorials. Thus when a news story quotes judgments—especially those representing only one side, from reputable sources, and not too contrary to accepted values—the readers do not erect the same defenses that they build when they read explicit opinion articles.

Most journalists try to abstain from exploiting this power by insisting that a judgment in one direction must confront one or more judgments in other directions. Even then, however, a problem may occur, not because of the full-time journalists but because of media manipulators who know how to twist the conventions of the press to their advantage.

As many scholars have pointed out, one of the persons most adept at using the media to his own advantage was Senator Joseph R. McCarthy of Wisconsin. About persons and institutions—especially the State Department—he would make judgments that the press thought it dared not ignore. And he warded off the desire of journalists to compose balanced stories by releasing his statements so close to deadlines that the reporters, driven by the fear of competition or the unavailability of other sources, thought they could not delay their stories long enough to obtain additional viewpoints. Jack Anderson and Ronald W. May (1952, 266) dramatize the situation that existed in the 1950s:

> Say you're an editor of a big afternoon paper. It's fifteen minutes before the deadline for the final home edition—the edition that goes into people's homes and makes up 95 percent of your circulation. And you've got no hot stories.
>
> Sure, there's an automobile wreck, and a mayor's announcement, and maybe a riot in faraway Iran—but these aren't exactly banner headlines in a big city. So what do you use for an eight-column black "line" in the Night Final?
>
> By this time you're scratching around, desperate. And then the wire editor pushes across a piece of yellow paper, marked WASHINGTON (AP). And you read: "Sen. Joseph R. McCarthy (R. Wis.) charged

> today that Ambassador-at-Large Philip Jessup had an unusual affinity for Communist causes. In a speech on the Senate floor, the Wisconsin senator said he has the proof for his sensational charge."
>
> Quickly you scribble a headline across the copy and mark it "P. 1." Then you stuff it in the capsule and send it up the airtube to the composing room. And you've got your Night Final banner headline!
>
> There, in a nutshell, you have 99 percent of the reason for Joe McCarthy's success.

The introduction of computers has made present-day newsroom procedures much different from those of the McCarthy period, but most of the pressures and many of the conventional beliefs still exist. In particular, the existence of deadlines is still used as a reason, and sometimes an excuse, for publishing incomplete stories, even in situations in which a delay would not place a publication at any conceivable disadvantage. Thus, when the *Milwaukee Journal* published a front-page article containing adverse criticisms of the local Roman Catholic archbishop by the leader of a small conservative group, reader-contact editor Thomas Heinen agreed with those who objected that the story was deficient, but then added (1988, 73): "That doesn't mean the story, which was written on deadline with limited time for additional telephone calls, was incorrect as published."

Most widely discussed, however, as the reason for journalists being trapped into reporting one-sided criticisms is their desire to be objective. Even when they personally believe that the judgments being expressed are grievously wrong, and even when they cannot obtain any counterbalancing statements, reporters believe the goal of objectivity requires that those "wrong" judgments be set forth without any indication of the reporter's own evaluations of them. This difficulty will be discussed in the chapter on objectivity.

Although the various types of journalistic communication sometimes raise difficulties, the solution to those difficulties does not lie in attempting to do away with them. Publishers, editors, and station managers could prohibit their reporters, commentators, editorial writers, critics, reviewers, and documentary producers from presenting disputable material. The result, if such discipline could be maintained, would not only be a devitalized, but also an unrealized, journalism. A great part of the ultimate achievement—providing the knowledge people need to make good, timely decisions—would be cut off at the knees. On many subjects, members of the public, in order to make up their own minds, need access to and consideration of the judgment of others.

Considerations of Persuasion

For many of the journalistic media, especially those that direct their messages to the masses of readers, listeners, and viewers, the persuasive genre is often employed reactively rather than actively, especially when public affairs issues are at stake. Instead of initiating their own proposals for solving current problems, too many editorial writers simply react to proposals made by others. If a community is suffering from poor student achievement or if a state faces a budgetary shortfall, the writers will usually wait for the governor or appropriate legislators to set forth possible solutions, and then will oppose or support those suggestions. If the State Department announces that a foreign country is not living up to international agreements, most editorial writers will wait until the President or other government officials describe a possible solution and only then will step in, launching their praise or condemnation.

Of course, the more complicated and distant the issue, the more reasonable it is for editorial writers to hesitate to leap into murky waters. Unfortunately, though, the tendency to be reactive rather than proactive often extends to local affairs.

Locally, editorial writers can often be as knowledgeable about the issues facing the city or the town as the elected officials of a community. Journalistic media pride themselves on being known as "the fourth branch of government." They can deserve that title if they contribute new proposals to the public forum and if they encourage the people themselves to join in the debate about public affairs.

Personal Affairs Persuasion

In matters of personal affairs, on the other hand, the journalistic media extensively advocate courses of action. Much of this is done by columnists, both syndicated and staff, by hosts on radio call-in programs, and by the writers of newsletters. The topics range over the gamut of personal concerns: finances, sex, child care, home repairs, etiquette, health, automobile maintenance, interpersonal relations, and the like.

Unfortunately, viewed strictly from a journalistic perspective, a good portion of this material involves an inefficient use of the mass medium. For example, Andrew Leckey, who writes on personal finance for the *Chicago Tribune*, led off one of his columns with this query from a reader: "I'm a newlywed and trying to get ahead financially. My husband and I own 400 shares of Burndy Corp. and wonder what its future looks like long- and short-term." Leckey replied that the stock was good, gave reasons for his thinking so, and advocated "holding or buying for short- or long-term goals" (1988). Other pieces in the personal-writing category can be almost voyeuristic. Ann Landers began one of her columns with a long letter from a woman who, nine years ago, had married a man she had known for four years. This was the man's third marriage, and she said he had supplied good reasons for his previous divorces. But the woman discovered that the man had lied to her, and she began to distrust him. He was making so many sexual demands that she became physically and emotionally ill. His high-school-age daughter was having sex in an open car in front of school, his son had stolen money and was thought to have burned a car to collect the insurance, and another son was living with a prostitute. Three years ago, she continued, the man had divorced her and moved in with a woman 20 years younger. The writer said she now doubted her ability to evaluate men and wondered what she should do.

Ann Landers suggested that, from now on, the writer learn a great deal more about boyfriends before considering marriage (Landers 1988, C9).

Two major problems are suggested by these and similar examples of personal affairs advice. First are the risks involved when a journalist gives personal advice to persons the journalist doesn't know and, except in live broadcasting, to persons the journalist can't question or engage in dialogue. The more personal the problem, the greater the danger the adviser might give counsel that is actually harmful, like the doctor who prescribes medicine over the telephone to a patient the doctor has never seen. One way to avoid this is by giving advice that is general and innocuous, but in thus doing something harmless, the writer also provides responses that are close to useless. Both generality and uselessness work against the goals of journalism.

The second problem grows out of a paradox. For the persuasive writer to give good personal advice, the writer needs to know the specific characteristics, situations, background, and objectives of the person seeking the advice. Thus it undoubtedly helped Leckey to know that the person he was advising was a newlywed concerned about her financial future, and the joint owner of 400 shares of Burndy Corp. And it probably helped Ann Landers to know the many details of the marriage of the woman who had asked her for help. But the more these columnists know those individuals and the unique details of their situations, the more the writers' advice about what should be done, if it is to be appropriate, applies only to those distinct individuals. Although a large number of persons may find it interesting to peek in on discussions of the personal concerns of others, catering to such interests is not the function of journalism. Strictly as journalism, therefore, much personal affairs persuasive writing involves, at best, an inefficient use of the mass media. Media that reach many thousands of persons are providing practical help, in some instances, only to very few persons. Among the thousands of readers of the *Chicago Tribune* there are not likely to be many other newlywed brides who are joint owners with their husbands of 400 shares of Burndy Corp, nor, among the much more numerous readers of Landers' syndicated column are there likely to be, many, even any, other readers who had experiences identical to those of the woman who wrote to Landers.

There are some exceptions, of course—some questions on such topics as home repairs or gardening that might have a degree of commonality—but, generally speaking, personal affairs persuasion does not contribute to the journalistic roles of the mass media. Such persuasion is best and most efficiently done on a one-to-one basis. People with sexual problems should go to sex therapists or doctors, those with financial problems to accountants or lawyers, those with family problems to ministers or social workers.

It is important to recognize, however, that the claim that the mass media are usually not the best place for personal affairs persuasion does not mean that all personal affairs journalism should be excluded from mass communications. The reportorial and, to a lesser extent, the interpretive genres of journalistic writing serve both public and personal affairs. But, since the ultimate question in personal affairs is "What is good for me?" (in contrast to the ultimate public-affairs question, "What is good for the community, for the commonweal?"), the standards for determining whether something is good or bad and for analyzing what should be done have a great personal and individual component. Taste, feelings, private inclinations play a great part, and these are not well suited to public debate. The person does need to know and understand what is going on in his or her life and in the surrounding world, and, having this knowledge, the individual may wish to consult experts of his or her choice, but this is best done within the boundaries of interpersonal communication and with respect for privacy.

An exception should be noted for the situations in which the personal welfare of a large number of individuals is so common and linked together that personal affairs persuasion is appropriate. Efforts to persuade young people to never start or to stop smoking, to promote exercise, healthful diets, and appropriate medical care could have far-reaching, beneficent effects.

Journalistic Genres

Perhaps it would be helpful to consider the point just made from another perspective. The four journalistic genres of reporting, explaining, evaluating, and advocating possess a logical, cumulative order. They provide the knowledge that we the people need, first, to know what is going on, then to understand what is going on, then to evaluate what is going on, finally to determine what should be done about what is going on.

Often journalists need to provide only the first type of knowledge; once we, the people, know what is going on we can often supply the rest of the knowledge ourselves. Once we have been informed that our favorite route from home to work will be under repair for the next three months, we don't need any journalist to explain to us what this means, to tell us whether, at least temporarily, it is good or bad, or to urge us to find a detour.

Less often we need both information and the interpretation that helps us understand that information, but, having that, we then can judge the event and decide what to do about it. If we read that a Thai restaurant that has opened in town serves food that is hotter than Szechuan cuisine, those who like spicy food now have information of which they can take advantage.

Still less often is there a need for persuasion after the public has received adequate reports, interpretations, and evaluations. This is most obvious in the area of the arts. If a drama critic, for instance, gives us information about a new play, explains portions that might confuse us, and gives a strong, reasoned evaluation of the play, the critic does not also need to try to persuade us to go see it if it is good or stay away if it is poorly done. On personal issues, we are usually quite capable of making those decisions for ourselves.

In fact, in the journalistic situation, one in which (by definition) the critic is addressing a mass of readers, viewers, or listeners, the critic is frequently incapable of adding any useful persuasion on personal issues. Each member of the public is an individual with a private good involving unique factors.

Let's say, for example, the critic gives the play a rave review. In spite of that, many people might decide, often for reasons the critic cannot penetrate, that the play is not a good one for them to see. One man may like only musicals, and this play is not a musical. One woman, who likes plays of this type, may have an ill parent whom she does not want to leave. One man may think the decor of the theater is so revolting that he cannot tolerate being there. One woman may think the leading man looks like an old boyfriend she now dislikes; another is planning to marry in six months and wants to save every dime for the wedding and honeymoon. The journalistic critic, the mass-communication persuader, cannot be aware of all these contingencies, and, even if he or she could become aware of them, there would be no efficient way in which the persuader could deal with all of them in one of the mass media. Of course, it is possible that all these people could be individually persuaded by friends or relatives to overcome their reluctance to see the play, but the means would not be journalistic persuasion but interpersonal persuasion.

Journalism and Personal Affairs

In some instances, on the other hand, idiosyncratic differences are ignored, and the journalist attempts to persuade masses of people on personal issues. In many such cases the good to be achieved seems so important that it transcends all individual objections. This occurs most often in a situation in which the public already agrees on what should be done; they are not yet, however, moved to action. We probably have all experienced the circumstance in which we know we should do something, yet we do not do it: stop smoking, show parents our love, exercise, wear our seat belt while driving, install a smoke detector in our home, aid starving children. One of the more famous examples of mass media, personal-issue persuasion was just such a piece. In an effort to dissuade automobile drivers from speeding, J. C. Furnas (1935) wrote, "—And Sudden Death." It was published in the *Reader's Digest* in August 1935, and millions of reprints have been distributed since then.

Journalism and Public Affairs

Yet the differences between public-affairs persuasion and personal-affairs persuasion are essential for an understanding of the broad field of journalism. The most important of those differences stems from this: public affairs issues are and ought to be publicly debatable. They are and ought to be subject to multi-person, public persuasion. They are issues that affect entire groups, entire communities, *even those members of the groups or communities who are not interested in the issues.* Many persons in the United States may not be interested in revisions in the Federal Tax Code, yet those revisions affect them whether they are interested or not. Even if a person's income is so low that he or she does not have to pay any tax, that person is affected by the provision in the tax code that exempts low-income people from having to pay income taxes. Even if the revision under consideration pertains explicitly only to those involved in offshore drilling for oil, all of us are benefited or disadvantaged, at least to a small extent, by any exemption or penalty applied to that small portion of the population. Good citizens will make their decisions on the basis of whether a proposed course of action is good, not solely for them individually but also for the group or community, for what is sometimes called the common good. Whether or not that is the goal in mind, however, the decisions on public issues, since they affect the welfare of the group or community, do, in fact, affect all who are members of that group or community. And thus it is good that any persuasion concerning those public issues comes at least from all who represent distinct positions on the issues.

This is not true when private affairs issues are involved. Should I learn to roller skate? My family, well aware of my physical capacities and temporal limitations, might try to persuade me that I should or should not. But this is no subject for public debate. Those who do not know me would waste their time trying to persuade me, and I would waste my time paying any attention to what they have to say. A company that rents roller skates might run ads aimed at convincing the public that skating provides ideal exercise and a way to share fun with friends and family. But if I feel compelled to resist those suasions, I do not also feel compelled to debate the issue in public with the advertiser. Private issues are often the basis for interpersonal discussions rather than general public persuasions.

Journalistic Genres: The Role of Advertising

Much advertising is primarily news. That is, many ads simply tell the public that some items or services are available for sale at a location that is open at specified days and hours or that can be ordered from a specific business. Most supermarket, catalogue, department store, automobile, and entertainment ads are of this type. Usually, of course, the item or services are described or pictured as attractively as possible. In general, in fact, advertisements are similar to many editorials or opinion columns in that the writers select and present the factual knowledge in ways that support the views of the writers or of the organizations that employ them. By the very fact that advertisements, editorials, and opinion columns are labeled as such, the readers are alerted to the possibility that the news content is selected to advance the cause of the writers. The reporting, in other words, is not what is often referred to as "objective."

Nevertheless, advertisements predominantly present knowledge in the form of information that helps large numbers of people make good decisions about issues that are facing them. To help compensate for the lack of objectivity in the reporting content of ads (and of editorials and columns), the reader or listener usually will be able to compare and evaluate other available ads or opinion pieces.

Many ads also include the journalistic genres of explanation and evaluation that are no different from what we find in other areas of journalism. But if they also employ explicit persuasion, that persuasion relies heavily on either the other journalistic genres or the later communications of sales people. The latter, being interpersonal, is not journalism as we have been using that term.

Thus, the more advertising aims strictly at *personal* affairs persuasion, the further it moves away from journalism. The more decisions need to be based on individual criteria the less the media of *mass* communication become the efficient means by which the grounds for making those decisions can be conveyed to readers, listeners, or viewers.

Let us take, for example, the merchants who are attempting to sell lamb chops, ten-speed bicycles, Picasso prints, or tickets to a rock concert. News, explanation, and evaluations may be of value, but persuasion, which aims at urging individuals to action, cannot take into consideration all the factors that may affect the decisions that those individuals will have to make.

Interestingly, advertising is often claimed to be enormously influential in the decisions that people make. And, to some extent, it is. But the influence in personal decisions, at least as far as journalism and thus the mass media are involved, comes rarely from the advertisers' efforts at persuasion. This surprises the many who recognize that advertising is a powerful and effective category of journalism. But its strength comes more from the attractiveness and selectivity with which the facts are presented and from the selective use of the other genres of journalism, such as explanation and evaluation, than it does from any explicit use of persuasion.

When we turn to public affairs decisions, as we will see in the next chapter, the situation is significantly different.

Prior to that, however, we need to bring to the surface two points that have so far been swimming under water.

First, although the journalistic genres are distinguishable, they are not always presented in separate articles or programs. In fact, critical and persuasive pieces almost always include some news and often include some explanatory material. This is most evident in newspaper and magazine editorials, in persuasive columns such as those by William Safire or Cal Thomas, in film documentaries such as Leni Riefenstahl *1937 Triumph of the Will*, in television documentaries such as the 1960 CBS Report "Harvest of Shame," and in books such as Allan Bloom *The Closing of the American Mind*. Efforts are often made to keep evaluation and persuasion (often simply called "opinion") out of news and interpretive reports, and some media, newspapers in particular, are criticized if they fail to do so. No efforts, on the other hand, are made to keep news and interpretation out of critical and persuasive articles. The 1987 revision of the Society of Professional Journalists' Sigma Delta Chi "Code of Ethics" states, "Sound practice makes clear distinction between news reports and expressions of opinion," but this usually works, if it is achieved at all, only in one direction: explicit statements of opinion may be excluded from news reports, but news reports are rarely excluded from opinion articles. The mere fact that two things can be and ought to be distinguished from one another does not necessarily mean that those two things must be separated from one another. Some of the consequences of efforts to achieve separation between news and opinion have already been discussed in the chapter on news and will be further analyzed in later chapters.

Decision to Print

Second, the same criteria used for evaluating what news is "fit to print" can be employed in determining what material in the form of the other journalistic genres ought to be printed, screened, or broadcast. For example, a piece of persuasion would be most fit to appear in a specific journalistic medium if it advocated a decision on an issue that was vital, that affected a large proportion of the audience of that medium, that had to be decided urgently involving something close at hand that could be effected directly, and that could reach the audience only or most probably through this specific medium. The only major qualification is this: these criteria apply primarily to personal-affairs journalism. Clear, thorough reporting often provides all the knowledge that readers, listeners, or viewers need to interpret the event or situation, evaluate it, and decide what needs to be done. Likewise, reporting plus interpretation sometimes make criticism and persuasion unnecessary, and reporting, interpretation, and criticism sometimes make persuasion unnecessary. If we turn this around, we then see another set of criteria for determining what is fit to print: the less reporting alone is adequate for enabling the public to make good decisions, the greater is the need for the subsequent journalistic genres; the less reporting plus interpretation are adequate, the greater the need for criticism and persuasion; the less reporting, interpretation, and criticism are adequate, the greater the need for persuasion.

These genres of journalism are most completely realized and most highly respected in public affairs journalism. Why is this so? And is the presentation of effective public affairs journalism an unattainable ideal for the mass media or is it a realistic and achievable goal? It is now time to try to answer these questions.

6

Journalism: Facts and Fiction

It is interesting that those who deny the existence of facts do not doubt the existence of fiction. In addition, almost all professional journalists agree that there are such things as facts: true knowledge of the world outside the mind and knowledge that can be accurately expressed. If the knowledge and expression of facts are not possible, they realize, then there is no need for journalism—or even for discussion of any kind. Now, then, let's look at some of the ways in which what are customarily known as fact and fiction have been combined.

Early newspapers in the United States (and, later, other media) attempted to win new readers to their publications primarily by appealing to what the editors thought were already existing areas of interest. Most of the editors employed this approach primarily to increase circulation, but they also had the hope that the growing number of readers would give increasing attention to the public affairs articles that appeared on the same pages.

The editors were aware that people liked to read stories, especially stories appealing to the emotions. Thus they began to devise ways through which their newspapers could take advantage of this widespread reader interest.

This storytelling type of journalism has been given many names: human interest stories (Hughes 1940), literary nonfiction (Weber 1980), new journalism (Wolfe 1973), faction (Shaw 1981), literary journalism (Sims 1984), and infotainment (Davis 1998) are some of the most popular. All of them have a few characteristics in common. All name some type of combination of journalism (or at least nonfiction) and fiction or literature.

The possible mixtures are numerous. Some of the blends have to do with content, others with style, mode of presentation, place of presentation, intention, or perception—and with many combinations of these and other factors. Many perceptive books have been written on these aspects, but the need still exists to narrow this broad field, to throw some new light on the realities that underlie many of the words, and to integrate this with some of the material already presented.

One way to limit the discussion is to ignore some of the areas in which fact and fiction are brought together. This can be done most conveniently by keeping in mind that this book is not concerned with all types of factual communication, but only with the type defined as journalism. Therefore, although scientific fact and fiction can be brought together in science fiction, and historical fact and fiction in historical novels, such combinations can be ignored here. Journalism involves communication of a type of knowledge that is quite different from the type conveyed by science or history.

Several additional genres—memoirs, autobiographies, biographies, true detective narratives, and true crime stories—often add fictional embellishments to primarily factual reports. When they deal with relatively contemporary persons and events, the resulting combinations may affect the practical judgments of people who read, see, or hear them. To the extent that they affect people's decisions about what should be done or avoided concerning the issues that do or should involve those people, they enter the field of journalism, and to the extent that journalism does become a significant element in the combination, they deserve some attention.

Also, our focus will be on the effects of the mixture of journalism and fiction on the journalistic side of the equation. The combination often can have and does have effects on fiction, but a full discussion of that important consequence will have to await another book.

Finally, what about such questions as these: Is there really any difference between fact and fiction? Is there any difference between what is literally true and what is invented, made up, imagined? Is there any difference between a statement in which the thought expressed conforms to reality and a statement in which there is not—or at least need not be—any such conformity? These and similar questions have been raised by many of those who are called deconstructionists, postmodernists, or poststructuralists (Himmelfarb 1995). They are, obviously, serious questions, but they will have to be given a full airing elsewhere. For now, emphasis will be on the most widely held view that there is a difference between what is conventionally called fact and what is called fiction.

Hoaxes and Other Deceptions

In the summer of 1835, two remarkable pieces of writing were published in the eastern United States. One, "Hans Phaall—A Tale," was authored by Edgar Allan Poe and appeared in Volume I, Number 10, of the *Southern Literary Messenger*, a periodical published in Richmond, Virginia, of which Poe had recently become the editor. It purported to be the story of Hans Phaall's exciting and astounding balloon trip to the moon. Written in a delightful tongue-in-cheek style (or, as Poe would later describe it, *jeu d'esprit*), the tale is rich with specific details and makes impressive use of scientific and astronomical terminology. In spite of the ingenious efforts at authenticity, however, there is no evidence that any reader was misled into believing that a moon journey had actually taken place.

Many reasons can account for the fact that no one was fooled: Poe included the words "A Tale" in the title of the story; he published it in a literary magazine, rather than in a newspaper; the "Editorial Introduction" to that issue of the magazine noted that "Mr. Poe's story . . . will add much to his reputation as an imaginary writer." And mixed with the many passages of scientific detail are others that mention, for example, that the balloon that brought Phaall's tale back to earth was "entirely manufactured of dirty newspapers."

Approximately three weeks after Poe's *Messenger* began to reach its subscribers, a small notice appeared on the second page of the August 21 issue of the *New York Sun*. The headline was simple: *"CELESTIAL DISCOVERY."* The story was brief: "The Edinburgh Courant says—'We have just learnt from an eminent publisher in this city that Sir John Herschel, at the Cape of Good Hope, has made some astronomical discoveries of the most wonderful description, by means of an immense telescope of an entirely new principle.'"

This brief announcement whetted reader interest, but nothing more was said for four days. Then on Tuesday, August 25, 1835, in three columns on the front page, the *Sun* presented the first installment of a story that was, eventually, to bring the newspaper a circulation greater than that of any other in the world. The *Sun* claimed that the source for this story was a supplement to the *Edinburgh Journal of Science* and, according to an editorial article, it "was very politely furnished us by a medical gentleman immediately from Scotland."

As Frank M. O'Brien pointed out in his history of the *Sun*, "It cannot be said that the whole town buzzed with excitement that day. Perhaps this first installment was a bit over the heads of most readers; it was so technical, so foreign" (O'Brien 1968, 44). Indeed, it contained a history of the work and telescopes of Sir William Herschel, the father of Sir John, who, it said, had made the startling discoveries. It provided details of the casting of Sir John's great lens, its packing and shipping to South Africa, where he confidently expected to study "even the entomology" of the moon. Even the claim that there would be revealed "wondrous secrets which had been hid from the eyes of all men . . . since the birth of time" (42), had only a modest effect on circulation.

But the Sun firmly grabbed the attention of the public the next day, August 26, 1835. In nearly four columns, the paper described the vegetation of the moon, animals (some like small bison, others like unicorns), and many types of birds. Even more amazing discoveries, the paper promised, would be revealed tomorrow.

By Thursday, August 27, people were gathering outside the Sun's building to snap up copies of the paper as they came off the presses, which were then running ten hours a day. Their reward was an introduction to a new region of the moon, accounts of lakes, volcanoes, forests, and many animals, including beavers that had no tails and the "invariable habit of walking upon only two feet." This, however, was nothing compared to the story spread before the readers the next day. On August 28, with its circulation already greater than even that of the *Times of London*, the *Sun* was able to report that Sir John, using improved lenses in his telescope, had sighted "beings in human shape. . . . They averaged four feet in height, were covered, except on the face, with short and glossy copper-colored hair, and had wings composed of a thin membrane, without hair, lying snugly upon their backs, from the top of the shoulders to the calves of the legs."

This moon story, which totaled 11,000 words, was later revealed to have come from the lively imagination of Richard Adams Locke, the *Sun*'s editorial writer. It was a sensation in New York and also in many other cities in this country and in France, England, and Scotland. It was believed not only by the general public but also by most of the other New York newspapers. Why?

Journalistic Hoaxes: The Nature

Aristotle said in his *Rhetoric* (2:21, 1400a), "The things which men believe are either facts or probabilities: if, therefore, a thing that is believed is improbable and even incredible, it must be true, since it is certainly not believed because it is at all probable or credible." That is to say, if one tells a lie so enormous (the "big lie") that no one would believe the person has the audacity to utter such an outrageous statement unless it were actually true, the lie will be believed. That may be one reason the great moon hoax was so widely believed: it presented a story so incredible that people thought the only reason it could be told was that, in spite of its improbability, it was, in fact, true.

In addition, of course, people have lingering in the backs of their minds the recognition that, now and then, some things that are enormously improbable actually do happen: toddlers fall out of tenth-floor windows and survive; the 200 to 1 horse does win a race; the Holocaust did take place. Knowing—or at least accepting as true—the reports that highly improbable events have actually taken place tends to block out the caution with which people normally greet accounts of unlikely events.

Yet it must also be noted that the moon hoax stories were not the first pieces of fiction to appear on the pages of the *Sun*. Its very first issue, September 3, 1833, contained a dialogue entitled "An Irish Captain," an imaginary discussion of the "glories" of dueling. In the third month of its existence, the *Sun* began a serial, "The Life of Davy Crockett," stories more notable for their thrills than for their accuracy. No one mistook or accepted any of these as factual accounts.

Why, then, did the readers accept the *Sun*'s moon hoax account as true, factual journalism? There are many reasons. The Sun spread the moon hoax stories across pages that, by 1835, were regularly devoted to news. Nothing in the headlines, the typography, or the writing style warned readers that these were anything other than news accounts. In fact, the newspaper published an editorial assuring its readers that the stories were true. The "facts" were attributed to reliable sources: the well-known Sir John Herschel, the *Edinburgh Courant*, and the *Edinburgh Journal of Science*. As many American astronomers knew, Sir John actually was in South Africa, and he was indeed at work examining the southern heavens as he had earlier studied the northern skies. The segments were loaded with scientific "information" and terminology. Scientists did not rush forth to attack the series as preposterous. The other New York newspapers either accepted the veracity of the accounts or kept silent. And the general public thought, as Aristotle had stated, that the stories were so unbelievable that they must be true.

Where, if anywhere, does journalism enter into the preposterous accounts of Sir John Herschel's great "discoveries"? The mere fact that the series appeared in a newspaper is not sufficient evidence, for newspapers have long contained non-journalistic materials among their contents: poems, fictional stories, comics, and similar nonfactual entertainment or fillers.

The moon hoax was finally revealed to be a piece of fiction, but, *if the moon stories had been true*, would they have had the characteristics we have ascribed to journalism? Would they have had any practical value? They were put forth as true. Were they also put forth as pieces of journalism?

Indeed, yes. The first brief announcement stated that the "Celestial Discoveries" had been made by virtue of "an immense telescope of an entirely new principle." If such a telescope had existed, it would have changed enormously the field of astronomical research. Later stories pointed out that Sir John's discoveries "solved or corrected nearly every leading problem of mathematical astronomy." Several of the *Sun*'s contemporary publications agreed that the stories had great practical significance: the *Daily Advertiser* wrote that "Sir John has added a stock of knowledge to the present age that would immortalize his name and place it high on the page of science"; the *New Yorker* added that "the promulgation of these discoveries creates a new era in astronomy and science generally."

Once the hoax was revealed, of course, it had no continuing practical effect on the readers, who, before the series was completed, extended around the world. It is interesting to note, however, that when a fire consumed about twenty blocks south of Wall Street in December of that same year, the *Sun*'s accounts of the disaster prompted an editor in Canton, China, to beg his readers to ignore the story and not to be alarmed by the new hoax (O'Brien 1968, 61). The principal long-range effect of this fiction posing as fact was to lower the public's confidence in the newspaper that had perpetrated the hoax.

Journalism and Fiction

Like some practical jokes, however, fiction disguised as journalism sometimes backfires and has serious harmful effects that may not have been intended. Many of these are recorded by Curtis D. MacDougall (1940), Joseph Bulgatz (1992), and other writers. Here we need consider only a few outstanding examples. On November 9, 1874, the *New York Herald* devoted all six columns of its first news page (page 3; the first two pages, as was the custom, were occupied with advertisements) to a story that began with the following headlines:

> *AWFUL CALAMITY*
>
> ——
>
> *The Wild Animals Broken Loose from Central Park*
>
> ——
>
> *TERRIBLE SCENES OF MUTILATION*
>
> ——
>
> *A Shocking Sabbath Carnival of Death*
>
> *SAVAGE BRUTES AT LARGE*
>
> ——
>
> *Awful Combats Between the Beasts and the Citizens*
>
> ——
>
> *THE KILLED AND WOUNDED*
>
> ——
>
> *General Duryée's Magnificent Police Tactics*
>
> ——
>
> *BRAVERY AND PANIC*
>
> ——
>
> *How the Catastrophe Was Brought About—Affrighting Incidents*
>
> ——
>
> *PROCLAMATION BY THE MAYOR——Governor Dix Shoots the Bengal Tiger in the Street.*

As the headlines indicate, the writer narrated a gruesome account of the carnage imposed on much of the city by the wild animals that had escaped from the Central Park Zoo the day before, a Sunday. In addition to lists of the many dead and injured, the story presented graphic word pictures: of the lion that had "jumped into a landaulet occupied by a nursemaid and her four young charges, mangling the delicate little things past all sign of recognition"; of a leopard "killing a little child and mutilating several women who strove to run before him"; of the rhinoceros that "attacked a party of young girls, killing the sewing girl, Annie Thomas, and frightening the others terribly"; of the "African lioness . . . saturating herself in the blood of eighteen victims—men, women and children"; of the "dead body . . . of a youth, fearfully disfigured about the head and face"; and much more. At the very end of this long story, the writer added one paragraph:

> Of course the entire story given above is a pure fabrication. Not one word of it is true. Not a single act or incident described has taken place. It is a huge hoax, a wild romance, or whatever other epithet of utter untrustworthiness our readers may choose to apply to it. It is simply a fancy picture which crowded upon the mind of the writer a few days ago while he was gazing through the iron bars of the cages of the wild animals in the menagerie at Central Park. Yet as each of its horrid but perfectly natural sequences impressed themselves upon his mind, the question presented itself, How is New York prepared to meet such a catastrophe? How easily could it occur any day of the week? How much, let the citizens ponder, depends upon the indiscretion of even one of the keepers? A little oversight, a trifling imprudence might lead to the actual happening of all, and even worse than has been pictured. From causes quite as insignificant the greatest calamities of history have sprung. Horror, devastation and widespread

> slaughter of human beings have had small mishaps for parent time and again.

Many subscribers, of course, had not read to the end of the story. But they had read the early part reporting that twelve animals were still at large, and they had read the proclamation by the mayor warning citizens to stay home. For many of them, the warning only sent them into a panic. Many parents had already sent their children off to school; many elderly grandparents had already left home to go shopping. The next day, the *New York Times* printed a scathing editorial and more than a column of letters attacking the Herald's "Heartless Practical Joke." One of the more moving letters, written by "A Husband," appeared in the *Times* two days later, on November 12:

> On Monday morning, this week, a lady who was very ill was sitting at the cradleside of a dying child, when the physician, who had in his haste glanced at the Herald's headlines, told her of the "awful calamity" at Central Park. This lady's husband had gone out early, and to her imagination was likely to be in danger. Something delayed the return of the gentleman, and meanwhile the child was passing to its death. For five hours this lady waited and watched, fearing, in her innocence, that she would lose her husband as well as her baby, and when at last he did return to tell her that the "awful calamity" was a hoax, he found her nearly a maniac.

Fiction posing as news had had serious deleterious effects.

Electronic Media and Problems

The newspaper is not the only medium in which material that is really fictitious is sometimes presented as though it were news. In this century, certainly one of the most exciting and affecting mixtures of fact and fiction was a radio program. At 8:00 p.m., Eastern Standard Time, on October 30, 1938, an announcer informed listeners, "The Columbia Broadcasting System and its affiliated stations present Orson Welles and the *Mercury Theatre on the Air* in *War of the Worlds* by H. G. Wells." Orson Welles was introduced, and he set the scene—the present time, in this country—for the drama that was to follow. By 8:03, the performance was under way, and it proceeded uninterrupted until the middle break at approximately 8:30.

The story begins with a weather report, then moves to a remote broadcast of "the music of Ramon Raquello and his orchestra" at the Hotel Park Plaza in New York. After a few seconds of music, an announcer interrupts to report that "Professor Farrell of the Mount Jennings Observatory, Chicago, Illinois, reports observing several explosions of incandescent gas, occurring at regular intervals on the planet Mars." More music, more interruptions, all in the style of the radio bulletins typical of those years. The listeners are told that a huge cylinder has struck the earth on the Wilmuth farm, Grovers Mill, New Jersey. Radio correspondents move quickly to the scene and give on-the-spot reports. The cylinder opens up. Unbelievable "things" emerge. Jets of flame leap out. State troopers, who arrived to control the crowd, are among those killed. The counties of Mercer and Middlesex "as far west as Princeton" are placed under martial law. Seven thousand infantrymen are brought in and surround the cylinder, but within seconds all but one hundred and twenty of them are killed by lethal heat rays. The station switches to Washington for a special broadcast by the secretary of the interior, but his plea for calm is ignored as bulletins report more cylinders hitting the earth, more invaders moving at express-train speed. Army bombers fail to stop them. They emit a poisonous black smoke as they move toward New York. An announcer on the roof of the broadcasting building describes millions of people dashing out of the city as the enemy is sighted above the Palisades: "Five great machines. First one is crossing the river. I can see it from here, wading the Hudson like a man wading through a brook. . . . A bulletin's handed me . . . Martian cylinders are falling all over the country. One outside Buffalo, one in Chicago, St. Louis. . . ." As the enemy moves closer, the announcer's voice fades away.

The program reaches its middle break, with the reminder to the listeners that they are listening to an "original dramatization of War of the Worlds by H. G. Wells." The second half-hour of the program lacked the fast pace and vivid immediacy of the first half, but by that time much of its effect had already been felt.

Fortuitously, just a year before the program was broadcast, the Rockefeller Foundation had given a grant to establish an Office of Radio Research, with Paul F. Lazarsfeld as director and Frank Stanton and Hadley Cantril as associate directors. The program provided an unexpected "experimental" situation in which they could study the program and its effects, and thus we have a more precise knowledge of the consequences than was possible with the moon or wild animal hoaxes.

In his book *The Invasion from Mars*, Cantril (1952, 47) summarizes some of the research findings:

> Long before the broadcast had ended, people all over the United States were praying, crying, fleeing frantically to escape death from the Martians. Some ran to loved ones. Others telephoned farewells or warnings, hurried to inform neighbors, sought information from newspapers or radio stations, summoned ambulances and police cars. At least six million people heard the broadcast. At least a million of them were frightened or disturbed.

What caused the panic? For one, people had begun to rely on radio as an accepted vehicle for important announcements. It was not unusual for musical or dramatic programs to be interrupted to alert the listeners to important news events. The style of such interruptions was carefully mimicked by the Mercury Theatre players. The program named real counties, cities, towns, highways, bridges, and other places. And the names given to experts and military organizations (although fictitious) had the ring of reality. Most important: other than the first brief announcement of the fictional character of what was to follow—an announcement missed or ignored by a large percentage of the audience—there were no other warnings during the first half of the program that the broadcast was anything other than enormously important news. Thus, although the media, the content, the organization, the style, the effects, and even the intentions might have been different, the moon hoax, the wild animal hoax, and the Martian invasion program had certain important elements in common. In all of them, fiction was presented as though it were journalistic news, and the public was not adequately informed that this was taking place. As a result, in all of them, people were misled. In all instances, this misleading had practical consequences, sometimes very serious ones.

Effect and Confusion

On November 15, 1983, many newspapers throughout the United States printed a column by Art Buchwald, distributed by the Los Angeles Times Syndicate. The first part of the column stated that New York City, instead of spending millions of dollars to wipe out urban decay, was using $300,000 of federal funds to drape the exteriors of burned-out, window-shattered tenements in the South Bronx with sheets of vinyl on which were painted "windows with curtains, shades and flowerpots, and nice varnished doors." "According to city officials," Buchwald said, "the facades will definitely improve the look of the neighborhood.

Buchwald devoted the rest of the column to his discussion of this event with "Humberto Cortez, a New

York taxi driver, who was trying to take me cross-town on 37th St. the other day." According to Buchwald, Cortez suggested that, instead of covering the blight with "vinyl decals," the government should invite Fidel Castro "to build a 10,000-foot airplane runway in the South Bronx." This would lead to war with Cuba, and, after the war, the Americans would have to send in foreign aid to help the Bronx get back on its feet. "The president will go to Congress," Buchwald quoted Cortez as saying, "and ask for millions of dollars to keep the borough from falling into the communist camp." Buchwald replied, "It's the wildest idea I've ever heard of," and quoted Cortez as saying, "It isn't half as crazy as covering up a city's urban decay with a bunch of phony vinyl fronts."

Even granting Buchwald some latitude because of his reputation as a humorist, most readers would be moved to wonder how much of this is a factual report. How much, if any, is made up, is a fiction? Readers with access to news sources such as the November 13, 1983, *New York Times* or the November 21, 1983, *New Yorker* magazine might have learned that the first part of Buchwald's column was generally true. But no one other than Buchwald himself (and Humberto Cortez, if he exists) can vouch for the later material. Buchwald (1981, 21) has claimed, "There are about three or four of us [columnists] whose poetic license is accepted by the reading public." Even if that unsubstantiated statement is true, it does not eliminate the confusion felt by readers of his column.

Confusion can breed distrust. That is, confused readers can resolve their confusion by deciding, "I can't tell what, if any, of this is true, so I simply won't take any of it seriously." They may thus protect themselves from being misled, but they may also prevent themselves from acquiring some of the knowledge they need as individuals or citizens.

One single column or even one single columnist will not destroy the trust that the news media must have if they are to contribute to fulfilling the goals of journalism. Mixture of journalistic fact and fiction and the attendant misdirection or confusion, however, are not limited to a single column or a rare broadcast or news story. Moreover, even if not prevalent, these combinations, when they confuse or are revealed to have been misleading, receive such extensive publicity that their adverse effects on public confidence are greatly magnified. One need think only of Janet Cooke *Washington Post* story about Jimmy or the Dateline NBC broadcast about a doctored General Motors pickup truck.

The Other Story

"Jimmy is 8 years old and a third-generation heroin addict, a precocious little boy with sandy hair, velvety brown eyes and needle marks freckling the baby-smooth skin of his thin brown arms." Thus began the 2,256-word story written by twenty-six-year-old Janet Cooke for the Sunday, September 28, 1980, edition of the *Washington Post.* That edition had a circulation of 892,220.

The dramatic, highly detailed story tugged at the hearts of many of those readers. The story did not contain the full name and address of Jimmy; thus many readers wanted to know where he could be found so that he could be helped. Washington Police Chief Burtell Jefferson launched a mammoth, citywide search. All schools, social services, and police contacts were asked for Jimmy's whereabouts. Reward money was made available. More than fifty letters were sent to the editor. Cooke was warned that she might be killed. The police threatened to subpoena Cooke and require her to reveal names and addresses. The *Post* editors stood behind her and the pledge of confidentiality she said she had given her sources.

On April 13, 1981, the news went out that Janet Cooke had won the Pulitzer Prize for local news reporting—for her story about Jimmy. The *Toledo Blade*, where Cooke had previously worked, noticed discrepancies between the biographical material that accompanied the story and the information the *Blade* had about her. The *Post* began a very thorough check. On the morning of April 15, Cooke wrote a longhand note for her employers:

> "Jimmy's World" was in essence a fabrication. I never encountered or interviewed an 8-year-old heroin addict. The September 28, 1980, article in *The Washington Post* was a serious misrepresentation which I deeply regret. I apologize to my newspaper, my profession, the Pulitzer board and all seekers of the truth. Today, in facing up to the truth, I have submitted my resignation. (Green 1981, A14)

The Pulitzer Prize was returned and Janet Cooke's promising career in journalism was ended. Dutifully, the *Post* invited its ombudsman, Bill Green, to tell the entire story, and he used more than three-and-a-half pages in the Sunday edition of April 19, 1981, to do so. The *Post* editors no doubt hoped this act of contrition would wipe away some of the shame they felt. The same edition of the paper also contained an article by *Post* columnist Haynes Johnson in which he confessed that Cooke's story "has left a grievous open wound that will be long in healing and never, I believe, forgotten." He added, "Certain techniques of the so-called 'New Journalism' . . . are eroding public trust in the reliability of reporting."

Dateline NBC

The November 17, 1992, news program Dateline NBC included a segment called "Waiting to Explode?" It purported to show what could happen when a car crashes into the side of a General Motors pickup truck. First, one car was shown crashing into a GM truck at "about 40 mph." Nothing happened. During a second test, "at around 30 mph," however, the truck burst into flames. This scene was replayed in slow motion.

The program was broadcast during the November "sweeps week," a period when the size of broadcast audiences is rated, measurements that help tell advertisers which are the most popular programs. Dateline NBC was on the screen in 11 million households.

The demonstration was both dramatic and, for many viewers, frightening. NBC, however, had neglected to tell those millions of people some important facts: that, to ensure there would be a explosion, Dateline NBC had overfilled the gas tank, used the wrong type of gas cap, and, most important, attached spark-producing and remote-controlled toy rocket engines to the pickup trucks.

General Motors Corporation sued NBC for defamation. NBC settled by making an on-air apology, stating that the demonstration was a "bad idea from start to finish," that it "was inappropriate and does not support the position that GM CK trucks are defective," and concluding "that unscientific demonstrations should have no place in hard news stories at NBC."

Both television executives and media analysts severely criticized the Dateline NBC program. Howard Kurtz (who writes for the *Washington Post*) summed up the reactions: "With one brief, fiery truck crash, NBC may have sent much of its credibility up in flames" (Kurtz 1993).

Belief and Journalsim

In what was almost a throw-away line, Samuel Taylor Coleridge mentioned in his *Biographia Literaria* (1817, 2:6) the "willing suspension of disbelief for the moment, which constitutes poetic faith." The expression "willing suspension of disbelief" was soon seized upon by literary critics and is quoted time and again to this day. It has become a dictum setting forth the precondition to our enjoyment of fiction and poetry: we must set aside, at least for the time of our reading or viewing, any misgivings we might have concerning the factual truthfulness of fictional works. The idea is quite similar to the notion that any artist must be granted his *donnée*, his "given," or starting point. The assumption is that anyone who wishes to enjoy a work of fine art must accept the world created by the artist and protest only if, within that world, the characters, feelings, actions, and other constituents of the fictional work are implausible. Thus, to enjoy Lewis Carroll *Through the Looking Glass*, we readers must set aside the disbelief that tells us there is no world on the other side of a mirror and that one cannot walk through the mirror and enter that other world. The role of belief in fiction is, of course, much more complex than this (Abrams 1958; Koelb 1984), but the very persistence of the notion of the willing suspension of disbelief helps certify the basic value of that viewpoint.

A corollary to the Coleridge dictum, unfortunately, has not been given equal attention. Just as the enjoyment of fiction usually presupposes the willing suspension of disbelief, so the good use of journalism assumes something quite different: an assumption of belief. That is, the recipient of journalistic knowledge must begin that reception with the assumption that what is being communicated is true and can be believed. Journalism itself requires a resistance to disbelief. No doubt, journalistic belief will be a wary belief, and there may be many instances in which the consumer of journalism will be disappointed, in which his or her faith in the strict veracity and accuracy of the journalist will be misplaced. Just as fiction does not always possess the plausibility or the verisimilitude, we rightfully expect after we have granted the creator his or her *donnée*, so also journalism does not always satisfy our assumption and expectation that every statement is literally true. Yet it is part of the very nature of journalism that we face each statement with the assumption and expectation that it is.

Why? One reason is that most of the knowledge conveyed by journalism is received by us as secondhand knowledge. It is knowledge that is first of all known by a journalist and then reported to us. Rarely do the recipients of journalistic knowledge have the opportunity to acquire the knowledge firsthand. Thus we, the recipients of journalism, must trust the accuracy and veracity of other people, of the journalists who are reporting to us.

Even in those instances in which we, the public, seem to be provided by the journalistic media with firsthand access to or "live" coverage of events, we must begin by believing that what we are hearing or seeing is, in truth, what the operators of the media tell us we are hearing or seeing. When a newspaper tells us that what follows is the verbatim text of a recent U.S. Supreme Court decision, we assume that, indeed, that is what we see set forth on the page. When a television station tells us that the next person we see and hear will be the President of the United States speaking on an economic crisis, we assume that what we next see is, indeed, the President and not some person impersonating him. When millions of people tuned into the O. J. Simpson trial, they all assumed that, indeed, that is what they were witnessing, not some piece of fiction.

We do not have the time or resources to check and attempt to verify every piece of knowledge that journalists set before us. The practical use we make of journalism requires that we have faith in the journalists. Whenever that faith is eroded—whether by lies, mistakes, or fiction—both journalism and the consumers of journalism suffer.

New Journalism

Even Tom Wolfe, whose name seems to be linked inextricably with the expression "new journalism," stated quite bluntly, "To tell the truth, I've never even liked the term" (Wolfe 1973, 23). Nevertheless, "new journalism" is a handy pair of words to designate those works that attempt to pull together the best of two arts: factual reporting and literary creation.

As already noted, the combination can pose a great danger to journalism. But does this mean that neither one can borrow and gain from the other? This is not the place to examine what, if anything, fiction can gain from journalism. It is the place, however, to consider the opposite, the possibility that, in spite of all dangers, journalism might gain something from incorporating at least some of the elements normally associated with fiction.

Paula LaRocque, writing coach for the *Dallas Morning News*, thinks the gain can be great:

> The word "fiction" often frightens people who deal in fact, but it needn't. Many of the devices that work well in fictional storytelling also work well in factual storytelling. Content rather than mechanics is the critical thing: One story may be actual and the other created, but both are more (or less) interesting because of how they're told. (LaRocque 1994, 55)

Such techniques as simile, metaphor, analogy, foreshadowing, and symbolism-normally associated with fiction—can, she says, add color, depth, and energy to journalistic writing. Wolfe, turning to the realistic novel for hints at literary devices that might be effectively used in journalistic stories, mentions scene-byscene construction, dialogue, point of view, and the detailing of status life (Wolfe 1973, 31ff). "Status life," Wolfe explains, encompasses "the entire pattern of behavior and possessions through which people express their position in the world or what they think it is or what they hope it is to be".

Of these literary techniques, only point of view, in which the journalist attempts to "penetrate the thoughts of another person," seems to pose an obvious danger, the danger of violating what John Hersey called the "one sacred rule of journalism. The writer must not invent" (Hersey 1980, 2).

In addition to the obvious danger that the journalist borrowing from fiction might stray into the fields of invention, there is another, much more subtle danger.

News and Appearances

Readers have become accustomed to seeing works of journalism appear in specific kinds of settings. This is most obvious, of course, in the newspaper, with its unbound sheets of paper, its large page size, and its special typography. The appearance of material in that distinctive location signals to us, "This is a place you can expect to find pieces of useful knowledge: reports, explanations, evaluations, exhortations regarding the issues facing you as individuals or members of groups." If a poem or a short story is inserted in a newspaper, we expect to be advised by format or label that this other material is not a product of journalism.

Even the media that have a great quantity or even a preponderance of fictional or entertaining material are normally careful to let the public know what is journalism and what is not. On radio, the news, talk show, and advertising segments usually can be easily distinguished from the classical or popular music programs. On television, such designations as 60 Minutes or Dateline or simply the 6 O'Clock News will be sufficient to enable viewers to separate journalism from entertainment.

Popular magazines pose a greater problem, but most of them label their contents in ways that enable readers to distinguish journalistic fact from other types of verbal or visual material. The table of contents of the *New Yorker*, *Esquire*, or the *Atlantic Monthly*, for example, will guide the readers through the forest of genres. And the scholarly journals, which constitute the overwhelming majority of periodicals, carefully distinguish their news notes (if any) from the material of perennial value. Where then, if anywhere, are the problems?

The problems exist, first, wherever there is not a match between what, because of appearances or usual modes of presentation, members of the public expect and what they are given. The "moon hoax" stories appeared in those sections of the newspaper where the readers expected to find news, and they were presented in the style of news stories. But these appearances did not match the reality: the moon hoax stories were fiction, not journalistic fact. The same was true of "Jimmy's World," the Dateline NBC segment about the truck crash, and, with a qualification to be discussed in a moment, the story about wild animals escaping from the Central Park Zoo. *War of the Worlds*, although it attempted to be fiction, had almost all the "appearances" of journalism and was accepted by the listeners as such, in spite of some effort to alert readers to the fact that it was not journalism. The Buchwald column appeared where readers usually expect to find journalism but was written as though it might be fiction.

In addition, even where readers or listeners were warned that the presentation was not what they ordinarily would expect, the warning was inadequate. In the story about the animals escaping from the zoo, the warning came at the very end of a long story, a place that many readers never reached. In the Orson Welles program, the warnings came early—before listeners had tuned in—or much later, after the most misleading segments had been broadcast and had already caused a panic.

"Appearances," therefore, establish certain expectations in the minds of the public. Those expectations result not only from distinctive format, typography, and labels (or lack of labels), but also from the style and arrangement employed by the journalist on the one hand and the fiction writer on the other. Readers, listeners, and viewers of news stories and programs, for example, have become accustomed to receiving the most important material first and the less or least important material later in the story or broadcast. This "inverted pyramid" structure applies not only to the organization of individual stories but also to the relative positions of stories within a publication or broadcast: the reports of what the editors judge to be the most important events are given the leading positions. But it is within the individual stories that, for purposes of our present analysis, this element of style plays an important role.

The journalistic inverted pyramid structure is just the opposite of that found in most fiction. In fiction, the most important material—the climax, the dénouement—is usually located at or near the end of the story. In at least a small way, therefore, one type of organization can signal to the public that the story purports to be a piece of journalism and another type that the story purports to be a piece of fiction.

The same is true of most of the techniques that LaRocque, Wolfe, and other "new journalism" proponents recommend. For example, comparisons (involving a relationship of like to like) fit in well with journalism; similes and metaphors (involving a relationship of things literally unlike one another) are more characteristic of poetry and fiction. Likewise, the public has come to expect quotations and paraphrases in news stories and tends to associate dialogue with a work of fiction.

Does this mean that works of journalism must be void, strictly and totally, of any stylistic or organizational devices normally associated with fiction? No. But they need to be used with care and only when appropriate. They are sparks that, if left uncontrolled, can incinerate a news story. The careful journalist can exert control by using the fictional techniques sparingly, not giving in to the temptation to employ all of them in a single story. For instance, consider the beginning of the following Knight Ridder story, reprinted by Fred Fedler in his book *Reporting for the Print Media* (1989, 117):

> SAN JOSE, Calif.—The man who called the state Employment Development Department last week said he wanted to hire 70 or 80 people to tear down a vacant house in East San Jose in a hurry.
>
> He got action.
>
> About 75 men, jobless and hungry for the job, offered $5 an hour, set about the task with zeal. By Tuesday morning, only the foundation and the floor remained—and the floor was disappearing fast.
>
> That's when the owner, Mark Campbell, showed up.
>
> "He asked us, 'Who gave you permission to tear my house down?'" said Robert Robinson, one of the workers. "He told us to get the hell off his property. We didn't know we were tearing down somebody's house we weren't supposed to."

The organization of the story is chronological. Unlike the normal journalistic story that would tell readers in the first paragraph that workmen had torn down the wrong house, this story delays that main point until the fifth paragraph. Otherwise, the style is that of a normal piece of journalism. It is not loaded with metaphors, similes, foreshadowing, dialogue, the detailing of status life, or other techniques often associated with fiction. Although some of the techniques associated with fiction writing are used in this story—probably with the result of raising reader interest in the report—they are used with restraint. Readers are not likely to be confused as to whether they are reading fact or fiction.

No doubt, an even greater use of fictional techniques than was used in the story just cited is possible without misleading or confusing the public. Consider, for example, the following story, printed in the *Minneapolis Tribune* and other newspapers in 1925:

> THE TALE OF A HORN AND A WISE JUDGE
>
> Chicago, Nov. 18—Now it came to pass in the reign of Calvin the Silent that two musicians brought a certain matter to a judge of the city for settlement. And the judge was John Richardson, and great was his wisdom.
>
> And with them they brought a cornet, and shewed it unto him. And one saith: "It is mine." And the other saith, "Nay, my lord, but it is mine, and this nutty bimbo hath swiped it from mine house."
>
> And the judge was sore vexed to know which of the twain spake the truth. But he had a hunch, and spake unto the one: "Let's hear you play it."
>
> And the one to whom he spake took the instrument, and swelling up like one sick with the dropsy, he blew it with all his strength. And it was a sour note, so that the judge lay as one dead and those who were in the court cried out to put the musician to death, saying he was a murderer as well as a thief.
>
> But he heeded them not, and blew a second time and the plaster fell like rain, and a centurion named

> Gilhooley came with certain of his men to carry him out to be stoned.
>
> But the judge awakened from his swoon and would not suffer them to kill him until his adversary had blown upon the horn.
>
> "But remember when thou blowest," he spake unto the other, "that if the note is not dulcet and easily harkened unto, thou shall be torn asunder and thy bones divided among the junkmen who have paid their tax."
>
> And the other blew, and lo, it was music, even as Alexander's Ragtime Band. And the centurions and those who were in court danced and made merry.
>
> Then saith the judge unto him who had first blown upon the horn: "Thought you could outsmart me, hey? Throw him into the hoosegow."
>
> And they cast him into a place of utter darkness. And his name was Walter Berry.
>
> But on the other, Preston Helm, he bestowed much praise and gave him the horn. And the fame of his wisdom was noised abroad.

What is fact here? What is fiction? (And does it really matter which is which?) Well, it is quite likely the following is factually true: that the police brought before Judge John Richardson in Chicago on or about November 18 two men, Walter Berry and Preston Helm, both of whom claimed ownership of a cornet. And the judge, to resolve the conflict, asked each to play the instrument, and Helm played it so much better than Berry that he was awarded the horn.Most of the rest of the story, a parody in both language and content of the Old Testament account of King Solomon's procedure for determining which of two women was the mother of the infant whom both of them claimed (1 Kings 3:16-28), is probably fiction.It seems likely that this story had no real news value, no practical value, for anyone reading it in newspapers published in cities outside Chicago; even for the readers in that city, the news value, if any, was slight. It found its way into the newspaper for its entertainment potential, not its journalistic value. It was a human interest story and, as Helen MacGill Hughes said, "Detachment from a practical purpose . . . characterizes the human interest story" (Hughes 1940, 253). That is certainly true of most of them. They are, like the comic strips, not intended to be informative, useful journalism.

Matter of Fact or Fiction

But the practice of mixing fact and fiction cannot be dismissed as though it were only an occasional and harmless distraction from the serious business of providing people with the knowledge they need to make good decisions about their personal and public lives. If we now bring together several of the points of this chapter, we can better see both the continuing dangers and the too frequent harm occasioned by these mixtures.

— So-called appearances (formats, positions, writing styles, labels or the lack of labels, and the like) arouse certain expectations in the minds of the readers.

— When these "appearances" tell the readers that they should expect that a message is a piece of journalism, then, appropriately, an assumption of belief is also aroused in the readers. Unless the reader is deterred from disbelief, journalists cannot effectively achieve the purposes of their work.

— Sometimes what the reader expects is not in fact provided; sometimes the factual truth and accuracy that would justify the reader's assumption of belief are not characteristics of the message. The substitution of fiction for fact is one of the ways readers' expectations can be thwarted.

— Sometimes when fiction is substituted for fact, great practical harm can follow for the public. Since the aim of journalism is to help, not harm, the public, such a substitution defeats the very purpose of journalism.

— Undue harm may sometimes not result from a mixture of fact and fiction, however, because, among other reasons, the public is not able to determine, which is which, or because the material has little or no news (practical) value. Little practical harm may be caused in either situation because the public, unable to trust the truth or relevance of the messages, does not make practical decisions or perform practical actions based on them.

— Neither public confusion nor public consumption of what is inconsequential, however, contributes to the goals of journalism. Furthermore, frequent confusion about what is journalism and a regular diet of material that appears to be journalism but has no practical value may habituate the public to refusing to grant the assumption of belief that journalism requires.

— The use of those fictional techniques that are usually harmless (chronological structure, dialogue, simile, detailing of status life, for example) may lead some journalists into those that are harmful (invention of dialogue, situations, and motivations).

— Thus, the use of fictional techniques by journalists is a risky business.

Some Considerations

When we consider what is sometimes called the "new journalism," therefore, we have at least two major questions to consider. First, is any employment of fictional techniques in journalistic messages worth the risk? Second, if the answer is affirmative, how can it be done to minimize the risks and positively contribute to the goals of journalism?

Fictional techniques can be used by journalists to benefit the media that use them; the techniques can also be used to benefit the public. Although these benefits are not mutually exclusive, the increase in circulation or audience share that was accomplished by such stories as the moon hoax, the Jimmy story, or the explosion of General Motors trucks greatly outran any public value. As they were presented, therefore, they have little reason for existence.

Is it not possible, however, for journalists to employ fictional techniques in writing stories that would clearly benefit the public and that the public might not pay attention to if the stories were written in the prevailing news style? That possibility was mentioned at the beginning of this chapter.

The first part of the question is easy to answer: We can find numerous examples of publicly beneficial stories that incorporate some fictional techniques. They appear frequently in columns one, four, and six of the *Wall Street Journal*'s front page, in the *New York Times Magazine*, in the *New Yorker*, on 60 Minutes on CBS, on National Public Radio, and in numerous other periodicals and broadcasts. But would members of the public have paid less attention to them if they had been devoid of literary embellishments? More specifically, would those who *did* read a story that, although factually true, was written in the style of a piece of fiction *not* have read the story if it had been written in the more typical news style? Although the evidence needed to supply a answer is not available, it does seem likely that, since people generally like to be entertained, many of them would be attracted by writing that has many of the qualities of interesting fiction.

Does this suggest that journalists should attempt to write all their stories in a fiction-like style? Not at all.

Most "new journalism" reports provide knowledge about "situations," about conditions that do not call for immediate action by the public. The more urgent the need of the people to know the knowledge that journalists communicate, the less likely is either the time or the need to employ literary devices to attract readers, listeners, or viewers to the report. Stories reporting that cryptosporidium has been detected in the municipal water system need no literary embellishments. In fact, in such situations efficiency requires the most simple, unadorned prose. The first sentence of Tom Wicker *New York Times* lead story on November 23, 1963, had to be plain and clear: "President John Fitzgerald Kennedy was shot and killed by an assassin today."

The use of the techniques of fiction is most efficient in "situation" stories. Because they lack the natural appeal of stories that require urgent decision and action, these are the most appropriate stories—assuming they also have practical value—for the combination of fact and fictional style. Stories throwing light on the character of candidates for political office, on problems underlying the surface of public affairs, on complex proposals for solving public problems might well welcome the attractiveness that the devices ordinarily found in fiction can supply. They can if one fundamental requirement is met.

Alerting the Mass

The unalterable requirement is not that fiction should never be combined with journalistic fact but that those who receive messages should always be able to determine what is fact and what is fiction.

From the very beginning of the moon hoax series, the *New York Sun* should have told its readers that the story was fiction. Even better, it could have reprinted, with suitable identification, Edgar Allan Poe's short story about a trip to the moon.

The *New York Herald* would have had to replace the headlines it ran with something like the following:

> *CENTRAL PARK MENAGERIE A DANGEROUS PLACE*
>
> Our Correspondent Describes What Might Happen
>
> *ESCAPED ANIMALS COULD CAUSE GREAT HARM*
>
> Writer Imagines Terrible Calamities

and then make sure that the first paragraph tells readers that what follows is a product of the writer's invention, that it is fabrication, not fact.

The Mercury Theatre on the Air would have had to interrupt War of the Worlds repeatedly, reminding the listeners they were hearing a dramatized story—as the television station in Charleston, South Carolina, did by superimposing "This is fiction" over the NBC show Special Bulletin a made-for-television movie exploring an act of nuclear terrorism as it would be covered by television news.

In his column about New York City's draping painted vinyl over burned-out buildings, Art Buchwald would have had to make clear to his readers what was fact and what invention, as *Miami Herald* columnist Dave Barry does by inserting into his generally humorous stories such expressions as "I am not making up Rancho Cucamonga: It's a real place." "The story appears on the *Daily Bulletin*'s business page. It begins, I swear, as follows." Or "I have here a document from an organization called the American Life League, titled "'Official Statement on Disney's Perverted Animation.'" The document states that Disney has been putting smut into its cartoon movies, and cites the following examples, which I still am not making up" (Barry 1995).

If, as Janet Cooke later claimed, the Jimmy of "Jimmy's World" was really a composite of several children she had seen or heard about during her research, she should have made that clear at the very beginning of her story.

Would such warnings, labels, and insertions weaken the dramatic, the interest quality of these and other similar reports? Probably yes. And sometimes even more than that. Dateline NBC, faced with showing viewers what had been done to bring about the General Motors truck explosion, would probably never have broadcast that program segment in the first place.

For most readers of Janet Cooke's story, being told that there was no specific, individual Jimmy; that there was not that single child who could perhaps be rescued and saved; that he was, at best, an invented composite of many (unidentified) children whom the reporter had come to know would have diminished the pity, the anguish, the heart-tug of Cooke's report. But the report would have gained the essential quality that her story had lacked: it would have been true.

Almost equally important, the journalists would have shown that they have the same confidence in their publics that they must demand those publics have in them.

Sometimes that confidence will be misplaced. On occasion, even journalists themselves ignore the warnings. When Dan Gillmor of the *San Jose Mercury News* wrote a column describing a financial conference at which analysts, stockbrokers, and executives said anyone buying Internet stocks at the current prices was an "absolute idiot," the *Milwaukee Journal Sentinel* printed the remark on July 20, 1998, page 6D. Overlooked, however, were the words with which Gillmor had begun his column: he was daydreaming, he said, "imagining a world where news stories were accurate because prominent people and institutions told us the unvarnished truth. Since that happens too rarely, unfortunately, I had to *make all of this up*."

Such oversights, however, are rare. Ordinarily, when the public (and professional journalists) are told what is fact and what is fiction, they are adequately deterred from disbelief. Unfortunately, however, as we will see later, the careless combination of fiction and fact is not the only situation in which secrecy, confusion, and misdirection take place.

7

The Objectives of Journalism

Those who say that journalistic objectivity is impossible because we cannot know the *whole* truth about any event, person, or circumstance are, of course, correct. None of us is omniscient. We see a man take a step toward the street. But we do not know the whole truth about him or this event. We do not know the clothing he might be wearing under the clothing we see, nor do we know the number of threads or stitches in any of it. We do not know the number of hairs on his head. We do not know where he is going or why he is going there (perhaps even he doesn't know). We do not know what effect that one step has on his muscles, his blood pressure, his nerves. Our knowledge of even this one, simple event is enormously limited.

Since we cannot know everything, we cannot report everything. More than that: it is quite likely, because of lack of space, time, pertinence, and other factors, we will not report everything that we *do* know.

If this is what is meant by those who deny the possibility of journalistic objectivity, they are correct, but they are also missing the point. It is true that we cannot know and convey the "whole truth" about anything. That, however, is not what journalists are trying to do. They seek to mine a limited piece of land. The task of journalism reporters is to obtain and communicate only the knowledge that would be practically useful in enabling people to decide what to do or avoid doing in the situations in which imminent choices need to be made.

Most reporting involves gathering and conveying knowledge about events, persons, or situations that are outside the reporters. Instead of gathering information about and writing about themselves, reporters usually attend to persons, activities and situations that exist independently of them, to something that for reporters is "out there."

Here we must confront two closely related questions. First, is it possible that reporters can ever know anything outside themselves as it really is, unencumbered and unaffected by the fact that it is they who know it? Second, is it possible that reporters can be sure that what they think they know outside themselves does, in fact, really exist? Perhaps a single example will answer both questions.

If one were a reporter covering a joint session of Congress on Tuesday, January 23, 1996, and a person who has been introduced as the President of the United States is speaking and says, among other things, "In our schools, every classroom in America must be connected to the information superhighway, with computers and good software and well-trained teachers," and no one has claimed that the person speaking is not really the President of the United States, and no one is claiming that what he is saying is something he would never say, is it possible that no matter what the reporter thinks of President Clinton, the Congress, computers, schools, the weather outside, the reporter's own family relationships, and much more—is it *possible* that the President is indeed speaking before a joint session of Congress? And is it *possible* that he is indeed saying, "In our schools, every classroom in America must be connected to the information superhighway, with computers and good software and well-trained teachers"? And is it *possible* that the reporter can know that the

President is speaking these words? And is it ever *possible* for the reporter to communicate at least what the President is doing in such a way that what he says corresponds to what he knows, which, in turn, corresponds to what is "out there"?

None of the critics of journalistic objectivity denies those possibilities. In fact, they might point out, unless there really are some things outside ourselves and unless we can really and truly know at least some things about those things and at least sometimes accurately state what we know, there would not only be no need to discuss objective reporting but also no need to discuss journalism itself. Or at least there would be no point in discussing journalism as it has now been frequently defined. The definition declares that there is such a thing as knowledge, that at least some knowledge conforms to reality and, once known, can help people make good practical decisions. If such is not what journalism is, those who say otherwise must furnish a new definition.

So far, therefore, we can say this much about the realities that underlie the words "objective reporting": it is an effort to know and communicate knowledge about events, persons, and circumstances outside the persons who are gathering and conveying this knowledge, and at least sometimes it is possible to do this so that what journalists think they know does in fact really exist and what they say does in fact really correspond to what they know. This does not contradict the notion that journalists can neither know nor communicate everything about anything. Nor does it even deny the widespread claim that it is impossible for reporters to do this all the time. But if it is possible to do it at all, then it still may be worth striving for.

Objective Reporting: Problems and Challenges

Not yet, however, have we reached the real difficulties implicit in the notion of objective reporting. If pressed on the point, nearly all those who question the possibility of objective reporting would admit that there are things that exist outside the individual person, that we can know at least some of those things, and that we can make statements that accurately express what we know about those things. But the complete operation of news gathering and news-writing is not that simple.

In a letter to *Quill*, Charles L. Klotzer (1984, 23) reminds us that "every reporter always knows more than is included in any report." Then he describes half of the additional difficulty: "The writer selects which facts to include and which to delete whether on the basis of irrelevancy or more suspect motives. Such selection is the core of subjectivity . . . and is the working practice of every reporter on every story at any time."

And the other half of the difficulty? In addition to the possibility of subjectivity due to judgments concerning the inclusion of some facts and the exclusion of others, there is also the possibility of subjectivity due to the organization of news stories. Which facts will come first or early in the story and which will come later or last? For more than a century, most newspapers have organized basic news stories according to the principle of the inverted pyramid, in which the most important material is presented first and the other material follows in order of decreasing importance. Thus, as part of the very nature of news gathering and news dissemination, reporters must choose what to include and what to exclude and, of what they choose to include, what will come first and what will come later.

Choices. Choices made by human beings, by persons who have different standards of judgment, different likes and dislikes, different feelings about and reactions to the events that are taking place. Events do not report themselves. Someone chooses which events to report, what to include in those reports, and in what order to present the elements of those reports. As no two persons are exactly alike, neither will their choices be identical. It is not possible, therefore, many maintain, that there can be any uniformity, any lack of bias, any absence of personal influence in this activity.

Is there any way to remove choices from the selection and organization of knowledge? Not, say those who deny the possibility of objective reporting, as long as human beings are doing it. And news reporting, they remind us, is done by people, not by machines.

Machine Vs. Man

We can contrast the work of the news reporter with its choices to the function of some machines that actually do a certain type of reporting. Automobile speedometers report how fast a car is traveling and odometers how far a vehicle has traveled. Grocery store scanners report what items were purchased, how much was charged for each, the total bill owed, the amount submitted, the amount of change, if any, and very often such other items of information as the date, the store at which the transactions took place, and the amount that was deducted if coupons were submitted,

We can have no doubt that these are objective reports. The one produced at the grocery store is particularly interesting because it not only normally records a number of purchases but also provides us with a printed record of the purchases, of the "events" that took place. In addition, although a machine is involved, people are also involved. The sales slip provided to us could be called an objective report for it lacks the qualities sometimes ascribed to subjective reports. Although a sales clerk prepares it, it is not about the clerk; it is about events that are "out there." It does not express the emotions, the likes or dislikes, the preferences, the values of the clerk who produced it. Although persons are involved in the event, the report itself is impersonal.

Positively and more important, the choices about what is to be included in the report and the order in which these items are presented are not in the hands of the clerk. These choices are determined by the program prior to the events themselves. The program can be designed to list the items purchased in the order in which they are placed on the counter or in alphabetical order or from the most expensive to least expensive. The program can be designed to include the time of the purchases, the name of the checker who was handling the purchases, the number of the counter at which the purchases were recorded. All of these and hundreds of other possible choices concerning inclusion and arrangement are made prior to the event itself. If there has been no malfunctioning in this entire operation, nearly all customers willingly accept the entire sales receipt as an objective report of an event: the purchase of items at a grocery store.

Thus, if "objective reporting" is taken to mean a type of news gathering and news presentation that is about a person, event, or situation that is outside the reporter rather than within or about the person who is the reporter and that is presented with choices concerning selection and arrangement unaffected by the preferences of the reporter, then the grocery sales slip is an example of that type of reporting. This statement does not include everything meant by objective reporting, but at least it is a start.

Even at this point, however, we may have merely pushed the source of subjectivity back one step, from the checkout clerk to the programmer. It is the latter who makes the choices, who decides which items and in what order those items shall be chosen for communication. And the programmer, objectors might point out, is subject to all the risks of bias and arbitrariness characteristic of subjectivity.

But that one step between programmer and clerk is important. Only the latter is in actual and direct contact with the event of the day. For the programmer, everything is conditional. *If* a can of salmon is purchased, the programmer decides, it will be listed in such and such a way, at a certain point in the record, with a specified charge. But the actual event may not include the sale of a can of salmon. The programmer is analogous to the grammarian. *If* one is going to write a complete sentence in English, the grammarian tells us, at least a subject and a predicate must be present and they must be in one order if the sentence is declarative and in a different order if the sentence is interrogative. But the grammarian does not produce the event, the written sentence. Only the author does that.

The grocery store sales slip, of course, is not an example of journalism, because, if for no other reason, it is not an example of mass communication. Is there, however, anything similar in journalistic news reporting to the sales slip with its predetermined selection and organization? Indeed there is, and in great quantity, although its existence is largely ignored in discussions of objective reporting.

Newspapers: The Fine Print

Newspapers publish a great amount of statistical data. These data were customarily printed in small, agate type (about 5.5 points) and were thus referred to as "agate material." Today, the kind and quantity of agate material vary greatly from newspaper to newspaper, of course, but publications that give heavy attention to business and sporting events devote much of their news space to this type of content. It is not unusual for metropolitan papers to devote three, four, or more full pages to reports of yesterday's activity on the stock exchanges, the bond markets, the mutual funds, and the commodities exchanges; and from many inches to many columns of space to box scores, team and individual standings, and many other athletic summaries and ratings.

Some publications also find room for birth notices, marriage license and divorce listings, the names of recent high school and college graduates, persons cited for driving while intoxicated, tables of campaign expenditures reported by political candidates, yesterday's high and low temperatures in cities throughout the country, and much else.

Many editors decide, for instance, that their papers will publish, in alphabetical order, the names of all the stocks traded on the New York Stock Exchange the preceding day and, for each one that was traded, information about the number of shares traded, the highest price, lowest price, and closing price. Once this policy has been determined, the papers continue to provide this information until readers are informed that some different policy will be in force. This information is provided to readers each day after a day in which the New York Stock Exchange was in operation, and the data are presented no matter what the personal, the subjective preferences of all those who are involved. One editor might be distressed, for instance, because the stock of the company that owns his or her paper dropped precipitously the preceding day; he or she might prefer that this information be concealed from the general public. But if objectivity is to prevail, that news will appear and in its predetermined order along with all the other listings.

Some newspapers make it a policy to publish, in a predetermined order, all the persons arrested during the preceding week for driving under the influence of alcohol. If the editor of the paper is one of those who were arrested, objectivity requires that his or her name be included with all of the others. Such publicity might shame the family, make the paper's campaigns in favor of sobriety appear hypocritical, cost the editor his or her job; journalistic objectivity will accept no excuses. The name will appear, and in the order that had been previously determined.

Does this seem to be mindless, fill-in-the-blanks journalism? Well, it is certainly very much like the machine reporting—the operation of an automobile speedometer or a supermarket scanner—referred to earlier. Much of the work, in fact, is or can be done by computers. For instance, in each instance that a stock is sold, the number of shares that change hands and the price realized are entered into a computer; these machines have been programmed to do all the rest.

However, there is a significant difference between the most mechanical of the machine operations and the most machinelike of human operations. Assuming that in neither case is any mechanical breakdown involved, the former—the operations of a speedometer or gas gauge—differs from the latter—the accumulation of information about stocks bought and sold—in this respect: only in the latter can human intentional misrepresentation be possible. In the operation of a speedometer, the information fed to the reporting instrument—the dial—comes itself from other mechanical operations. A person controls the event being reported by controlling the speed at which the automobile is traveling, but the *reports* of the events are, thereafter, totally mechanical. In the stock market example, however, people enter in at two stages: first, they do the buying and selling, thus determining the event: the number of shares traded and the price involved. Second, a person, by entering these data into the computer, also carries out the first step of the reporting. In both, unintended inaccuracies are possible, but the very fact that inaccuracies can exist in both situations prevents inaccuracy from being a clearly differentiating factor.

If all of the equipment is working properly, the speed at which an automobile is traveling—the event—must be reported as it is actually happening. Because no human intervention is involved, no lie is possible. But under the same conditions, the price at which a stock is traded—the event—can be entered by a person as some number different from the true number. Or a person, by deciding not to enter into the computer any reference at all to the stock, can fail to do what the person and the paper promised to do. Either directly or by omission, therefore, the person can choose to lie.

One of the most stringent forms of journalistic objectivity, therefore—the one in which both order and selectivity are predetermined—remains a peculiarly human activity, for falsification is still a possibility.

The criteria used for determining inclusion and organization are, of course, regularly subject to fine tuning. In the 1990s, for example, many business-page editors began to use boldface type to emphasize those New York Stock Exchange issues whose prices, as the *Wall Street Journal* explains, "changed by 5% or more if their previous closing price was $2 or higher." In general, however, these refinements tend to increase the usefulness—or at least the interest value—of this objective reporting.

This strict type of journalistic objectivity is exemplified in still another class of news presentation, that in which the event is verbal and is re-presented in its entirety. Widely employed by mid-nineteenth-century newspapers (Bovée 1986, 251-59), this form of story still appears in those media that consider themselves publications of record. Complete verbatim texts of presidential inaugural addresses, Supreme Court decisions, budget messages, and the like, would be instances of this form of journalistic objectivity. In such material, no portions of the verbal event are omitted, and it is the presenter of the material, not the journalist, who determines the order in which each sentence is to appear.

Possibilities of Objective Reporting

But such agate material and verbatim texts are not what journalism scholars usually have in mind when they discuss the possibility of objective reporting. Instead of looking at the areas where objective reporting might be located, they focus on the types of stories in which it is probably impossible to find it.

Indeed, objective reporting is not likely to exist in the reports of events that involve a great amount of controversy. Political campaigns, economic disputes, foreign and domestic policy disagreements, environmental debates, religious arguments, and similar events lack any consensus either on what particular data should be included or excluded or on the order in which the included items ought to be presented. In addition, those issues often arouse strong feelings not only among the participants in the discussions but also among the journalists covering the events. Furthermore, except for the re-presentation of complete speeches or other texts, the closer the event comes to being broadly unique the smaller the possibility that there would be any predetermined agreement about how it should be covered.

On the other hand, routine weather, auto accident, house fire, metropolitan burglary, obituary stories—the very ones that come closest to the agate material and verbatim texts discussed earlier—are not the examples chosen by those who deny the possibility of objectivity. Why this happens is not difficult to understand. Routine stories do not win Pulitzer Prizes. They pose little intellectual challenge. Most often, they are handled by neophyte reporters. One story is so much like all the others of the same type that they lack any distinctiveness; they hardly seem worth discussing.

Most of them, in addition, are concerned with what was previously described as personal affairs—rather than public affairs—news. News helps the public make good decisions about what should be done, but personal affairs news assists in the making of personal decisions, decisions that each person can make for himself or herself; personal affairs news does not lead to decisions that require a consensus. Heated controversy, therefore, is less likely to occur.

But personal affairs news *is* a type of news. It can be useful to enormous numbers of people. The media give it large amounts of space and time. More important, the possibility of objective reporting in at least this type of news keeps alive another, much more important, issue: if objective reporting is at least sometimes possible, must we also conclude that it is, therefore, desirable?

"Objective reporting" can be used as a shorthand term to describe a way of gathering news and a manner of conveying news. News gathering can be considered objective when the knowledge is about persons, events, or situations outside the reporter, when that knowledge does correspond to what is really "out there," when it is gathered on the basis of criteria established prior to the time when this particular knowledge is acquired, and when the criteria are made known to and are not rejected by those to whom the knowledge will be communicated. News presentation can be considered objective when the type of knowledge just described is conveyed truthfully and in a manner that is detached, impersonal, and devoid of any additional value judgments. This is possible.

But the mere fact that something is *possible* to do does not, of course, necessarily imply that it is good to do.

Perhaps some of those who say objective reporting is impossible really mean that objective reporting leads to such harm that it would be best to abandon it. In other words, for them, what is impossible is not objective reporting but rather the *good use* of objective reporting.

And, indeed, in many situations it is not possible to achieve the totality of objective reporting. Thus, when we consider whether objective reporting is desirable, it would be helpful if we considered possibility and desirability separately. In the situations in which it is not possible to achieve the totality of objective reporting, we can ask whether it is desirable to aim at as much of it as *is* possible.

Objective Reporting and Controversial Public Affairs

One of the great problems of striving for objective reporting when controversial public affairs are involved is that, although reporters themselves may be truthful, unbiased, and impersonal in reporting an event, they may still communicate one or more falsehoods to the readers or listeners. This can happen because the quoted portion of the report contains one or more lies. Many critics leveled this accusation against the late Senator Joseph McCarthy (R.-Wis.) in the early 1950s. Senator McCarthy, they claim, perpetrated many falsehoods that journalists, maintaining their sense of objectivity, dutifully and accurately conveyed to the public. The reporters did not lie; McCarthy, it is claimed, did. The reporters merely extended the source's lies to a much wider public.

In a strong attack on this and some other characteristics of objective reporting, Theodore L. Glasser (1984, 15) says, "Objective reporting virtually precludes responsible reporting, if by responsible reporting we mean a willingness on the part of the reporter to be accountable for what is reported." But journalists are aware that they have two stages of responsibility in reporting a verbal event. One is the responsibility for reporting the event itself accurately, for conveying to readers or listeners the actual words used. The other is the responsibility for the truth of the statements made by those words. Objective reporters do not assume the second responsibility, but they do assume the first. Thus objectivity does not totally preclude responsibility.

Nevertheless, we dare not ignore Glasser's criticism. Indeed, can any good come from those reports that, under the claim of objectivity, communicate lies? If the job of the reporter is to provide knowledge that will help people make good decisions, how can they make good decisions when what they are being told is not true?

Perhaps the best reply was given by John Stuart Mill (1859, ch. 2) in his essay *On Liberty*. Mill reminds us that, sometimes, what journalists consider to be lies may not be lies at all; the speaker may be right and the journalists wrong. Or, Mill adds, even if the statements are lies, there may be some truth mixed in. Or, even if the statements are total lies, the public must know about them so that they can be refuted and so that the liars can be accurately judged for their defects of character.

Mill was assuming, however, that there were both time and opportunity, first, to reveal what truth, if any, was embedded in the quoted statements or, second, to set forth the evidence that would show the people the falseness of those statements. And many public liars know that, in the rush of practical affairs, neither adequate time nor opportunity may be available. Often, the truth never seems to catch up with the falsehoods.

Yes, say the adherents of objective reporting, but at least sometimes we can unveil a falsehood by turning to another source who will speak the truth. We can maintain our own impartiality and detachment by quoting other people "out there." If the Democrats say one thing, we simply turn to the Republicans for a reply. In fact, we don't have to determine who is speaking the truth; we merely set forth the opposing viewpoints and then let the public decide.

But this assumption that journalists can provide their publics with the truths they need to know by presenting "both sides" of a disagreement outrages some critics of objective reporting. Narrowing ideological disagreements to only two sides distorts the realities of actual situations. In fact, it tends to elevate the dominant viewpoints and ignore the unconventional ones: presenting only the views of those who favor and those who oppose a balanced budget omits the views of others, for instance, who want a budget surplus. As J. Herbert Altschull (1984, 128) says:

> [T]he code of objectivity assists power in the capitalist world to maintain social order and to fix limits to departures from ideological orthodoxy. . . . [I]t safeguards the system against the explosive pressure for change. So long as "both sides" are presented, neither side is glorified above the other, and the status quo remains unchallenged. Dissent is permitted, even encouraged, under the code of objectivity, but its limits are proscribed.

Even when the media present more than just the pro and con positions, they often fail to present a truly balanced account of alternatives. For instance, sometimes the supporters of one or a few positions are well organized, well financed, and insistent upon having their viewpoints publicized, whereas others lack one or more of these qualities. In the 1990s, the National Rifle Association was one of the former, while organizations opposed to the private ownership of handguns lacked some of these characteristics. In addition, editors may find it difficult to locate a person who will set forth a particular point of view. Edward W. Conlon, for instance, who has written about the daily grind of a New York City police officer for the *New Yorker*, has done so under a pseudonym. Sometimes, no recognized spokesman exists, as has long been true of the United States prison population. Or people are afraid to step forth and offer themselves as spokespeople, as was long the case for the gay rights community and for victims of sex crimes. In other instances, speakers for one position—such as Federal Bureau of Investigation or State Department officials—are restrained by the need to preserve confidentiality, whereas opposing speakers are not. In addition, in trials and ethics hearings, the accusers are given the opportunity to present their viewpoints before—sometimes days and weeks before—the defenders can assert their positions. Also, the glib or well educated usually do a better job of communicating their viewpoints than do the halting or uneducated.

It is understandable that, with all this in mind, many people would cry out against the desirability of objective reporting. Ignoring the routine stories in which it can be achieved, they point to the complex public affairs in which total success is impossible and claim that any attempt to cover those stories objectively is only a pretense. For such major and important stories, in fact, objective reporting is not only impossible but even, they say, misleading.

Objective Reporting and Criticism

Gaye Tuchman faces many of these objections with the suggestion that claims of "objective reporting" are merely tactical devices by which journalists ward off criticism. In a highly respected article, she says that "the correct handling of a story, that is, the use of certain procedures discernible to the news consumer, protects the newspaperman from the risks of his trade, including critics" (1972, 661). Thus, to minimize the penalties imposed by deadlines, libel suits, and superiors' reprimands, the reporters will adopt procedures that they can claim mark their work as "objective." They will set forth conflicting possibilities, pile up facts to support truth claims, use quotation marks to distance themselves from any opinions, and structure stories according to an accepted sequence, such as beginning with the usual formula: who, what, where, when, why, and how.

Tuchman says these procedures do not actually guarantee objectivity. But linking them with a respected professional quality helps journalists compensate for the fact that their special professional knowledge is not respected by news consumers. In doing this, she says, journalists are like members of other occupations who "develop ritualized procedures to protect themselves from blame" (Ibid., 676). Journalists are using a word, "objectivity," as a means of defense.

Although her argument is interesting and deserves the attention it has received, she sets forth objectivity as a defense and not as a possible journalistic goal. Defenses, of course, are intended to be temporary. Once an attack or an evident threat of attack has ceased, there is no longer any need for the defense. On the other hand, if the attack continues unabated and, in fact, even seems to grow larger and more fierce—as the growing accusations of media bias would indicate is taking place—then it is not a good form of defense and ought to be discarded. (This might account for the disappearance of the term "objectivity" in the Society of Professional Journalists' Code of Ethics.) If objective reporting—at least as much of it as is possible—does have any truly positive and journalistically intrinsic value, therefore, we must search elsewhere in order to find it.

Journalistic Objective Reporting

Much of the controversy over journalistic objectivity arises from the failure to recognize that there is more to journalism than news reporting. News reporting is so highly esteemed by members of the Fourth Estate that the words "reporter" and "journalist" are often used interchangeably. But news reporting is only one ingredient in the cake. Explanation, evaluation, and persuasion are also part of the mix. To ignore them is, often, to produce a totally inedible concoction.

Indeed, the more complex and controversial the event, the more likely will be the public need for something beyond the presentation of facts alone. As Douglass Cater (1950, 46) said in his detailed analysis of the media's handling of the Senator Joseph McCarthy accusations, "Faced with a phenomenon as complex as McCarthyism, the 'straight' reporter has become a sort of strait—jacket reporter. . . . His initiative is hogtied so that he cannot fulfill his first duty, which is to bring clearer understanding to his reader." Altschull (1984, 128) said criticisms of Senator McCarthy were limited to the editorial pages, and, because few people read the editorial pages, their influence was limited. But news analysis and news comment stories—by-lined and printed on news pages but separate from the objective news reports—are common. It is not beyond possibility to place editorials, suitably identified, on page 1. For instance, when the *New York Herald Tribune* on October 25, 1951, wanted to convince its readers that Dwight D. Eisenhower should be the Republican candidate for President, it did so with an editorial at the top and center of page 1. On April 11, 1951, the *New York Journal American* devoted two front-page columns to expressing its outrage when President Truman removed General Douglas MacArthur from his Far East commands. And on March 22, 1991, the *Milwaukee Sentinel* began a page 1 editorial with the reminder, "For seven days, the Milwaukee Sentinel has published front-page editorials urging readers to pressure their elected representatives to support a seven-day waiting period for the purchase of a handgun."

In fact, exclusive reliance upon objective reporting has been declining since the 1950s. One reason is the need by the broadcast media to fill time during the nonstop coverage of major events. Instead of repeating again and again the limited available facts, those media turn to experts and partisans for explanations and evaluations of what is going on. This was particularly evident during the early days of the Gulf War. During that period the print media also broke away from the limitations of objectivity and began to add—usually in by-lined stories—background and critiques not only of the events but also of those who had control over information about those events. The people were repeatedly warned that the war news was censored, and they were cautioned to read, watch, and listen with that in mind. Commenting on government restrictions concerning information about military operations in Iraq and Kuwait, for instance, Max Frankel, executive editor of the *New York Times*, was quoted as saying, "We are not getting any information that really fully and properly describes the magnitude. . . . We don't know how many are participating, how much ordnance is being dropped. It's hard to remember this is a nonstop, massive operation, the likes of which we may not have seen before" (Rosenbaum 1991, 10).

It is significant that this and other similar material (see Lamke 1991, 2) were appearing in the *news* sections of newspapers. It was not restricted, as it had been during the Senator McCarthy period, to comments "buried" on littleread editorial pages.

In general, it is not objective reporting that prevents journalists from providing us with the knowledge we need to make good decisions. Rather, it is the failure of both journalists and their publics to make good use of *all* the journalistic resources.

Benefits of Objective Reporting

To say that objective reporting is not necessarily counterproductive still leaves unanswered the question: What good, if any, is it?

It is true that now, in the coverage of complex public affairs, it is not possible to achieve the totality of objective reporting. At the present time we do not have a publicly accepted set of criteria on the basis of which the selection and organization of facts can be arranged. But what is possible is for reporters to turn their attention to persons, events, or situations outside themselves, to acquire knowledge about them that is accurate, to convey that knowledge truthfully, impersonally, and devoid of any explicit or intentional value judgments. This is not the whole of objective reporting, but it is a good part of it and a goal that is worth striving for. The people are well served if they are provided with information gained in this way. Even in the most controversial events, such bare facts are the material the public needs for active citizenship. As Jorgen Westerstahl (1983, 407) has said:

> The requirement of objective news reporting is intimately related to Western democracy and to one of its basic principles, the freedom of opinion . . . citizens need to be informed of what is happening in the world around them. News reporting must be factual and impartial in order to provide a foundation for independent and rational decision making.

It is important to mention that, although it may often be advisable to segregate the objective reporting from other genres of journalism—explanation, evaluation, persuasion—this is not a universal necessity. We can recognize this most easily if we view journalistic work from the perspective of the journalist who sets out to write a piece of persuasion, an editorial, for example. A persuasive editorial explicitly expresses opinions. It is not objective in the sense described here. Nevertheless, that editorial will normally include some content that sets forth the factual situation upon which the writer's opinions are based. That reportorial portion of the editorial can be—and should be—objective reporting. That is, it should have those portions of objective reporting that are possible to incorporate in even the most contentious material. And what is true of the editorial is equally true of all journalism. Magazine articles, in particular, are most likely to be a combination of journalistic forms, as any glance at the *Nation*, the *Atlantic Monthly*, or the *New York Times Magazine* will reveal. In all those instances in which reporting is involved, that reporting should be as objective as is possible.

Emotions and Objective Reporting

It is sometimes said that, in attempting to be as objective as possible, journalists should strive to be dispassionate (Merrill and Lowenstein 1971, 228). Whether it is possible and desirable for objective reporting to be free of feeling, to be free of emotion, depends on the meaning one assigns to these words.

Most helpful is what Aristotle says about the emotions. If one follows the Aristotelian tradition, then no truly human and alert person is ever free of emotions. In the *Rhetoric*, for example, Aristotle defines emotions as "those states which are attended by pain and pleasure, and which, as they change, make a difference in our judgments" (2:1, 1378a). Thus, if a person is not angry, that person is calm, but *both* anger and calmness (one painful and the other pleasant) are emotions. Likewise, if a person is not fearful, that person is confident, both of which are emotions. Every person, he said, must be one or the other. If everyone, including both journalists and their readers, viewers, or listeners, must always be in one or another emotional state, how, then, is it possible to avoid emotions in the presentation of news?

To answer, one must distinguish between the existence of emotions and changes in emotions, and between the data that cause emotions and the persons who present those data.

Let us say that a fictitious Mr. Jones is retired and has all of his funds invested in a single company. The dividends he has been receiving from the company's stock are the principal source of his income. For years, the stock market listings have informed him that the company is doing quite well. Thus, today, when he opens his newspaper, he feels confident.

But then he notices that the price of the stock has dropped precipitously, and when he turns to another objective listing, he learns that the company has omitted its usual dividend. His confidence changes to fear. He will probably have to endure painful financial strictures.

Were all of the stock market listings prior to this fateful day unemotional? No. His study of the stock market report each previous day had given him a feeling of confidence. If anything, the repeated reassurances he had received from reading the financial pages probably increased his confidence. Moreover, the day's news, which changed his emotion from confidence to fear, did not change his state from an unemotional to an emotional one. All along, he had been in an emotional state, and he now continued to be in an emotional state.

Thus, when we say that an objective news report is unemotional, we cannot mean that it has no effect upon the feelings of readers and listeners. The report is a stimulus that either maintains an existing feeling or changes that feeling to another feeling. It does not move people from a nonemotional to an emotional state. And what applies to the reading and listening public can be said equally about the journalists themselves. They, too, when normal and alert, are never unfeeling machines.

Both journalists and public, however, are sometimes affected in such a way as to bring about a change in the *type* of emotions they are feeling. Painful emotions sometimes motivate evident exterior actions that will liberate people from painful feelings and replace them with pleasant feelings, as when one escapes from a fearful object. The dash to safety replaces painful fear with pleasant confidence. In some other situations, merely the passage of time can bring about a change of feeling, as when a feeling of anger, as days go by, is replaced by a feeling of calm.

What is the cause of these changes in emotion? For the reading, listening, and viewing public, it could be the journalists themselves, as is most evident in television news reporting. In addition to the spoken words, facial expressions and other body language also convey the reporter's feelings to the public. The American television journalists who reported the assassination of John F. Kennedy, for example, found it enormously difficult to control indications of their own feelings, and the feeling of shared grief intensified the sorrow felt by their viewers. But even if the reporters had controlled indications of their own feelings, they would still have affected the emotions of their viewers, this time by holding somewhat in check the degree of their personal feelings.

In most instances, however, instead of the messenger, it is primarily the content of the message that affects the people's emotions, as when, to use our previous example, Mr. Jones receives word that the company on which he has relied for much of his income will no longer pay a dividend.

It is also true that reporters can intentionally shape the telling of the message so that the very process of communicating affects the feelings of the public. The use of emotionally loaded words, for instance, shifts matters so that the cause of emotions is neither the content of the message nor the messenger but the very phrasing of the message itself. If a newspaper reporter would say, for instance, that a source "replied with a sneer," the word "sneer" might arouse anger in the readers who admire that source. Thus objective reporters attempt to use emotion-neutral language: they simply write, for instance, that the source "said" something and then quote what was said.

But what if the source did, in fact, reply with a sneer? Then we must rely upon something beyond objective reporting to let the readers know this fact. Objectivity alone does not guarantee that everything that needs to be said is, in fact, said.

When we say, therefore, that an objective news report is unemotional we mean that whatever effect it has on the public—and it will have *some* effect—is not due primarily to the reporters but rather to the data outside the reporters that the latter communicate to the public in otherwise emotion-free language. Not everything can be conveyed in such a language, but, as inspection of agate material reveals, it is possible to do so with some types of content. That is enough to establish it as a possible goal for which journalists can strive.

Violations of Objective Reporting

Because objective reporting directs the public's attention to persons, events, or situations *outside* the reporter, there will be some situations in which objective reporting is not desirable. This will happen most clearly when the reporter himself or herself is a part of the event being reported. For example, the September 9, 1940, issue of the *Chicago Daily News* carried Helen Kirkpatrick's account of the bombing of London during World War II. It began this way:

> London still stood this morning, which was the greatest surprise to me as I cycled home in the light of early dawn after the most frightening night I have ever spent. But not all of London was still there, and some of the things I saw this morning would scare the wits out of anyone.

This account violates several of the characteristics of objective reporting. It is partly about the writer instead of being totally concerned with events outside the writer. It is expressed in the first person, and it sets forth the writer's feelings and judgments about the event. But this subjective report provides useful knowledge about the consequences of warfare, knowledge that objective reporting would not have been able to convey.

Similar characteristics can be found in the story by United Press reporter Russell Jones that was published on November 15, 1956, about the Hungarian rebellion:

> Life as the only American correspondent left in shattered Budapest is sometimes frightening, sometimes amusing. But mostly it is a continuous feeling of inadequacy both as an American and as a reporter who helplessly watched the murder of a people.
>
> For the first time since I was a boy I wept.
>
> I saw a former British soldier break down completely. The situation was worse than the Warsaw uprising into which he was parachuted in 1944.

At other times, what the public most deserves is not objective reporting but rather temporary or partial silence. For example, when one party in a dispute launches a criticism against a second party, the entire story can sometimes (not always, of course) be delayed until the journalist has obtained a reply from the latter. Lou Cannon of the *Washington Post* suggests that this is what Daniel Schorr, then of CBS News, might have done when, in July 1975, Air Force Colonel L. Fletcher Prouty told Schorr that Alexander Butterfield had been a CIA spy in the White House. Butterfield could not be reached immediately for a reply because he was on the West Coast looking for work. Schorr did not wait; he put the story on the air immediately. He gave the competitiveness of his network with NBC as his reason for not delaying the broadcast of Prouty's remarks (Cannon 1977, 47-50). But rarely is the public served (in fact, the public is usually not even aware of, and thus not impressed) by the game of "me first." *By itself* objective reporting is not always fair. It may need to be supplemented by other journalistic genres. But it should not be made even less fair than it has to be.

Reconsidering Objective Reporting

Critics who claim that objectivity is impossible because no reporter can know the whole truth about any person, event, or situation are partly correct. No reporter is omniscient. And, of all that is knowable, reporters never attempt to know everything but are selective in the knowledge they attempt to obtain. If they are good news gatherers, they make their selections on the basis of what they judge will be most useful for the public to know when making practical decisions. And, just as they do not attempt to know everything, normally they also do not communicate everything they do know, and for the same reason: some of it is not useful knowledge for the public.

Those who say that objective reporting is possible are also partly right—if they mean that there are some things about a person, event, or situation that reporters can truly know. They can know that a certain senator said, "I am a candidate for the presidency of the United States," and can honestly and accurately report that statement—and much else that they know.

Even in the selection and organization of what they choose to know and of what they choose to communicate, reporters can be objective journalists if we mean by this that they establish *prior to* the events that they cover the criteria on which they base their observations and communications.

Let's consider, for example, the sports reporters who will communicate to readers the information normally included in the box scores for a basketball game. From experience they have learned what the readers want to know and thus, among all the possible bits of knowledge, the specific pieces that they should choose to include: the names of all the players for both teams who actually participated in the game, the number of field goals attempted by each player, the number of field goals made, the number of free throws attempted, the number made, and so on. Although these journalists have feelings, desires, and biases, this format helps them set aside those subjective elements as they go about carrying out an objective investigation. No matter how much they like a certain player, his name will not be included if he did not play in the game. And if the format dictates that the players will be listed in the order in which they are announced to the crowd, then the organization of this material is also determined. Even if a reporter has a favorite player and would like to list him first, the objective journalist will not do so if that player is not the first one whose name was announced.

In doing this, reporters can be objective in the same sense that scientists and other objective data gatherers and communicators are objective. Before conducting any experiments, a biologist, for example, will choose a number of options that he or she knows from experience will be accepted by his or her peers: that measurements will be made according to the International (metric) System rather than the U.S. Customary System; that a certain number and type of class intervals will be employed; that a certain degree of accuracy will be used in measuring continuous variables; that a certain level of significance will be acceptable; that the report will be written in English or in some other chosen language, and the like. As the mathematician R.T. Hayslett Jr. (1968, 83) has said about his own field, often thought of as one where great objectivity can be achieved, in all computations "some assumptions need to be made." Likewise, in the choices and organizations predesigned for agate material, journalists can accomplish the same degree of objectivity that most people find acceptable in scientific endeavors.

Even those who say that objectivity is impossible but worth striving for are partly correct. For the coverage of complex and controversial public affairs, total objective reporting is not possible because there are no accepted criteria for the selection and arrangement of material. But objective reporting is a complex process; thus, even when achieving the totality is not possible, it may be possible to achieve some of the elements. Even in the most contentious affairs, reporters can be accurate in their observations and truthful in their statements. They can direct the public's attention to the object of the story rather than to the writer. They can exclude any explicit statements of judgment or advocacy. Thus, even when insuperably difficult, objective reporting—at least that much of it as it is possible to achieve—may be a goal worth pursuing, for objective news underlies nearly all the other types of journalistic writing.

But whether it is achieved completely or only partially, objective news is not always fair. For example, agate material may show that a quarterback on a professional football team completed only three of the eighteen passes he threw. But if seven of those passes went right into the hands of intended receivers but were dropped, the agate material, though accurate, does not give a fair account of his ability.

And even where fairness is not involved, readers often need more than completely objective material. On November 16, 1996, for instance, many papers reported in their stock market listings that, on the previous day, International Business Machines stock advanced $8.125 to close at $145, a nine-year high. Why this leap in price? The agate material did not give investors the answer. They had to turn elsewhere, perhaps to interpretive reporters, who pointed out that, on the same day, Merrill Lynch & Co. announced that it was raising its target price for the stock from $150 to $195.

In general, therefore, journalistic objective reporting can be both possible and desirable. But, by itself, it is not the paragon of all journalism.

8

Journalism and Democracy

By "participatory democracy" it means a type of direct democracy, a system in which political decisions are made, not by elected legislators, but by the entire electorate, the people as a whole. According to Naisbitt, the public would not "vote on *every* issue, only the ones that really make a difference in our lives" (Naisbitt 1984, 145). Of course, the issues that really make a difference in our lives are the very issues to which legislators now devote a major portion of their time: taxes, defense, education, health, environment, agriculture, and similar public matters. All of them affect our pocketbooks and our own or our families' physical or mental well-being.

If it were true that we the people actually do (or should) decide these and the almost countless other issues that "really make a difference in our lives," the responsibilities of our political leaders, our governors, would be greatly diminished and the people's responsibilities would be increased to a level that they could not possibly attain. Let's look for a minute at what would happen.

The governors would become coach drivers (a metaphor that Yves Simon [1951, 146 ff.] borrows from Paul-Louis Courier). That is, our governors (our congressmen, for instance) would be like the drivers of coaches whom we hire to take us where we want to go. "Go straight ahead," we might say, and they would do so. "Turn to the left," we would order, and they would follow our orders. "Vote for this bill," we would demand, and that is the way they would vote. We would be in charge. They, the governors, would simply certify the decisions that we, the people, would make. In fact, we would become the real decision makers, the real governors. Should the maximum tax rate for personal income be set at 25 per cent? The people would decide. Members of Congress might vote on the issue, but they would vote only as their constituents wanted them to vote. Consequently, of course, the responsibility and the agony of deliberation would shift from the shoulders of our governors to our shoulders.

Personal Welfare

Most of us know that this coach-driver theory does not prevail in the United States. Almost always, it would be impossible. The reason is not that the people in general lack the ability to govern but that the people do not have the time to take care of both their own personal goods (being good electrical engineers, good high school teachers, good grocery store managers, or good nurses) and of the common welfare (being good county supervisors, good members of the state assembly, or good United States senators). The common welfare cannot be achieved unless we all take care of our personal goods. That is, for example, there will be no good city unless that city has not only good city council members but also good doctors, plumbers, teachers, and car dealers.

Not everyone understands this. For example, some people write angry letters to newspapers to complain that their senators or members of the state assembly are not voting as the majority of their constituents think they should. And some elected officials may consistently and slavishly follow what they think are the wishes of those who voted them into office. Sometimes we close our eyes and permit our minds to be invaded by nostalgic visions of small New England towns where the people *do* gather and decide that a new fire engine is needed or that a street should be resurfaced. But those episodic actions do not reflect the reality of this country as a whole. Even if we did not pay much attention to the social studies textbooks assigned to us in high school, a large majority of us do understand at least this much: although we elect our legislative and top executive leaders, and although we can attempt to influence them through letters, telegrams, demonstrations, and other types of persuasion, it is they—not we—who make the political decisions we call our laws.

Edmund Burke's statement about a member of Parliament's (MP's) relations with his constituents is as appropriate for a twentieth-century American legislator as it was for an eighteenth-century English MP:

> Their [the constituents'] wishes ought to have great weight with him [the Member of Parliament]; their opinion, high respect; their business, unremitted attention. It is his duty to sacrifice his repose, his pleasures, his satisfactions to theirs; and above all, ever, and in all cases, to prefer their interest to his own. But his unbiased opinion, his mature judgment, his enlightened conscience, he ought not to sacrifice to you, to any man, or to any set of men living. . . . Your representative owes you, not his industry only, but his judgment; and he betrays, instead of serving you, if he sacrifices it to your opinion. (Burke 1774)

Almost two centuries later, John F. Kennedy, in his book *Profiles in Courage* (1957, 14), reiterated the point:

> The voters selected us, in short, because they had confidence in our judgment, and our ability to exercise that judgment from a position where we could determine what were their own best interests, as a part of the nation's interests. This may mean that we must on occasion lead, inform, correct and

> sometimes even ignore constituent opinion, if we are to exercise fully that judgment for which we were elected.

In spite of what Naisbitt and some other commentators on our political system say, representative democracy is not obsolete, nor is it being replaced by participatory or direct democracy. On the contrary, rather than becoming more closely and extensively involved, the people are becoming increasingly distanced from those who are actually the decision makers. The public, for example, has no direct control over the vast and growing personnel of federal, state, and local executive departments, much less over the decisions made by those officials. We do not elect military generals, for instance, but they establish rules and procedures that affect the lives of thousands.

Even more significant is the vast growth, on both federal and state levels, of relatively independent executive and administrative agencies. They possess both legislative and judicial powers (Schwartz 1955, 285), and yet those decision makers are not elected by the voters. The Civil Aeronautics Board, Equal Employment Opportunity Commission, Farm Credit Administration, Federal Communications Commission, Federal Trade Commission, Nuclear Regulatory Commission, and U.S. Commission on Civil Rights are only a few of the more than fifty such agencies on the federal level alone. And, despite efforts in the mid-1990s to streamline government, most of them still exist. They affect nearly all areas of American life, yet the American people have no direct voice in determining either their membership or their policies.

Thus when influential people seem to accept as true what they describe as "one of the primary assumptions held by the American citizen," namely, that "In a democracy, it is the people who rule" (Altschull 1984, 18-19), we have the right to object. In fact, if we are properly to understand the role of journalism in contemporary America, we *must* object, for the communication needs of those who rule are qualitatively and quantitatively different from the communication needs of those who are ruled. Those who rule, who govern, ought to be thoroughly informed about the issues upon which they must make decisions. In large, complex political communities, those issues are so numerous and complicated that the general population cannot attend to both what they need to know in order to decide them properly and also what they need to know to take care of the needs of their personal lives. The sheer magnitude of the task of governing (at least on the international, national, and state levels) requires a division of labor by which a relatively few persons devote themselves to making decisions about the public welfare and relatively many persons go about the various tasks by which they achieve their personal welfare.

Even for our elected political leaders, the task of governing has become so immense that they can no longer handle all of it by themselves. They must delegate great slices to staff aides, cabinets, committees, independent agencies, and similar assistants. In many instances, an executive or a legislator will still make or participate in making the final decision—as when a congressman votes to approve a bill advanced by a House committee, or when the President approves the recommendation of his Secretary of State—but often the elected official has control only over the appointment of the persons who actually make the decisions. Once federal judges are appointed by the President with the advice and consent of the Senate, for instance, those appointees make decisions that do not have to be submitted for the approval of the persons who appointed them.

Thus in spite of such ringing declarations as Lincoln's "government by the people," the reality is that, in the United States—or even in any other sizable and advanced nation—the actual governing is not in the hands of the people. It is true, of course, that no government can long survive against the united opposition of its people; thus the people do give, at least by passive non-action, consent to their governing. But, except in the rare instances of initiative or referendum (and on the national level we have neither of these), or of jury trials, the people themselves do not directly decide public affairs.

The Role of Public

This does not mean that the role of the people in public affairs is either minuscule or unimportant. On the contrary! In addition to the obvious point that the governors themselves are drawn from the people, we the people play a major part in public life through the choices we make in elections and through the influence we exert as a part of that force called public opinion. The quality of our performance in all those areas depends greatly on the quality of the journalism that is available to us. Let us turn, first of all, to consideration of the people as electors.

Unfortunately, the mistaken view that we the people govern stands in the way of our doing a good job of selecting those who actually *do* govern. If we think *we* are the governors and that the office seekers should drive the coach of state through the twists and turns that we dictate, then *we* want to know, as specifically as possible, what the various candidates for office intend to do once they are elected, for then we can choose the issues we want to support and vote for the candidate whose intended choices best match our own.

The discussion of issues during a political campaign is important, but not for the reasons sometimes advanced. It is not important so that we can choose among those issues, as though we ourselves were going to decide them. An election is not a referendum. In elections, we vote for (or, at least, we *should* vote for) *persons* whom we want to have as our governors. We pay attention to issues and to what the candidates have to say about them not because we will be able to vote on those issues but because of what the discussion of those issues reveals to us about the character of the candidates.

"Look to character first," James David Barber (1972, 445) said when identifying a better way to select our presidents. That guideline for electing presidents applies equally well to all candidates for public office.

Character is those developed and relatively stable qualities of people which, when known, enable us to trust (or distrust) them and their judgments concerning what should be done. Character is not appearance or the other superficial aspects often implied when people say political campaigns should focus on "issues, not personalities." Character refers to something deeper and weightier than personality. Voters should attempt to determine the character of candidates in order to examine what the candidates have to say about issues. Voters should pay attention to candidates' personalities only to the extent that personality is being used to conceal character.

Members of the judiciary, especially those elected at the municipal and district court levels, normally do not propose laws but rather make judgments on the basis of already established statutes. The qualities the electorate look for in making selections among judicial candidates therefore require consideration of professional qualities, such as legal expertise, not required by executive and legislative officials.

The Character of Political Leaders

To what aspects of character should journalists, acting in their function of providing useful knowledge to the people, give principal attention in order to convey them to their readers, listeners, or viewers? An answer was given more than two thousand years ago by Aristotle.

In the most practical of his many books, *The Rhetoric*, Aristotle describes three means of persuasion, but to one, he says, the politician should give special attention: "That the orator's own character should look right is particularly important in political speaking" (2:1, 1377b). And he quickly adds, "There are three things which inspire confidence in the orator's own character: good sense, good moral character, and goodwill" (2:1, 1378a).

He does not describe these three qualities of character in detail, but from many scattered references and the general context one can pull together what Aristotle had in mind. To our understanding of each of these it is also essential that we try to add the ways journalists can look beneath the appearances to help voters judge the extent to which the politicians actually possess these characteristics.

Good Sense

Let's look, first of all, at good sense. People of good sense know how to get things done. They are practical, efficient, down-to-earth. The opposite would be the dreamers, the idealists, those who stubbornly butt their heads against the stone wall of reality.

Thus, to mention only a few of the characteristics of sensible people, they have the ability not only to determine what means will achieve an end but also to select the *best* of those means, the one that averts the greatest number of obstacles and deficiencies.

They know the world and the particular situations as they actually are, and they deal with them as they are. For any issue that faces them, they seek out the relevant facts. They know that everything has its cost, immediately or eventually. They recognize that some things take time, that almost everything is gray rather than black and white, that the total of advantages and disadvantages is often nearly even. They learn through both their mistakes and their successes; thus experience becomes an important ingredient in the development of good sense. They can determine when one should hold firm on principle and when it is better to compromise.

They realize that some issues are more important than others, and they give each the time, attention, and resources that it deserves. They don't precipitously leap for the first option that comes along, but they also avoid undue delay. Once they have made a decision, they don't abandon it without a sound reason, but neither do they stubbornly stick to a choice that has proved to be unwise.

Although advanced education is no detriment to good sense, neither is it a guarantee of it. Some people with many advanced degrees are so impractical that they cannot open a can of sardines or remember to put their rubbers on before going out in the rain.

Moral Goodness

If we are going to trust people to be good political leaders, what moral qualities do we expect them to possess? One, certainly, is honesty. We need to be confident that they are telling us the truth. This is not always easy for anyone; we all are tempted to lie in order to avoid embarrassment, protect ourselves, or advance our personal welfare. But, as Sissela Bok points out in her book *Lying* (1979), politicians face a special temptation. Not only do they sometimes want to lie for selfish reasons, but they also sometimes think they must lie for the sake of the common welfare. They think, in some instances, the country, state, or community will be harmed if they speak the truth. Bok reminds us (178), however,

> We cannot take for granted either the altruism or the good judgment of those who lie to us, no matter how much they intend to benefit us. We have learned that much deceit for private gain masquerades as being in the public interest. We know how deception, even for the most unselfish motive, corrupts and spreads. And we have lived through the consequences of lies told for what were believed to be noble purposes.

Another political virtue, important even though not always widely appreciated, is courage. In *Profiles in Courage* (1957, 8), John F. Kennedy describes the many ways in which public officers face a special challenge. He says that the "most significant sources of pressures which discourage political courage in the conscientious Senator or Congressman . . . is the pressure of his constituency, the interest groups, the organized letter writers, the economic blocs and even the average voter." The temptation to become merely a "coach driver" is enormous.

Of course, no virtue comes amiss to good political leaders. In fact, all the moral virtues tend to meld together, as, for instance, courage is often needed in order to be willing to tell the truth. In addition, at least in the Greek tradition, all the moral virtues are means between extremes of excess and defect. As Abraham Edel (1967, 135) reminds us, "Aristotle is careful to point out that it is not an arithmetical mean but a mean relative to the individual. If ten pounds is too much for a person to eat and two pounds too little, it does not follow that the trainer will recommend six! It depends on the person and the purpose." Thus, courageous people will avoid both cowardice and rashness, but exactly what they will do in the face of danger can vary greatly, depending upon the situation and their abilities. Likewise, temperate people choose neither total abstinence nor perpetual indulgence, but something in between; liberal people are neither spendthrifts nor misers;

the properly angry are neither apathetic nor short-tempered; and the strictly just person distributes to everyone what is his or her due, neither more nor less.

Goodwill

Finally, the person who possesses goodwill is one who wishes good to others and does whatever he or she can do to help those other people achieve their good. This quality is sometimes called friendliness. The opposites of goodwill are selfishness and indolence.

Thus, first of all, the primary concern of political leaders who possess goodwill is not themselves; it is others. These leaders work for the welfare of the people, for the good of those whom they are governing. This does not mean they always agree with those others (friends will often disagree), but whether they agree or not, political leaders who possess goodwill place the common welfare ahead of their own personal welfare. They carry out the duties of their office to serve the people, not to promote their own fame, fortune, pleasure; nor for the advancement, prosperity, gratitude of their personal friends; nor for the prestige, well-being, reputation of their family.

In addition, they work hard at their job. They sacrifice their own rest and leisure to meet the demands of their political positions. They give up golfing or pinochle or a night at the movies to find more time to serve their constituents.

The three characteristics of good sense, moral goodness, and goodwill must be considered together, for each, in a sense, throws light on the others. For example, those who possess goodwill might be so devoted to the welfare of others that they would be tempted to work to the point of sacrificing their own health, but good sense would warn them that sick or exhausted political leaders cannot accomplish as much for others as healthy leaders can. Leaders with good sense possess the ability to devise means for accomplishing a great number of things, but moral goodness would tell them that some of those things are not right and proper to do. Morally good and friendly leaders will think of many benevolent goals that good sense tells them cannot be achieved with the resources available now or in the foreseeable future. A tax cut may be a right and friendly step, but good sense may warn that this is not the right time to do it. It is not enough, therefore, for political leaders to possess one or two of these qualities; they must possess all three. Or, as the historian Allan Nevins put it in his introduction to Kennedy *Profiles in Courage* (xvi):

> Moral courage is great and admirable in itself; but it must be pointed out that it almost never appears except as part of the greater entity called character. A man without character may give fitful exhibitions of courage. . . . But no man without character is consistently courageous, just as no man of real character is lacking in consistent courage. In short, moral courage is allied with the other traits which make up character: honesty, deep seriousness, a firm sense of principle, candor, resolution.

Elections and Journalists

How do journalists help the electorate determine whether or not candidates for public office do possess these characteristics?

First of all, they report to the people those things that the candidates have done and are doing that evince the presence or lack of character. Since *everything* that people do reveals, at least in a tangential way, something about their character, this reporting must be highly selective, focusing on those actions that most clearly and crucially show capabilities for the specific political position for which the candidate is competing. The fact that a candidate for state assembly has been a member of the Veterans of Foreign Wars tells us very little about that person's character—unless he falsified his military record in order to gain admission to the organization. The fact that a candidate obtained all of her education in private schools tells us very little about her character—but might be relevant if she is running for a seat on the public school board.

Isolated events from a candidate's distant past often are not reliable indicators of his or her present character. St. Augustine was quite a hellion as a young man, but turned out all right in his later years. Past transgressions should be significant only with evidence they still exist or if the grown person refuses to acknowledge errors or mistakes.

In many instances, the electorate need more from journalists than the mere reports of candidates' actions to judge their character; often, the panoply of journalistic genres must be employed, especially interpretation and criticism. For example, let's say that as an incumbent governor is running for another term, the governor's son is arrested for selling cocaine. The governor immediately hires the best defense lawyer in the state to defend the young man, all the time maintaining that the boy is innocent. It would take more than news reporting to remind the electorate that it is not a character flaw for a parent to love his or her son, to want to help him in his difficulty, and to maintain that he is innocent, at least until proved otherwise.

In addition to reporting and commenting on what the candidates have done and are doing, the journalists must make available to the people, and then analyze, what the candidates are saying. In particular, the electorate must know what the candidates propose to do when they gain office and how and why they propose to do it. Not everyone agrees that such detailed position statements are desirable. James David Barber (1980, 314), for example, says:

> Pressed for specifics during the campaign, the candidate and his aides and advisers expend their intellectual energies composing tedious position papers. They are not frequently cited after inauguration day. The fundamental reason is not that the candidates lie, though some do, but that such detailed blueprints for government action are drawn up abstractly, disconnected from an as yet unknown context of forces and chances in Washington and of necessity shaped for an immediate purpose: to win the election. . . . To center campaign debate on specific candidate plans is to shift the conversation away from evidence and toward opinions that cannot readily be tested, however sincerely they are advanced.

But Barber and those who agree with him ignore two essential points.

First, the situation that he describes as existing prior to an election is not temporally different from the situation that exists after a candidate has been elected to office. The interval between a campaign and an election is not much different from the time between the introduction of a legislative proposal and its enactment. In both instances, the person is advancing "opinions that cannot readily be tested." In both situations, whether candidate or officeholder, the person is making presentations in the midst of contingencies that are always in a state of flux. If a proposal is enacted into law, it is only after its enactment-sometimes long after—that adequate evidence appears to enable the public to determine whether or not the original proposal was a good one.

Second, and more important, the value of candidates' setting forth specific proposals lies not in thereby enabling voters to choose the items they find most appealing and then voting for the candidate who affirms the greatest number. Elections are not choices among proposals. Elections are choices among persons. As S. I. Benn and R. S. Peters (1959, 408) have put it:

> It is sometimes assumed that the job of a democratically elected government is to implement the electors' wills, by enacting as quickly as it can the programme on which it was returned to office. But this is quite untenable. The electors' will is limited to the single question decided at the poll: Who shall govern? Nothing can be inferred beyond that.

Why, then, should candidates for office advance detailed proposals? Assuming that the details include the *reasons* the candidates have for the plans they are recommending, this process enables both voters and journalists to judge the character of the candidates. For their part, the journalists can be particularly helpful when they not only report the reasoning of political candidates for office, but also analyze and critique that reasoning.

What Barber calls "tedious position papers," therefore, may present exactly what journalists and the people in general need to know. Those papers can tell us what goals the candidates have in mind. They can indicate for whom the plans would be beneficial, what means would be employed to achieve them, what obstacles might rise up, and how they would be handled. Good plans, journalists can point out, require a grasp of both facts and principles. The very effort to devise programs indicates a dedication to the requirements of the position being sought. The reasons reveal whether the proposals are workable, whether they are being set forth honestly and courageously, and whether they are designed to benefit the political entity that the candidate wishes to serve. By providing an account and analysis of candidates' programs—in addition to presenting information about candidates' past and present activities—journalists help the people make good choices among those who offer themselves for public service.

Political Campaign and Advisers

Some people worry about the role that public relations advisers, media consultants, and other staff members play in political campaigns. Candidates for office, increasingly in recent years, are helped, guided, advised by the people the candidates gather around them. But as was pointed out earlier in this chapter, the same is true of those who have already succeeded in gaining office. One of the major responsibilities of persons in public life today is to locate and appoint, or approve the appointment of, those who can collaborate with the elected officials in governing. Thus, candidates need to be judged not only on their own qualities but also on the character of the persons whom they choose or permit to advise them. For better or for worse, candidates for public office are subject to the same influences as those who are successfully elected to public office.

Political Public Affairs

Typically, of course, the electorate must choose between two or more candidates for every public office. Thus the role of political public affairs journalists is not limited to setting forth the character of individual candidates; it also extends to comparing, contrasting, and making relative evaluations of candidates. Since the choice is seldom between a paragon and a miscreant, this is not an easy task.

It would not be unusual, for instance, for one candidate to evince great good sense but to show only moderate amounts of moral goodness or goodwill, and for a second candidate to be almost ideal in moral goodness and goodwill but deficient in good sense. Unfortunately, no one of the three characteristics is so paramount that the others can be ignored. There may be a time in the history of a community, of course, when it needs a person who is dominant in one of the qualities—as when a town that has suffered years of political lassitude, nepotism, and benign neglect is in desperate need of a person of goodwill—but, again, this is not the typical situation. Most often, the electorate, with the aid of journalists, must make decisions at sixes and sevens. They must weigh and balance, influenced always by the tug of private interests and the appeals that candidates make to them, but finally seeking, if they are truly good journalists and good citizens, a match between the character of the candidates and the requirements of the common welfare. For the journalist to achieve this, newswriting alone is not sufficient. Although it is fundamental, interpretation, criticism, and persuasion must be added.

Non-Political Public Affairs

In addition to political public affairs, other types of public affairs deserve and often receive journalistic scrutiny. One type comprises the personnel and activities of the tax-exempt, nonprofit organizations that receive public funds, subsidies, or exemptions and are required to file Form 990 with the Internal Revenue Service. As Felix Winternitz has pointed out (1995, 40-1), these include not only charities and some religious groups but also hospitals, museums, public radio and TV stations, colleges, cemeteries, labor unions, trade organizations, city clubs, public housing agencies, festivals, credit unions, zoos, farm cooperatives, and many other groups—totaling one million organizations nationwide and employing 6 percent of the American work force.

The general public, of course, does not elect the leaders of nonprofits, but, because those organizations spend at least some public money, the people deserve information, evaluation, and recommendations about those leaders and their organizations' affairs. When a symphony orchestra board of directors is in the process of choosing a new conductor or when a hospital selects a new director, the opinion of the public can be a force of considerable importance. Public oversight can help increase the probability that nonprofits will be successful and also contribute to the public welfare, the latter being the principal grounds upon which they are granted their nonprofit status.

The characteristics that leaders of nonprofits should possess are the same as those for political leaders, with one major addition: those who head nonprofit organizations should also possess demonstrated expertise in the area in which they are employed. The curator of an art museum, for example, in addition to being a sensible, morally good, hardworking, and friendly person, should also be knowledgeable in the field of art.

Even more distant from the area of political public affairs are those activities and officers of large private corporations, especially the companies that serve large proportions of the public or the government itself. The auto, airline, food processing, pharmaceutical, entertainment, and mining industries would be just a few examples. Many of them are already subject to some type of government regulation, and for that reason alone they deserve public oversight. In addition, however, their impact on the general welfare warrants journalistic attention. The public has no direct power over the leaders of these corporations, but the influence of public opinion, especially through the boycott, can help shape the directions in which they move. Consider, for example, the boycott against Shell Oil products in the summer of 1995 when that organization planned to sink an oil platform in the North Sea. Under public pressure, the company reversed its intended course of action.

Private organizations also take on a public affairs aspect when we view them from inside, from what is often the perspective of the relationship between the executive and operating personnel and the employees, stockholders, customers, and suppliers. For all of them, privately owned corporations constitute a special type of community that share some of the characteristics of political communities. They have goals that their various members work toward in common. And, to the extent that they do, all of the members need the knowledge necessary to enable them to progress toward those common goods.

Understanding Democracy

Our understanding of the nature of the United States political system and the means by which journalism serves it requires at least one more confrontation with reality. We proudly say that we live in a democracy, and in constitutional structure and in intention we do. But it would be more accurate to say that democracy is something we are progressing toward but have not yet achieved. It is essential that we recognize this. Failure to do so leads to a misevaluation of the obligations and accomplishments of American journalism.

The political system that has been *achieved* in this country at this time is not Lincoln's "government by the people." It is not, unfortunately, even government with the full participation (through decision and advice) of all the people. It is rather a government (through decision and advice) of only a portion of the people, yet a government in which many more are eligible to but do not, in fact, participate. It is a type of oligarchy. Or it could be called a self-selecting aristocracy combined with democratic controls.

The United States, among democratic countries, is not distinct in this respect. As Yves Simon (1951, 106-8) has pointed out:

> Any regime, in order to work well or merely to survive, needs or may need the operation of principles distinct from, and opposed to, its own idea. Ancient monarchies were kept in existence through extensive concessions to the aristocratic principles, and, in modern times, association with rather radical democracy is the only thing which proved capable of assuring the survival of monarchy. . . . Modern democracies can be described as mixed regimes with a predominance of the democratic element (at least according to constitutional law; for so far as actual practice is concerned, the oligarchic element predominates in some of them).

It is not easy to specify exactly the oligarchic characteristics of the United States. No regular and complete system exists, for example, for reporting the total number of elections at all levels of government throughout the country; it is obvious, however, that the number of public officeholders is a small minority of the total population. The number of people who lobby, petition, demonstrate, write letters, send telegrams, submit their views to the mass media and otherwise attempt to be active members of the political society is also impossible to estimate. We do know, however, that, at least in this century, no presidential election—which, except for occasional highly contested local elections, normally draws the greatest voter turnout—has attracted as many as two-thirds of those who are eligible to vote. The best record was in 1960, when 62.8 percent of the eligible voters cast ballots. Some primary elections fall far short of this. Commenting on some of the 1988 results, Graham Allison and Katie Smith (1988, 27) pointed out: "Only some 23 percent of voting-age Texans showed up at the polls to give away Super Tuesday's biggest prize: 294 delegates. In Florida, about 22 percent of those eligible to register and vote bothered to vote despite expensive courtship from Vice President Bush and Bob Dole on the

Republican side and nearly all of the Democratic front runners."

Public of USA

Who, then, are "the people of this country" who rarely govern in any determining fashion but are often asked to select and advise those who do govern? It would be helpful for journalists to recognize that there are several major peoples, several major publics.

The "Object Public"

Those we can call the "object public" are all the persons who simply occupy space under the jurisdiction of the United States of America. They may be newborn or elderly, imprisoned or free, dirt poor or billionaires, retarded or genius. Most are native-born or naturalized citizens, but some may even be, perhaps only temporarily, aliens. Most live within the boundaries of this country, but some dwell abroad. They are all those for whom the leaders of the country feel responsible because all of them are presently or potentially subject to the laws of the land. They are the population that the Bureau of the Census attempts to enumerate every ten years.

The "Ineligible Public"

Within this object public is a group who can be called the "ineligible public." These are the people who, temporarily or permanently, wholly or partially, are not permitted to take an active role in political affairs. Most completely excluded are the severely insane, retarded, and senile; they neither vote nor contribute to the deliberations of public opinion. Partially excluded are felons in institutions and young people up to the age of eighteen who cannot vote, but, if they are able to communicate, can add their views to public opinion. The normal very young, adults with curable mental and psychological defects, and pardonable felons may eventually be able to gain all the privileges of citizenship.

Almost concealed within this ineligible public is the large section of the adult object public unable to read: the 35 million who cannot read a life insurance form, understand the instructions on a federal income tax return, or grasp the antidote instructions on a bottle of lye, and the 25 million even more severely handicapped who read at less than a fifth-grade level or not at all. These 60 million adults—more than one-third of all American adults—are, Jonathan Kozol argues persuasively, "substantially excluded from the democratic process and the ordinary commerce of a print society" (Kozol 1985, 10-11).

The illiterates, and also some immigrants whose native language is not English, are not totally excluded from the political process. Through radio and television both groups can acquire some understanding of political issues and candidates. Many immigrants are served by publications in their native languages. Both groups can stand up and speak at some public forums and voice their views through the aural media. And, since literacy is no longer a criterion for voting, illiterates can, given some preliminary assistance, cast their ballots in referenda and elections. Although all of these activities are possible for the illiterates, Kozol says they are not likely to perform them:

> Illiterate citizens seldom vote. Those who do are forced to cast a vote of questionable worth. They cannot make informed decisions based on serious print information. Sometimes they can be alerted to their interests by aggressive voter education. More frequently, they vote for a face, a smile, or a style, not for a mind or character or body of beliefs. The number of illiterate adults exceeds by 16 million the entire vote cast for the winner in the 1980

> presidential contest. . . . Democracy is a mendacious term when used by those who are prepared to countenance the forced exclusion of one-third of our electorate. So long as 60 million people are denied significant participation, the government is neither of, nor for, nor by, the people. It is a government, at best, of those two-thirds whose wealth, skin color, or parental privilege allows them opportunity to profit from the provocation and instruction of the written word. (Kozol 1985, 23)

The "Potentially Eligible Public"

Since the deficiencies of many members of the currently ineligible public are remediable, a large portion of this second group can be identified as a "potentially eligible public." This is a segment of the population in which the journalistic media, especially the print media, have a great interest, but about which they can directly do very little. The task of remedying mental, physical, and psychological weaknesses belongs to such fields as education, medicine, and psychiatry, not to journalism. But journalists can, and for their own self-interest as well as for the public interest must, encourage action and progress by these other services. Newspapers, for example, are not read by 45 percent of the adult population, but the figure is so high because 35 percent of those adults are simply incapable of achieving the reading level at which news stories and analyses are written.

The "Active Public"

The public with whom political affairs journalism is primarily concerned, therefore, is the remaining one, the "active public." Members of that public exhibit, of course, a great range of activity. The least active of that group—and they are no more than two-thirds of the object public—merely vote every two or four years. The most active run for public office, read widely and carefully both the general and the specialized public affairs journals, listen to and watch programs that specialize in public issues, speak and write on current affairs, and attempt to induce other citizens to support their candidates and causes. This latter group, sometimes referred to as the opinion leaders, probably constitutes some 10 percent of the object public. It is primarily to this active public, from least active to most active, that the journalism media ought to direct their messages.

The other publics cannot be ignored. The permanently ineligible public need journalistic oversight, assuring that their basic human rights are being protected by the governors of the political society. The temporarily ineligible public need the same oversight but also the assistance of the *media* to remedy their deficiencies. Although this remedial, primarily educational task is not true journalism, it is a job that can be carried out by the same media that communicate the work of journalism. "Sesame Street" is not journalism, but it is a worthy part-time use of a journalistic medium.

It is for this active public that the genres of journalism focusing on public affairs ought to be most specifically intended. The journalistic works concerned with personal affairs have a wide, attentive audience and readership, but public affairs journalism ought to be aimed at an engaged, active public. Newspapers should not do less than they are now doing; they must do more. They must satisfy the serious needs of the active public: more information, better explanations, keener and more strongly supported evaluations, and much better argued persuasions. If the journalistic media do not better serve the active public, then the dynamic core of our governmental system is deprived of its vital nourishment. Those who water down the soup to make it palatable for the masses, risk thinning it out to the extent that the active public die of starvation.

Thus William Greider (1983, 7), the astute national correspondent for *Rolling Stone*, while recognizing many of the realities of the situation, seems to go along with what he admits is a bit of press hypocrisy:

> Among my models for the way I think newspapers ought to do lots of things are the best European newspapers. . . . They assume a much broader charter of what it is they're doing. But there's a big difference between those newspapers and American newspapers in terms of audience. The best newspapers in Europe are elitist. They speak only to a very narrow band of the population. They make no attempt to speak to everyone. They presume that the rest of the population wouldn't understand anyway.
>
> An American editor or publisher starts with a very different premise, which is that his audience is the whole spectrum of society, regardless of education, income and everything else. While there's always some hypocrisy in that, it's the premise of metropolitan newspapers in America, and I think it's right.

But does it make sense that American newspapers should be written and edited for that sizable segment of the population that cannot or does not want to read them? If the ineligible or only potentially eligible public do not buy the newspapers, there is not even an economic or an advertising advantage to doing so.

The eligible public should, of course, be given every opportunity to become part of the active public. Newspapers should not be priced so high or distributed so sparsely as to be unavailable to all those who want them. And the papers and other media, by satisfying the need for knowledge about important personal affairs, can do much to draw readers' attention to knowledge about public affairs.

Furthermore, since the economic well-being of the mass media requires that they maintain a certain level of audience or readership, comics and other types of entertainment might have to find space or time to assure survival. But at the heart there must be public affairs journalism adequate in both quality and quantity adequate to satisfy the needs of the active public. Not every publication has to do everything; the responsibility is shared. But the active public of every community must have access to the knowledge they need for the welfare of that community and of whatever other communities those people can realistically affect. Lacking that, our political system will not survive.

Even the active public, because of the range of their activity, need a variety of attentions by journalists. To achieve this is not easy, for the steps taken to encourage the least active to become more active may distract the most active, the group upon whom democracy basically relies.

Of the many means suggested for increasing attention to knowledge about public affairs without cheapening or watering down the content of journalism, one entails both great promise and great risk.

9

Journalism and Freedom of the Press

Most people make a rough distinction between facts and opinions. A fact, they think, is an assertion that something is or is not true of something else. For example, if Ms. Jones had said, "I weigh 120 pounds," most people would take that to be a factual statement. Even if it were not true, it would still be a statement set forth as a fact.

On the other hand, if Ms. Jones had said, "California is the best state in the Union," most people would take that as an opinion. Even if they agreed with her, it would still be an opinion. She would be saying, in effect, that something is good (or bad) about something else.

And if Ms. Jones had also added, "I should buy a house in California," people would also take that to be an opinion, a proposal that something should (or should not) be done. Again, whether or not others agreed with her makes no difference.

As the journalistic genres of criticism and persuasion have their counterparts in the thoughts of people generally, all of us evaluate persons, events, and situations. All of us think that it would be good to pursue some courses of action and to avoid others. And most of us would accept the statement of these evaluations and proposals as opinions.

Admittedly, such definitions are rough. They do not satisfy legal requirements, especially not in the area of defamation, where the statement of most opinions is protected whereas some defamatory expressions are not. In fact, even the courts have found it virtually impossible to distinguish between statements of fact and statements of opinion. For example, one criterion used by the courts to determine whether a statement is an opinion is the very imprecision of language. Thus the courts decided that to call a person a "fellow traveler of Fascists" is to utter an opinion, for there were various interpretations of the word "Fascists" (Middleton 1988, 157). The definitions mentioned earlier would not resolve such a problem. The sentence "Bill is a fellow traveler of Fascists," has the form of a statement of fact. But in the context, it asserts a negative evaluation of Bill, and thus has the character of an opinion.

For the purposes of this book, it will suffice to say that an opinion is a mental judgment that some person, event, or situation is good; or that some person, event, or situation is bad; or that some course of action would be either desirable or undesirable.

The Public Opinion

Now let us return to Ms. Jones. If we would agree that her view about automobile gasoline mileage is an opinion, we next can ask what type of an opinion it is. Many people would say it is merely Ms. Jones's personal opinion, and let it go at that.

It certainly is her personal opinion. Even if others also have the same opinion, this one is hers. It may not be hers exclusively, but it is hers.

Is there any reasonable way, however, by which it might also be referred to as a public opinion?

One possibility, of course, is that she make her opinion public. That is, she can express her opinion so that others become aware of it. She can shout it aloud in a situation in which others will hear it, or she can publish it. She can join an organization dedicated to the same cause that she upholds. She can march in a demonstration that supports her opinion. In general, her private opinion can be made public if she pushes it out of the recesses of her mind into the light of the world, where others can know it and examine it.

Making an opinion public, however, seems insufficient to designate it a public opinion. If we were to take some of the other opinions she has, for example the opinion that she should buy a house in California, we could reasonably maintain that making it public would not transform it into a public opinion. Even if she were to buy space in a newspaper to announce, "I, Mary Jones, am of the opinion that I should buy a house in California," we would be hesitant to agree that it is a public opinion. It seems to be much too personal.

If an opinion is not about personal matters, however, but rather is about public matters—what was described in earlier chapters as public affairs—it would seem safer to refer to it as a public opinion. Such an opinion would be concerned with the workings, the institutions, the directing personnel, the opportunities, the plans of a political community—whether local, state, national, or international. As long as a person has in mind an evaluation or a proposal about any of these, that person has in mind a public opinion.

We can go one step further. Those subjects that can be described as quasi-public affairs also seem to fall within the realm of public opinion. They do so, at least to begin with, because they are opinions on issues concerning the welfare of an organization rather than on issues affecting only the welfare of a private person. Thus, a manufacturing company, an athletic team, a union, a private college, a religious body all can be the subjects of public opinions.

Once again, let's return to Ms. Jones. Even if we were to say that her view on gas mileage is *a* public opinion, we would not say that her public opinion on gas mileage is the equivalent of *the whole* of public opinion on gas mileage. In other words, "public" refers not only to the content of the opinion but also to the number of persons who hold that opinion.

How many people need to have an opinion about gas mileage in California to enable us to say that public opinion about the subject now exists? And does it make any difference who those people are?

Normally, the persons who hold public opinions are those who are affected by, those who have some stake in, the subject of that opinion. Thus the public of the public opinion about gas mileage in California could include, among many possibilities, all the adult people in California, all the executives of companies that manufacture automobiles, all new car dealers, all the state legislators. And, usually, those discussing the matter would let us know. They might say, for example, "Public opinion among California voters is . . ." or "Public opinion among General Motors executives is . . ."

But this still leaves us with one enormous problem: What number of people or what proportion of people need to hold one or another opinion before we can claim, for instance, "Public opinion opposes (or favors) a proposal that all automobiles sold after 2001 in California be able to travel a minimum of fifty miles per gallon of gas?"

Multiple Public Opinions

That question has evoked a multitude of answers. Many scholars have charted them out and provided a reason for the diversity. Marbury B. Ogle, for instance, cites several of them and then explains that the reason for the variety is the desire of all the users to find a meaning that suits their special field of interest: psychologists one way, sociologists another, political scientists still another (Ogle 1950, ch. 3). That is understandable: a runner would find one meaning for the word "dash," a telegrapher another, a punctuator still another. What, then, might public opinion mean for the professional journalists who provide useful knowledge about public and quasi-public affairs?

It is not surprising that, for those journalists who view the press as the fourth branch of government, the answer would be one appropriate to the field of political science. Many of them find their answer in the words of Lord James Bryce, an English statesman and historian writing near the end of the nineteenth century. Bryce focused on two possibilities. The term "public opinion," he pointed out, is used "to denote, sometimes everybody's views—that is, the aggregate of all that is thought and said on a subject—sometimes merely the views of the majority, the particular type of thought and speech which prevails over other types" (Bryce 1899, 2:247).

Bryce opted for the second meaning. He almost had to if he was to maintain his underlying viewpoint that it is really public opinion—not legislators or executives, but public opinion—that governs in the United States. He said, "[I]n America public opinion is a power not satisfied with choosing executive and legislative agents at certain intervals, but continuously watching and guiding those agents, who look to it, not merely for a vote of approval when the next general election arrives, but also for directions which they are eager to obey, so soon as they have learnt their meaning" (Ibid., 270).

But Bryce realized that, if public opinion were realistically to determine the course of governmental affairs, it would have to be known directly and quickly. This was not possible at the end of the nineteenth century, but he foresaw a day when it would be possible. That stage would be reached, he said, if

> the will of the majority of the citizens were to become ascertainable at all times, and without the need of its passing through a body of representatives, possibly even without the need of voting machinery at all. In such a state of things the sway of public opinion would have become more complete, because more continuous. . . . [T]his informal but direct control of the multitude would dwarf, if it did not supersede, the importance of those formal but occasional deliverances made at the elections of representatives. To such a condition of things the phrase, "Rule of public opinion," might be most properly applied, for public opinion would not only reign but govern. (Ibid., 258-59)

As might be expected, public opinion pollsters were quick to assert that they could provide the mechanism for the achievement of this final stage. Particularly during the decade following 1935, the year in which George Gallup founded the American Institute of Public Opinion and Elmo Roper began the *Fortune* Survey (Cantril 1951), a certain euphoria swept through those who thought direct democracy in the United States was not only appropriate but also possible.

Although public opinion does not direct the day-by-day governing of large, complex political societies, it does play a major role in the establishment and maintenance of those societies.

A people has to agree with explicitly or at least acquiesce in certain founding opinions for a national political society to exist at all. In this country, those opinions are set forth in the Preamble and Articles of the Constitution. There one finds expressed the objectives of our political system and the general means by which, we hope, those objectives will be achieved. This country did not come into existence until its people, sometimes directly, sometimes indirectly through elected agents, endorsed a broad, general policy of ends and means.

Those principles must remain alive in the beliefs and aspirations of the people. Some of this is done quite explicitly, as when immigrants pledge allegiance at naturalization ceremonies, when public servants take their oaths of office, when schoolchildren are taught the meaning of their full participation in citizenship. More often it takes place less explicitly and completely in the course of parades, rallies, the singing of anthems, the display of symbols, and other patriotic observances. For some members of society, it exists simply in their decisions not to rebel. But no matter whether expressed or not, it is public opinion, not police or military compulsion, that glues a society together.

In addition, on some rare occasions public opinion acts like a huge boulder. At times, as during Prohibition and the Vietnam War, it refuses to roll in the direction the political leaders order it to go. Another time, as during the Gulf War, it tumbles along, pulling at least some of the political leaders along with it, regardless of subtleties or consequences of the course of action. In other words, now and then, the people simply refuse to be governed objects. Not waiting for elections, not asking for a national referendum, not employing any of the constitutional means by which they can control their governors, they attempt to govern themselves.

This last is a dangerous state of affairs. Even when the people are right, even though their choices are broad and thus still dependent on the governors for specification and enactment, the people are attempting to do what they pledged not to do. As Yves Simon (1951, ch. 3) so precisely explained, the people do have a power greater than that of their governors. And when the people transmit that power to their governors, they do not lose it, *but they do agree that they will no longer use it*, except when there is some dire and immediate threat to the welfare of society. Perhaps in the examples mentioned above, such a dire and immediate threat existed. Even if so, however, any instance in which the people attempt to snatch back the power they have transmitted to their governors is a time of danger.

For purposes of clarity, let's refer to those broad, prevailing opinions by which the members of a society form and maintain the bases of a society and, on rare occasions, sweep that society in one direction or another as general public opinions. And let us call the views of the members of a society on the almost countless specific issues that must be decided for a society to move toward the achievement of the public welfare particular public opinions. It is important to note that on any given topic a general public opinion is the single, prevailing position on that topic. But particular public opinions are all the diverse views on a topic.

Based on this division, some examples of general public opinion would be these: It will probably work out well to have the government of this society divided into three branches; it will probably work out well that each state, no matter what its size or population, will have two United States senators; it will probably work out well to forbid the government from establishing a state religion; and, increasingly during the years from 1969 to 1975, it would be best for the United States to discontinue fighting in Vietnam.

General public opinions tend to persist over a long period. Many of them are communicated more through formal education than through journalism. And, of course, these views of the people either already are or do become strongly prevailing. They become settled in a single direction, and most can be best expressed as a probability: "It will probably work out well or best."

Particular public opinions are also probabilities, of course, but they have not yet achieved any common agreement. Because they continue to express diversities of viewpoint, they are best introduced as issues, as practical questions concerning what should or should not be done.

Thus, examples of the issues upon which particular public opinions are formed would include the following: How should the federal budget be balanced? Should the United States attempt to establish a colony on Mars? How can states improve the quality of primary and secondary education? How can hospital and medical care be provided for all the people? Should airport air controllers be permitted to go out on strike? Should there be a ceiling on the salaries of major league baseball players? How can we protect our natural environment? Depending on the days and the places, one could cite thousands of additional public issues upon which the people form opinions.

The public's opinions on all of these issues can be enormously important. All of them, therefore, ought to be known.

In upholding this view, Simon and many others choose the meaning of public opinion that Bryce rejected: they see it as "the aggregate of all that is thought and said on a subject." Particular public opinion, therefore, is not a single position on an issue. Rather it is a great variety of opinions, united not by *the* position on an issue but rather by the *issue* itself. What is public opinion about capital punishment? It is all the arguments—for, against, and in between—concerning the undesirability or the desirability of capital punishment.

Yves Simon calls the opining public a "deliberating assembly" (Simon 1951). The people of some community, society, organization, or other group discuss and offer their opinions and advice to those who actually make the decisions concerning what is best to be done to solve the current problems of the groups of which they are members. The members of these publics need not be within the physical presence of one another; instead, they usually come together through and in the media that service their organizations.

No longer is the emphasis on how many persons hold this or that opinion; instead, it is on the opinions themselves and the reasons that the public gives for them. Thus "public opinion" points to something that really exists, and, important for the purposes of this book, it enables us to see the many ways in which public opinion and journalism are related.

Journalism and Public Opinions

Journalism serves public opinion, first of all, by alerting the public to the issues that deserve their attention. Journalism then provides the people who constitute the deliberating assembly with the knowledge they need to make judgments about public affairs.

Especially through the exercise of their reporting and interpreting functions, journalists alert the public to people, events, and situations that require political action; they provide background information; they point out what, if anything, is being done elsewhere, what options exist, what the admitted likely consequences of various actions might be, what choices their political leaders are considering.

One of the principal roles of journalism is to inform public opinion.

It is important to recognize that this journalistic function need not be, in fact cannot be, totally satisfied by every individual journalistic medium. No one newspaper, magazine, or broadcast program can provide all that the many deliberating assemblies of the people need to know on every public issue. National media are unable to provide all the knowledge that the people of all cities, counties, or even states need. And no one local medium can satisfy the needs of the people in other distant local communities. The CBS Evening News cannot keep the people of Iowa up to date on the public affairs of that state, but the Des Moines Register can. The *New York Times* cannot enlighten the public opinion of Cook County, Illinois, but the *Chicago Tribune* can. *Newsweek* would find it impossible to inform the people of Augusta, Maine, on all the public issues facing that community, but the *Kennebec Journal* can.

The responsibilities of local journalistic media begin with their localities, and they extend outward to the county, state, nation, and world, in that order and with decreasing urgency, to the extent that time, space, staff, and finances permit. The responsibilities of national journalistic media begin with the nation, and they extend toward localities or toward the international scene, with decreasing urgency, to the extent that time, space, staff, and finances permit.

Some people lament the lack of attention given to world affairs by many of the mass media in this country. The nations of the world, they quite rightly say, are interdependent; then they add, unrealistically, that public opinion is deficient if it is not well informed about the problems of these nations. But the United Nations of this planet comprises more than 150 sovereign states, no one of which is free of problems. Some of the problems are so momentous and dependent upon worldwide response—as the massacres during the 1990s in African nations—that they should not be ignored by American public opinion. Some others impinge so directly on this country—as does the drug traffic out of Colombia—that they dare not be ignored. But it is just as impossible for a medium in one country regularly and adequately—adequately, that is, to permit the formations of sound opinions—to inform the deliberating assembly of that country about the public affairs of all the other nations of the world as it is for a medium in one city, regularly and adequately, to inform the deliberating assembly of that city about the public affairs of all the other cities in this country.

Such realism need not lead to isolationism. To remove from the popular mass media the impossible burden of providing worldwide practical knowledge is not to promote a know-nothing attitude about international affairs. It is simply to allocate the obligation where there is some chance of its being fulfilled. That place is the specialized media.

Those interested in the affairs of Mozambique can satisfy their curiosity by subscribing to AIM, published by the Mozambique Information Agency. If worried about the accuracy or completeness of the information supplied by that agency, they can turn to specialized magazines and books, to CNN and SCOLA and other channels on cable television, to National Public Radio's worldwide coverage, to the Internet and World Wide Web on their own (or the library's) computers. Those interested in the events, people, and situations in the Republic of China on Taiwan can read the *Free China Journal* or refer to some of the alternative media just mentioned.

The number of persons who would do this would be probably quite small. But as long as the information is available for those who want to seek it, the fact that only a few persons do seek it is no disaster. Those few are likely to be those whose opinions will be well formed and most influential. Of the public affairs to which most of us can afford to devote some attention, it seems reasonable that the events and issues closest to us should receive first consideration. It is more useful for most of us to know about the situations in our own towns—where we can more easily contribute to the public deliberations concerning what can be done—than to know about the issues in Chile or Singapore or Bangladesh, whose problems we have little chance to affect.

Reporting Public Opinion

Journalism serves public opinion, second, by reporting it. Since the people as a deliberating assembly cannot advise their political or other public leaders unless the latter can know what the former have to say, it is essential that there be means by which public opinion can be communicated. Often the communications proceed directly from the people to the leaders, as when letters, telegrams, petitions, and various lobbying activities are employed. But there are instances in which the expressed opinions of the public would not be known by governors unless the manifestations were observed and published or broadcast by journalists. This is particularly true when meetings and demonstrations are involved. If journalists are not present, such activities result in little more than people talking to themselves. Those engaged in civil rights movements, Vietnam War protests, pro-life and pro-choice activities, and many other causes recognize, if they are to reach the eyes and ears of those whom they want to reach, the importance of the presence of journalists.

The task of reporting public opinion is particularly difficult when the people's evaluations and proposals are still in their minds, when they have not yet entered the external world. In such situations, someone must go to the people and ask them what they think. At the present time, most of the efforts to do this are carried out by public opinion pollsters, either those employed by organizations independent of the press (whose findings are then reported by the mass media) or, increasingly, by the media's own research departments. Unfortunately, the most publicized polls often fail to report what most needs to be known.

Once again, the problem arises because decision making is confused with advising. In elections and referenda, the people do decide matters. But as members of the consultative assembly, as public opinion, they do not. Polling is often used in both situations: to predict the outcome of elections and referenda and to reveal internal public opinion. In the former, numbers are of prime importance. In providing advice, however, what are needed are argument and evidence: of prime importance is not the quantity of numbers but rather the quality of reasons.

Some of the questions that currently concern public officials are these: Should the number of terms of elected officials be limited? Should people afflicted with AIDS be publicly identified? What should be done to decrease the use of illegal drugs? Should subsidies for tobacco growers be continued? Should English be declared our national language?

On such matters, our governors need to listen to what the people have to say, not because the people should decide these issues but because the people may be able to advance reasons for their being decided one way or another. The prime purpose of public opinion is to enlighten the prudence of the governors. Obviously, elected officials cannot totally ignore the numbers who would prefer that decisions go one way rather than another, for the people who advise are usually the same people who vote at election time. But, although the process of acquiring public office is a necessary condition of governing, it is not the act of governing. Good governors give attention to public opinion, but they do not kowtow to it.

When the people do make a decision, as in an election, the difference between 49 percent support and 51 percent support is crucial. But when the people are being consulted for advice, such precise differences are meaningless. Even a poll revealing that 54 percent of the people prefer increased military spending and 46 percent oppose it—figures which, allowing for the typical plus or minus 3 percentage points for sampling error, would show a high probability that, if the people were deciding the matter, they would choose increased spending—means only, as far as the consultative assembly is concerned, that the people are about equally divided on the issue. As far as numbers are concerned, that rough estimate is all the governors really need. Much more important, the governors need reasons, arguments, and alternatives. Why are some in favor and others opposed? How can we obtain the additional funds if increases are made? What can be done to ensure national defense if they are not?

And when the poll results are overwhelmingly one-sided? All the more do public officials, especially those on the other side, need access to the reasoning of the deliberating assembly. There can be no rational debate without it.

Pollsters will sometimes list what they have found to be the major reasons for an opinion and the major options available, and they will ask a sample of the public to indicate which of these choices they prefer. By listing these closed-end options, the polls can report what positions the people support. Furthermore, through the use of intensity scales, pollsters can even reveal the strength of that support. But such procedures do not reveal any truly original arguments or alternatives. To accomplish that, such open-end questions as "What do you think ought to be done?" or "Why do you think so?" need to be asked. The answers to these would be most helpful to those who need to make practical decisions about practical affairs, but, as

Philip Meyer (1979, 131-32) points out, pollsters are reluctant to ask such questions:

> Open-end questions are not currently as fashionable as they used to be. Sociologists liked them because they do not limit the range of responses. An open-end question can tap attitudes and ideas that you never thought to ask about. The trouble with them is that they leave so much room for error in recording and coding.
>
> Interviewers do not take shorthand. . . . When a respondent has a long answer, only part of it is going to be recorded and even then the part that gets written down may not be the most important part. Moreover, the part that is recorded might not be recorded correctly or with the proper nuances.
>
> Later on, the open-end response, to be subjected to analysis, must be classified and coded. Working out a coding scheme is time consuming but not technically difficult. However, consistent application of a coding scheme is difficult. . . .
>
> Finally, the whole process of coding open-end responses adds to survey costs and delays the analysis, both near fatal disadvantages for news applications.

This does not mean that all polls and surveys are useless or impractical. They can have great value, especially when underlying situations need attention. For example, polls revealed a strong public concern for some form of firearms control from 1988 onward. Even the passage of the Brady Bill did not significantly ease the pressure that the public continued to exert on political leaders. Because of this pressure, efforts to find solutions to the domestic havoc caused by handguns still occupy an important place on the national political agenda. But even when polls reveal a hunger for solutions to widespread problems, they have little value in bringing forth from the people the original ideas, arguments, and proposals that are needed to achieve solutions for those problems.

Moreover, the random sampling necessary for reliable public opinion polling assumes that all members of the public being polled are equals. As eligible voters, they are equal. As advisers to public leaders, however, they are not. Some will have a strong and broad interest in public affairs, a sophisticated understanding of the complexities of those affairs, and original ideas about what should be done to make them better. It is this latter group that needs to have an opportunity to emerge from among the disinterested, uninformed, and inexperienced. Even polls with open-end questions are not likely to pick out, in a random sample, these most valuable members of the deliberating assembly.

Respecting Public Opinion

The third means by which journalism serves public opinion attempts to take care of the eventuality just discussed. The managers of many journalistic media provide time and space so that those most interested members of the public can express ideas that will reach the leaders who can most profit from them.

This role of the media is widely referred to as the forum function. The association of that function with the ancient Roman Forum, especially as it existed during the period of the Republic, may be a bit of romanticizing. It is true that the Forum did exist as a popular gathering place for the diverse people of the city and that within the Forum the Roman people often assembled to discuss public affairs. At one end was the rostra, a platform ten feet high, eighty feet long, and forty feet deep, from which orators (most notably, Cicero) would address the people. But the available evidence tells us little about the extent to which the common people—the book sellers, sandal makers, wine merchants, and the like—climbed the stairs to the rostra to speak their views (Grant 1970). Nevertheless, the Forum has come down to us as a symbol of public discussion of public affairs. Where does the public forum exist today?

There are some public hearings where people physically gather together and discuss public issues. But these are rare and often not convenient for many members of the public.

Much more common are the talk and call-in shows on radio and television, which have the advantage of voice-to-voice and, on television, face-to-face exchanges of viewpoints. They can convey tonal nuances and, on television, physical expressions as well as words. But the fact that broadcast messages exist in time rather than, as in the print media, in space poses several major obstacles to their success as a means of communicating the views of the people as a deliberating assembly. Whether members of the forum are attempting to persuade other members or the governors, the oral media send out their broadcasts at a set time, one that may not be convenient for the intended audience. Moreover, listeners can attend to only one broadcast program at a time. The relative impermanence of broadcasting makes it difficult for listeners to review and reconsider what was said. They cannot underline, annotate, clip, and file. If their attention is interrupted, they may lose, with no chance of regaining it, the whole trend of a discussion. And the rate of presentation may be faster or slower than the listeners desire; the medium, rather than their own judgment, controls the rate of their perception.

Thus, although the electronic media have great popularity, immediacy, timeliness, and ability to reach even the illiterate—all great advantages for the presentation of urgently important news—they are not the best means for providing a place for the public discussion of public affairs.

Even magazines are of limited value for this purpose. Not only are they relatively expensive and infrequently published, but most of them are specialized in content and national in scope. They are not likely to be able to provide a forum for deliberations about local and state issues. What the Internet may accomplish has yet to be determined.

It is to newspapers, therefore, that we most often turn to find the public forum. Only the literate, of course, can participate, but literacy is likely to benefit, not harm, the quality of the advice the forum provides. Within the newspapers, the forum that is open to the public is most often found in the editorial section. This does not mean it is efficiently handled there. On the contrary, as the next chapter will discuss, by not looking under the surface of what they are doing, most newspaper editors and editorial directors fall short of providing a resource greatly needed by all of us.

Contribution of Journalism to Public Opinion

Finally, journalists themselves serve public opinion by expressing their own views on issues and thus making their own contributions to the deliberating assembly.

Here, of course, we are referring to a special kind of journalist. Chapter 2 pointed out that any literate person who wants to be a journalist can be a journalist, for, broadly speaking, journalists are simply members of the public who happen to engage in the activity of providing, through mass communications, useful knowledge about public or personal affairs. Thus any members of the deliberating assembly who make use of the time and space provided by the media to contribute to the public discussion are journalists.

But the same chapter also noted the special few who make their living by providing this useful service to society: the professional journalists.

These professional journalists, since their livelihood requires that they attend to public problems, are likely to possess a background and understanding greater than those of individuals who must devote their working hours to repairing roofs, keeping books, ballet dancing, and so on. In addition, because they work in the field of communications, they probably express their knowledge more clearly and effectively than could the average citizen. Moreover, because they work for the mass media, they probably have greater and more immediate access to the means of communication. Finally, some of these people are specifically hired by media managers for the very purpose of deliberating about and then expressing their views on public issues. It is this last group of professional journalists who deserve special attention. Whether called editorialists, columnists, commentators, or spokespeople, they occupy special seats in the deliberating assembly of public opinion.

In newspapers, these journalists normally restrict the expressions of their opinions about public affairs to signed columns and to editorials. (The present references to columnists are not intended, of course, to include those who only amuse or titillate their readers.) Sometimes these pieces are directed to the political leaders, sometimes to the readers of the newspapers, sometimes, unfortunately, to no one in particular, being then only ventilations of an inflated sense of self-importance. But when they focus on public affairs and are designed with either the governors or the public in mind, they can make a valuable contribution to the political process. For, no matter how vigorously column writers and editorialists are sometimes scorned, most of us will agree that most of them are intelligent, widely informed persons. Moreover, those who work for the largest newspapers are like the governors to the extent that their very job and primary source of income is to inform themselves about, to think about, and to express their views on public affairs. To this extent at least, there is some legitimacy in referring to the press as the fourth branch of government.

To the governors, they can offer additional arguments in favor of or in opposition to courses of action that are under consideration. They can help the governors see all aspects of public issues, thus enriching their political prudence. Sometimes, although much too rarely, they even propose original courses of action for consideration by the governors.

When the messages are directed toward the people, these writers can, in ways such as those just mentioned, likewise nourish public opinion. The more mature public opinion is, the more useful it will be when brought to the attention of the governors.

These writers can also serve two additional functions. First, they can take the part of watchdogs, and alert the public to inadequacies that may range from laziness, stupidity, and moral flaws to gross malfeasance on the part of the governors. If these weaknesses are not too great, they can be lodged as factors for the people to consider at the next election. If they are severe or if the political leaders are appointed rather than elected, the writers can attempt to rally the public to support immediate censure or, in extreme circumstances, deposition.

Second, journalists can make it easier for the governors to govern. Editorialists can help persuade the public to support their governors in the difficult decisions the latter sometimes have to make. A choice that congressmen think is the most prudent but that a majority of the voters initially oppose, for example, may fall in defeat if the people cannot be persuaded to reverse their stand. Only the representatives who are not seeking reelection, who are in the early months of their terms of office, or who possess extraordinary fortitude will persist with a course of action, no matter how wise they think it is, that meets strong public opposition. To attempt to change public opinion in such a case is first of all, of course, the responsibility of the political leaders themselves, but the press can provide valuable assistance. And, although newspapers also need public support, their occasional opposition to public opinion is not as risky for them as it is for politicians: It is more difficult to vote a newspaper out of existence than to vote a governor out of office.

In most newspapers today, the forum—the place where these professional editorializing journalists are likely to publish their knowledge—is located in the editorial section. Unfortunately, however, it is not a place where one can find a clear, equal, and wide-open battle of ideas. Instead, in most newspapers, it is a place where the discussion is chaotic. In addition, in most newspapers, the discussion is stacked in favor of the newspapers themselves. This latter point derives to a great extent from the American newspaper practice of publishing unsigned editorials. This, as will be shown in the next chapter, is a custom based in great part on a faulty understanding of the nature and function of editorials themselves.

Forum and Freedom of Press

Once we understand the forum as the place where the people exercise the democratic function of the deliberating assembly, we again recognize that the newspaper editorial page is a forum only in a metaphorical sense. That page is not literally a place where an interested public gathers. It is not a place where one can stand up, wave a hand, shout, or in some other way attract attention and announce the desire to be heard on an announced topic. It is not a place where other members of the public can give immediate response to a speaker, or where an individual can successfully insist that a fresh item be added to the agenda. Even when the newspaper forum discussion is well organized, it is still a place much more under the control of the directors than was the great forum of ancient Rome.

The newspaper forum is not only directed; it is also owned. It is a private, not a public place. The persons who will be granted access to the editorial page, the topics on which they will be allowed to speak, the length at which they will be permitted to set forth their views, the time at which those views will be made available to the general public—all this and more are controlled by those who are in charge of that page. In the contemporary newspaper forum, not all of the participants have equal freedom to say what they want to say. As A.J. Liebling said years ago (1961, 30), "Freedom of the press is guaranteed only to those who own one." It is important, therefore, that we examine the relationship of the forum to freedom of the press.

An examination of the legal concept of freedom of speech and of the press is unnecessary. Hundreds of books and articles have already been devoted to that important subject in attempts to determine what, if any, are the limits to these First Amendment rights.

It is also unnecessary to repeat the debate concerning whether the First Amendment should be extended to guarantee a legal right of the people to have access to the mass media. Jerome A. Barron (1973) argued forcefully and extensively in favor of such a right, especially in his book *Freedom of the Press for Whom?* But scarcely a year after the publication of the book, the U.S. Supreme Court made moot Barron's basic arguments. In the 1974 case of *Miami Herald Publishing Co. v. Tornillo*, the court issued a unanimous decision that there was no constitutional access right to private communications media. To Barron's claims that such a right exists, the court held that such an interpretation of the First Amendment had, in the words of Benno C. Schmidt, Jr., "no support in historical understanding, in the constitutional text itself, or in the uniform holdings of courts that have considered the question" (Schmidt 1976, 240). That seems to settle the legal status of public access.

Both before and after the *Tornillo* decision, however, other writers proposed extralegal means of assuring some degree of public access to the newspaper forum. In 1969, for instance, Ben H. Bagdikian recommended that, among other possibilities, there be "a national press council that would . . . investigate and make public findings on claims of gross malpractice" (1969, 13). And in 1977, Peter Donaghue proposed that the press accept a voluntary code that would include attempting "to provide an outlet for the expression of all segments of the public on a wide range of subjects from diverse points of view." Media compliance would be enhanced by their cooperation "with local, state, regional and national press councils studying press policies and practices" (Donaghue 1977). Instead of relying on the law to enforce access, these writers saw the pressure coming from the public through the mechanism of independent councils that would pronounce judgment on the adequacy of newspaper forums.

Newspapers and magazines, however, have proved reluctant to accept even this type of pressure. A major effort to improve the press, the National News Council, lasted only from 1973 to 1984. During these eleven years, the council investigated 242 complaints, of which it decided only 82 were "warranted," that is, deserving of condemnation. More importantly, almost all of the complaints dealt with accusations of reportorial inaccuracy or bias; less than a half-dozen were even remotely related to media access. Even a longer-lived council, therefore, would probably have had little influence on expanding the people's participation in the public forum.

Accuracy and fairness, of course, are important journalistic attributes. Moreover, the council was also a national voice in support of many First Amendment causes. But as of the end of 1978, only thirty-two media and media foundations were providing financial support (National News Council 1979). And some major publications, including the *New York Times* and *Time* magazine, declined even to cooperate with the council. Its demise, therefore, though regrettable, was not unexpected.

Some of the regret was very strongly expressed. For example, Margo Huston, a Pulitzer Prize winner and member of the council for six years, lamented, "Now that the nation is without the news council, the nation's press is without a conscience" (Huston 1984).

But neither the death of the National News Council nor the earlier legal decision in the Tornillo case deprived the nation's press of its conscience. Conscience directs from within, not from without. Law and public opinion are exterior influences; they are not one's conscience. Laws and councils, it is true, are powerful forces. One or both may sometimes deter editors from doing what they would prefer to do or, more rarely, incline them to do what they would prefer not to do. But neither one is a substitute for an editor's conscience.

Moreover, law, public opinion, and other exterior influences are unlikely to provide the initiative, the ingenuity, the detailed and protracted action necessary for great accomplishments. If there are to be truly major enhancements of the public forum, they will be motivated and achieved, not by outside powers, but by journalists themselves.

Freedom of the Press: The Positive View

At some time in our lives, many of us are struck by the realization once expressed by the English journalist G. K. Chesterton: "From the first vaguely, and of late more and more clearly, I have felt that the world is conceiving liberty as something that merely works outwards. And I have always conceived it as something that works inwards" (1936, 103).

Chesterton's comment applies to that freedom known as freedom of the press. Often we think of it, discuss it, battle for it primarily as a release from exterior pressures. The wording of the First Amendment—"Congress shall make no law . . ." —probably inclines us in that direction. Moreover, it is certainly true that little can be accomplished unless that initial freedom, the freedom from exterior control, does exist. One cannot race to glory when one is chained to the starting gate. Many have realized, however, that freedom from ought to exist in order to achieve a more important freedom for. Laws and councils do not bring about the creativity required for that more positive type of freedom.

With very rare exceptions, laws and councils punish wrongdoing rather than reward excellence. They prevent actions from dipping below a minimum level of tolerability. But that is insufficient for achieving an effective public forum. The forum requires initiative and ingenuity. These cannot be imposed from the outside, nor are they automatically released when outside restraints are removed. But once we have achieved the freedom to act, they can come from the free exercise of the dedication and labor of journalists themselves.

Where and how well professional journalists direct their acts depend in great part on their goodwill and on their understanding of what journalism is and what is required to practice it well. Goodwill, in most journalists, already exists. History has shown that most of those persons who practice the arts of journalism have used that freedom well—not only for their own good but also for the public good. This may be less true of some of those businessmen who are only media owners. But they, too, are not opposed to good journalism if it will also pay a dividend. Fortunately, the journalism that serves the real needs of the public does not require a vow of poverty.

As a further contribution to understanding the work of journalism and, in particular, the newspaper forum as a place where the people act as a deliberating assembly, let's take a closer look at what is generally considered to be the essence of that forum: the editorial and the place where editorials appear.

10

Conclusion

Since journalism itself comprises many elements, it is not surprising that these factors, too, would develop chronologically before coming together to constitute the total work that is journalism. What were those elements, those realities, those early necessary conditions? For one, people had a need for the kind of practical knowledge that would enable them, as individuals or as a group, to make good decisions about what to do or avoid doing.

Even the most primitive people needed that knowledge. If some members left the others to seek food for all, the others needed to know they left for that purpose, not to fight enemies or to do something else. Food was needed; if some had not gone to find it, others would have had to go.

In addition, it was also necessary to have some means by which knowledge could be transferred from the mind of one person to the mind or minds of other persons. This, too, undoubtedly existed very early in the prehistory of humankind. This early communication, probably oral or tactile, was like wisps of smoke in the air: we have no record of it.

We do know, however, that graphic signs of knowledge were employed in Sumer about 3300 B.C., and instances of movable type printing have been found in the island of

Crete and estimated to date from 1700 B.C. (Mooradian 1972).

But one more characteristic had to be in place before *journalism* could exist in the sense the word is being used in this book. There had to be, not merely communication, but *mass* communication: the conveyance of knowledge to many more people than those from whom it originated, to so many people, in fact, that the one or few who originated the communication did not know all of those who were capable of receiving it, and those many were so situated that they were not able to provide an equal response.

Here we must distinguish two types of mass communication. One type, the one with which we are most familiar today, takes place when the message is *sent out* to the many recipients. Another type, important but often ignored, is that in which the many recipients *come to* the message. In the latter, the message is placed somewhere, and many people, more than the message maker knows and more than will normally respond, come to wherever the message is placed. Today, billboards are probably the most widespread example of this latter type of mass communication, although it is also importantly evident in the notices and declarations pasted on walls in many low-technology countries.

This "come to" type of mass communications existed early in human history in an interesting variety of ways: in the signs that informed people that food, drink, lodging, care of animals, and other services were available at designated premises; in the signs and displays that weavers or pot makers used to inform those who needed such wares; in the designs of buildings—of churches, for example—that informed people of the use for which they were intended. Some of the very earliest journalism, in other words, was the type that later was given the name "advertising."

"Come to" mass communications also existed by 59 B.C., during Caesar's first consulship, when the *acta diurna* or "daily gazette" began to chronicle events both momentous and trivial in Rome and the empire. The acta, which extolled the workings of the government and continued for more than two centuries, were posted in public places, where the literate could read them and sometimes narrate the contents to those who could not read. As C. A. Gifford has pointed out, "They were copied in manuscript and sent to distant provincial outposts, where they were eagerly perused," especially by those who needed to know what was going on, as when the outcome of wars might lead to loss or profit (Gifford 1975, 106). Today we would give this journalism that projected an image of a country or institution the name of political or commercial *public relations*.

But much of advertising and public relations is, to a great extent, personal affairs journalism. That is, it provides knowledge that is useful to people to satisfy their business, recreation, health, and other personal needs.

What about public affairs journalism, the type that collections of people need to achieve and maintain the welfare of the groups, societies, and other organizations of which they are members? That type of journalism also came into being at least by the time of the Roman Empire. It existed in the Forum, which was a "come to" type of mass communications, a place to which the people came to discuss laws, trials, and elections (Ibid.). Although the medium of communication was oral, it satisfied all requirements of mass communication.

What about the persons who produced these various types of journalism? Most of them, of course, were only part-time or amateur journalists; their livelihood was gained by doing something else. The people who produced or made copies of the *acta diurna*, however, might have been different. The acta were produced daily and probably required full-time journalists, and, although the names of most of them have not survived, Cicero does refer to a man named Chrestos whom Gifford describes as "the first by-lined reporter . . . who apparently made his living by gathering and selling news" (Gifford 1975, 107).

Western and Eastern Journalism

But the march of journalism did not follow an even and clearly marked course. Especially irregular was the type of journalism that depended on "sent out" mass communications, the kind in which messages are duplicated and then made available to large numbers of people. Although copies of the *acta diurna* were made and delivered to many persons, they were handwritten; the expense of this kind of production deterred others from attempting a similar venture. In addition, the acta depended upon the existence of a highly literate upper class. With the fall of Rome in the fifth century, however, the arts of reading and writing began to wither away, surviving only in the monasteries (Ibid., 132). The fall of Rome also brought an end to the public forums and, consequently, the disappearance, even in an oral society, of places where people could gather and listen to speakers discuss public affairs. Thus, at least in the West, all that survived for a long time was the advertising journalism that could get along with come to" mass communications.

In the Eastern world, however, printed communications continued to develop during the very centuries in which they were nearly dormant in the West. Pi Sheng, in China, reinvented movable earthenware type in the eleventh century, and by the fifteenth century, cast metal type was being widely used, first in Korea and soon after in China and Japan. Because paper, needed for any extensive and relatively inexpensive circulation of publications, had existed in China since the second century, one might therefore think that everything was available for a vast expansion of journalistic communications (Carter 1955). But this did not happen. Although many works were published, they were almost exclusively works of literature and education rather than the practical works of journalism.

With one major exception: Beginning as early as A.D. 750, the Chinese emperor began to collect information about the welfare of the country and, twice a year, sent copies to designated officials. Later these publications were printed and distributed once a month. The publication became a weekly in 1361 and a daily in 1830 and became known as the *Peking Gazette* (Desmond 1978, 17-18). But this was a unique, official publication, another example of political public relations.

In the Far East, two special factors limited the spread of written journalism: lack of an alphabet and a printing press. Because of the former, the Chinese had to carve and cast a distinct character for virtually every word that might be used. A thousand words might require nearly a thousand different characters. This was so formidable an obstacle that, by the nineteenth century, the far eastern countries had almost altogether abandoned printing from movable type and returned to the older block printing (Carter 1955, 233). (A Korean alphabet—using twenty-four characters—was invented in 1443 but did not become immediately popular.) These handicaps discouraged the publication of anything that large numbers of people could afford and that had, at the same time, only the temporary value of timely, practical knowledge.

Even when, near the middle of the fifteenth century, Johann Gutenberg made use of an alphabetic language and adapted the wine press to the task of printing on paper, no great surge of written journalism ensued in the West, for no extensive public was capable of reading such material. "Down to the end of the seventeenth century," S. H. Steinberg (1961, 166) reminds us, "both literacy and leisure were virtually confined to scholars and 'gentlemen.'"

Included among the literate were, of course, the clerics, whose greatest interest was in books—products of enduring value restricted in their circulation by their expense.

Thus print journalism of any type was relatively rare until the fifteenth century on the Continent, the sixteenth century in England, and the eighteenth century in America. Among the few exceptions was a broadside—a large poster-issued in 1480 by William Caxton in London to advertise one of his books. This instance of advertising journalism preceded newspaper journalism in England by 140 years (Emery and Emery 1978, 42).

For a long time after Gutenberg, most trade and commerce were still conducted reasonably well through oral communications or through interpersonal correspondence. Governmental and military information traveled primarily in one direction: from the leaders to the followers. There seemed to be little need for a discussion of public affairs by the common people and even less need for any medium by which the people could convey their reactions and proposals to the leaders. Even as late as 1621, King James I was issuing proclamations against "the great liberty of discourse concerning matters of state" (Ibid., 8).

Professional Journalism: The Beginning

Although, early on, some individuals may have been designated by emperors, kings, or popes to spend their working hours collecting information about current happenings, and although other individuals, such as town criers, may have made it their business to circulate information of this type, such people were, until around the seventeenth century, exceedingly rare. By then, however, the number who made their living by acquiring knowledge useful for making everyday personal and public decisions and by distributing that knowledge to the public began rapidly to increase.

The number of professional journalists began to grow when their survival ceased to be dependent upon the largess of a relatively few wealthy or powerful individuals. The increase took place when reader-supported journalism was added to what had been predominantly public relations (that is, institutionally supported) and advertising journalism.

What caused this increase? As far as print journalism is concerned, many things. Literacy spread from the prosperous and scholarly to the middle classes. As Steinberg points out, both the commercial middle class and women acquired a taste for reading during the eighteenth century, and the growth of lending libraries made it possible for these parts of society to satisfy this appetite without spending a great amount of money (Steinberg 1961, 166-67). Later, free public libraries and compulsory school attendance spread literacy to those living at even lower economic levels. At about the same time, the use of wood pulp (instead of rags) for the making of paper, improvements in presses, and the automation of type casting all helped reduce the costs of printed products and thus made them available to increasing numbers of people (Desmond 1978, 85).

But these changes might have led only to a vast growth in public relations, advertising, and personal affairs journalism were it not for other social and political developments that occurred in the centuries following the Gutenberg period. Most important among these were the Reformation of the sixteenth century, the English "Glorious" revolution of the seventeenth century and the subsequent enactment of the Bill of Rights, and the eighteenth-century revolutions in France and America. "No taxation with representation" became a powerful cry for those eager to advance ideas, and Thomas Jefferson's assertion that "All governments derive their just powers from the consent of the governed" reaffirmed the public affairs obligations of all the people. Such incentives awakened, in the increasingly literate public, recognition of opportunities to make significant decisions affecting the welfare of the many communities of which they were members. Public affairs journalism burst into full blossom.

Along the way, more and more men (and a few women) found it possible to earn a livelihood by supplying people with the knowledge those people needed to make decisions concerning timely issues, both personal and public. In many instances, professional journalism depended upon and grew out of the business of printing, but by the early eighteenth century in England and only a few years later in America, it was possible for people to depend upon journalism alone as a source of income and thus as an occupation to which they could devote themselves.

By the eighteenth century, therefore, a number of realities had come into existence: mass communications, public relations journalism, advertising journalism, personal affairs journalism, public affairs journalism, amateur journalism, and professional journalism. In all instances, the realities were in existence before names were coined to identify them. The naming, alternate naming, and renaming are still going on, but the realities persist.

Journalism and the Media

Several other characteristics existing by the end of the eighteenth century deserve at least brief attention. For instance, although today many people tend to associate journalism with newspapers, in the early centuries of the printing age journalism was most frequently published in books, magazines, and pamphlets. Some were works of public affairs journalism, such as John Milton *Areopagitica*, a fervent argument for unlicensed printing, published in 1644, or Daniel Defoe's many persuasive articles which appeared in *Mist's Journal* from 1717 through 1720 (Emery and Emery 1978, 11). Others were pieces of personal affairs journalism, containing "practical advice for home and garden and field," as S. H. Steinberg (1961, 166) points out.

In addition, in great part due to the existence of advertising journalism, that public affairs journalism was able to be produced by professional journalists, especially by those working for newspapers. Advertising journalism was so highly esteemed by the owners of early American newspapers that many of them incorporated the word "Advertiser" in their titles, such as the *Boston Weekly Advertiser*, the *Salem Gazette and General Advertiser*, and the *American Recorder and Charlestown Advertiser*. These names remind us that, even though those communities that depend upon the consent and participation of the public could not endure without public affairs journalism, the public itself has always been reluctant to pay the full price for the knowledge which that consent and participation require.

Finally, it is interesting that the growth in print journalism temporarily signaled the end of oral journalism. Not until the twentieth century were means invented to extend vastly the range, first, of the human voice and then, along with it, pictures of speakers and their surroundings.

Public Affairs Journalism: The Scope

The scope of the public affairs function of journalism grew gradually through the centuries, becoming stronger as the people's roles in governing expanded. Many of the stages in this progress are linked with landmark documents: Magna Carta in England, the American Declaration of Independence, the United States Constitution and Bill of Rights. But to the extent that these documents had anything explicit to say about journalism, they spoke out more for the value of journalistic freedom than for the nature of its functions.

Some early commentators on the press in the United States, however, recognized not only the value of its liberty but also at least some of the purposes for its existence. For example, Tunis Wortman, a New York lawyer prominent in Tammany politics, a vigorous defender of Thomas Jefferson, and, in 1813-14, publisher of the *Standard of Union*, presented a closely reasoned defense of freedom of the press (Wortman 1800).

As Wortman saw it, the role of the federal government was exceedingly limited, most would say too limited. "The true utility of Government," he wrote, "is to suppress crimes and afford protection to the community: every other interference [with the states and with individuals] is pernicious, and will be continually liable to abuses" (Ibid., 130). Thus the federal government, he believed, had no business restricting freedom of speech or of the press.

But Wortman did see virtue in the free discussion of public issues. Recognizing that societies exist not only to prevent violence and offenses but also to improve people, he affirmed: "To promote the improvement of Society it is essential that Mind should be free. Unless individuals are permitted to reflect and communicate their sentiments upon every topic, it is impossible that they should progress in knowledge" (Ibid., 133). In words very similar to those that John Stuart Mill would use more than a half century later in his essay *On Liberty*, Wortman continued:

> Shall I be permitted to express in conversation what I am prohibited from publishing through the medium of the press? If my impressions are true, their circulation will be beneficial; if they are false, it will be the means of destroying them. . . . The publication of those errors will eventually produce a beneficial tendency; it will infallibly be the prelude to their detection. But if my sentiments are founded in Truth, why should they be concealed? (Ibid., 142-43)

In addition to the value of unrestricted discussion for the general sorting out of truth and falsehood, Wortman identified more specific roles for the free press in a representative democracy. For example, since any member of a representative democracy may be selected for public office, all persons need to know enough about the public situation to determine whether they themselves should run for office. He continues, "It is . . . absolutely indispensable . . . that each individual should be furnished with all the means of obtaining political information, and be permitted to exercise his faculties in the pursuit of such knowledge without interruption or restraint" (Ibid., 199). Likewise, the people need to be furnished with information in order to exercise their elective right, and this information should include not only what the candidates stand for but also the reasons they have for those positions: "It is to be presumed that the elector, who prefers between contending candidates, *decides from the influence of reasons which are present to his understanding*" (Ibid., 200, emphasis added). Moreover, the people's need for knowledge about public officers, Wortman emphasized, must be continuous. Whereas other forms of government can deal with the misuse of power only by submission or by violent resistance, representative governments provide peaceful alternatives: expressed criticism of the governors while they are in office with the hope of their improvement, or, failing this, replacement of the offenders by others through an election. The people need to know not only what candidates for office and officeholders themselves are doing, but also their character:

> Surely, if my suffrage is requested in favor of any individual, it is my duty to enquire what are his qualifications? What his morals? Is he entitled to public confidence? What are his pretensions to the virtue of Integrity? . . . Character and general Conduct are, therefore, correlative. An examination of the one implies an examination of the other. (Ibid., 203)

Thus, the people need from the press a great amount of information about public officials themselves as well as about the decisions they make and the reasons for those decisions.

Concerning the knowledge needed by the people to formulate sound public opinions, Wortman presented an amazingly sophisticated understanding of the nature, causes, and functions of public opinion. He delineated the differences between general opinions, which establish and sustain the very bases of social institutions and have broad support, and particular opinions, upon which there is great disagreement. He noted that the evidence of public opinion "may be either positive or presumptive. In the former case it may be gathered from the express declarations of the people; in the latter it is to be implied from their silent acquiescence" (Ibid., 119). Although Wortman did not specifically mention that the voices of the people, particularly in the early stages of inquiry, could contribute to good governing, he did see that "diversity of sentiment" would help achieve "the eventual reception of Truth":

> It produces Collision, engenders Argument, and affords exercise and energy to the intellectual powers; it corrects our errors, removes our prejudices, and strengthens our perceptions; it compels us to seek for the evidences of our knowledge, and habituates us to a frequent revisal of our sentiments. In the conflict between opinions we are enured to correctness of reflection, and become taught in the school of Experience to reason and expatiate. It cannot surely be visionary to predict the ultimate triumph of Truth. (Ibid., 123)

And it was the press, he saw, that could provide a stimulus and location, a public forum, for such "collisions."

The Editorial and News Contents

At about the same time that Wortman was writing, editors such as Noah Webster in the *American Minerva* and David Denniston in the *American Citizen and General Advertiser* were beginning to insert into their newspapers special pieces that we now designate as editorials. These items usually appeared on an inside page under a heading, now known as a "masthead," that included the name of the newspaper and the city in which it was published. Today, editors often assert that editorials are a means of separating opinion material from the news content, and, indeed, they frequently serve that purpose, particularly when the opinions expressed are not shared by all or nearly all of the readers. (When readers and editors happen to be of the same mind, the latter frequently do not bother to separate opinion from the news: see, for example, the coverage of "our side" during World War II or the reporting of the hometown athletic team versus an out-of-state rival.)

Such separation, however, was not the original purpose of editorials. Rather, editorials were simply the material that was written by the editor, the person who was responsible for the contents—and usually also for the printing—of the newspaper. And, since normally the only material written by the editor was that dealing with local events, that material would appear under a heading identifying both the place where the paper was published and the locale of the news events. Most of the stories printed in these local columns were simple, straightforward reports devoid of opinion or advocacy. For example, the first items under the "Boston" heading of the March 5, 1770, issue of the *Boston Gazette and Country Journal* were these:

> Thursday last Capt. Paddock, in a Schooner, arrived here from London.
>
> Last Thursday Se'nnight [a week ago] was married at Roxbury, JOSEPH OTIS, Esq. of Barnstable, Son

> of the Hon. JAMES OTIS, Esq; to Miss MARIA WALTER, Daughter of the Rev. NATHANIEL WALTER of Roxbury.

But when a local event happened also to be an occasion of unusual importance and high emotional quality, the editors did not hesitate to express opinions and to let their feelings be known. For example, in the same paper a week later, the "Boston" column began its account of the Boston Massacre in these words:

> The Town of Boston affords a recent and melancholy Demonstration of the destructive Consequences of quartering Troops among Citizens in a Time of Peace, under a Pretense of supporting the Laws and aiding Civil Authority; every considerate unprejudic'd Person among us was deeply imprest with the Apprehension of these Consequences when it was known that a Number of Regiments were ordered to this Town under such a Pretext, but in Reality to inforce oppressive measures; to awe & controul the legislative as well as executive Power of the Province, and to quell a Spirit of Liberty, which however it may have been basely oppos'd and even ridicul'd by some, would do Honor to any Age or Country.

In fact, near the end of the eighteenth and the early part of the nineteenth centuries, little deliberate effort was made anywhere in newspapers to separate news from opinion. Both could be found almost anywhere, whether in the column that bore the name of the city in which the paper was published or in any of the other columns. But in the half-century after 1830, numerous developments began to interact and change the character of the columns that had once been the prerogative of editors: inexpensive papers began to be published; circulation increased; advertising income increased; additional people were hired to produce the larger papers; press technology permitted ever larger press runs; events that had never been covered before—such as sports and society—began to receive attention; departmentalization of the contents began to occur; the telegraph permitted the sending of information over vast distances in a short time; newspapers began to cooperate in the gathering of news; news coverage of the Mexican and Civil wars emphasized quickness, conciseness, and factuality over the expressions of opinions. Although it may seem that a single gestation, such as the organization of news services that provided stories to many newspapers with differing opinions, might have been sufficient cause for deemphasis on the expression of opinions in the news stories and the gradual public acceptance of opinion pieces as more appropriate for the editorial pages, this is probably an oversimplification of what occurred. All the factors mentioned and many others as well, although some only very remotely and indirectly, played some role in the change.

It is important to recognize, however, what that change was. It was not a total elimination of all expressions of opinions from news stories. Those opinions that an overwhelming majority of the readers were willing to accept continued to squirm their way, unnoticed because inoffensive, through many news stories. But the expressions explicitly intended to *change* the minds of numerous readers gradually worked their way out of most news columns and found a welcome home only in editorial, or other explicitly opinionizing, columns. The editorial column was no longer a place to which readers would turn to find the local news or an article that readers could assume was written by the editor. Editorials, not only those that appeared under the masthead but also those published elsewhere in the newspaper, became disembodied voices expressing opinions and advocating actions, most of them, especially in large metropolitan papers, written by persons unidentified to their readers.

Participation of the Readers into Public Affairs

One might think that an increase in the opportunities for people to take part in political public affairs would lead to increased participation in those affairs and that this, in turn, would bring about a growth in the public affairs journalism that is needed to fuel that participation. This does not seem to have happened.

The most dramatic increases in political opportunities involved the extension of suffrage. Although the Fifteenth Amendment, ratified in 1870, proclaimed that the right to vote shall not be abridged "on account of race, color, or previous condition of servitude," it brought about only a brief increase in the number of black voters. By the 1890s, southern white Democrats were using the grandfather clause, poll taxes, literacy tests, all-white primaries, and even physical intimidation to keep black men from the polls.

Thus it was not until the twentieth century that a genuine expansion of the franchise took place. In 1920, the Nineteenth Amendment extended suffrage to women and virtually doubled the number of eligible voters. The Twenty-fourth Amendment barring poll taxes and the Voting Rights acts of the mid-1960s finally gave the franchise to minorities, and the Twenty-sixth Amendment, lowering the voting age to eighteen, added more than ten million young people to the ranks of eligible voters.

Yet in spite of the fact that the road to the polls was opened to vastly more people, there was no corresponding swell of marchers along that road. Whereas three out of four eligible voters regularly went to the polls during most of the nineteenth century, in the election of 1924, only four years after women were granted suffrage, less than 49 percent of eligible voters cast ballots in the race among Calvin Coolidge, John W. Davis, and Robert M. LaFollette. In 1988, in spite of the opportunities made available to minorities and to eighteen- to twenty-year-olds, the total turnout for the election in which George Bush defeated Michael Dukakis was less than 51 percent (D. Rogers 1992), and for the eighteen- to twenty-year age group alone it was less than 34 percent (Cultice 1992, 223).

In 1996, according to the Committee for the Study of the American Electorate, a nonpartisan Washington, D.C., group, the rate of eligible voters who went to the polls was 48.8 percent, the lowest since 1924. It is difficult to know what effect, if any, journalism had on all these developments. As one set of scholars put it: "It is the paradox of mass politics in the United States: despite a 200-year-old tradition of public participation, an intense and virtually uninterrupted barrage of video, audio, and print information on local, national, and world events, one finds a conspicuously large number of citizens with only marginal interest in and information about public affairs" (Neuman, Just, and Crigler 1992, xiv). As these same writers pertinently note, what the people come to know about public affairs is the product of many sources: the knowledge, and twist to that knowledge, provided by sources; the ways in which journalists turn their knowledge to what they think are appropriate public purposes; and, important but often overlooked, the manner in which the people incorporate that journalistic knowledge into what they already know from their experience and from other sources (Ibid., ch. 7). In addition, public affairs must compete with personal affairs for our attention. Combine this with the fact that public affairs knowledge does not necessarily cause political action—not even the seemingly simple political act of voting—and perhaps we should not be surprised that, according to the February 1, 1993, *New York Times*, more persons (an estimated 120 million of them) watched the Super Bowl football game on television in January 1993 than, a few months earlier, turned out to vote in the presidential election.

The reasons for this state of affairs cannot be loaded exclusively onto the backs of the mass media. As W. Russell Neuman noted, "Political information is available in great richness to all in the United States who wish to pay attention. Those who blame the media for the ills of the modern American polity tend to confuse the characteristics of the medium with the characteristics of its audience" (Neuman 1986, 134). The Jim Lehrer News Hour, the Cable News Network, National Public Radio, the *New York Times*, the journals of political analysis, and much more are available. They are just not attended to by the majority of Americans.

Thus the spirit of public nonchalance has many causes. But when we look beneath the surface of journalism, we can find a few that are of special importance.

The Commercialization of Journalism

Although amateur journalism—the infrequent participation in the public debate by persons for whom journalistic work is not their main occupation—makes enormously important contributions to the public discussion of public affairs, the products of the amateurs would have few places to go if it were not for professional journalists. The latter not only do journalistic work on a steady, ongoing basis but also provide most of the media of journalism, the places where the amateurs can occasionally find an outlet for expressions of their own deliberations.

Media, of course, need money. Ideology, enthusiasm, dedication, energy-each by itself or even all of them in combination—have not been sufficient to assure the survival of mass communications. Subsidization, as with the political party press of the early nineteenth century or the religious media today, can keep a newspaper or broadcast station afloat, but their appeal is usually only to those who adhere to the beliefs of the subsidizers. Such media have not been a successful means for assuring a wide debate, a consultative assembly for public affairs.

Thus those interested in providing public affairs journalism have found it necessary, if they want to increase the odds for survival, to turn to an old companion: advertising journalism.

In the days when advertising was achieved through "come to" mass communications, those who wanted to inform the public about products or services did not need the mass media. The merchant or provider simply put up a sign. Persons traveling by saw the sign and, if they wished, took advantage of whatever was offered.

When the mass media did come into existence, however, advertisers quickly took advantage of these "sent out" mass communications. No longer did a merchant, for example, need to hope that an occasional passer-by would both see his posted message and have a need for whatever was advertised. The mass media made it possible for the merchant to take the initiative to seek out a great number of prospective customers. And, as communities grew in size and people dispersed, this became an enormous advantage. For many merchants, the number of potential customers who would see their messages was important: the more the better. If several general circulation newspapers were available, therefore, the one with the greatest number of readers had the upper hand.

How does a journalistic medium attract the masses? Usually by adding material in which people have an easy, natural interest. As Aristotle said, a person "will be ready to attend to anything that touches himself, and to anything that is important, surprising, or agreeable" (3: 14, 1415b). Even editors who had never read Aristotle seemed to recognize that if the contents of their newspapers had these attributes, some of which constitute human interest journalism, people would buy the publications.

Journalism and the Human Interest

The early history of journalism suggests that, at first, the inclusion of human interest material in what was otherwise practical, useful news was more an effort to maintain, rather than to expand, an existing readership.

This way of using human interest existed in Europe even before the development of journalism in America. In the sixteenth century, for example, the House of Fugger made Augsburg, Germany, the information center of Europe. Intended primarily to provide the Fugger business interests with useful information, a stream of news reports from Europe, Spanish America, Mediterranean Africa, and the Orient flowed into Augsburg. But, like the news service reports that come into a publication office today, the Fugger correspondence was unedited and covered an enormous variety of topics, not all of them of practical use.

For instance, the June 8, 1579, letter from Seville begins, "Of news we have none of import to give you these days. But a curious occurrence recently took place five miles from here, in a village, St. Ginar by name." The writer then narrates the story of a man, lodged in a church to escape his creditors, who was persuaded to leap from the church door onto a cart and there take the part of Jesus in a mystery play. One of the creditors arranged with the man playing Judas to push the actor out onto the street, where he could be seized and marched off to debtors' prison. This done, a turmoil ensued; the many participants were brought before a judge, who decided, among other things, that the man who played Jesus should be freed of his debt for all eternity. "Of this," the report ends, "for lack of better news, have I wished to give tidings unto you" (Matthews 1959, 57-8).

In America, more than two hundred years later, the situation was similar. Newspapers, especially those west of the eastern coastal areas, typically would have only four small pages. Crowded onto those pages would be advertisements, federal laws (the contract to print and thus "make public" these laws was often the financial linchpin of frontier newspapers), material borrowed from other papers, opinions and exhortations from the readers, and a little local news and editor comment. But if the papers had insufficient "news of import" to fill those few pages, it was not unusual for an editor to print a poem, story, or other entertaining material.

In the 1830s, a new type of newspaper began to appear. These papers usually cost only a penny (compared to the six cents charged by their existing competitors), and they thus found favor with a whole new segment of the population. The appeal lay not only in the lower price but also in the attention given to events not previously covered by the more expensive papers read primarily by shippers, businessmen, political leaders, and professional people.

No longer did editors add interesting material merely to fill space. Instead, the aim was to expand readership. Increasingly, editors would brag about the size of their newspaper's circulation, not only as a mark of prestige but also as a bait for advertisers. Activities in the municipal courts, sporting events (mostly boxing and horse racing), and the parties and balls of the socially elite attracted the interest of the expanding readership. Some of the knowledge provided by these new areas of coverage had no useful value to most of the growing number of readers. In particular, knowledge of the bustlings of high society or the emotional conflicts in municipal court was no more news—timely, useful knowledge—than were the romantic novels that were also attracting attention at this time. The stories were published not because they were journalistic news but because they were interesting. Thus the first issue of the *New-York Daily Times* (September 18, 1851) devoted front-page space to the story *"Death in a Cell"*:

> At a late hour on Tuesday night, policeman Coalter, of the Fourth Patrol District, found an unknown female, aged 35 years, lying in Madisons st, laboring under the effects of delirium tremens, and apparently lifeless. A dray was procured, and the poor woman was conveyed to the Station-house, where she seemed to somewhat revive, but was yet under the influence of strong drink, and was accordingly placed in a cell in the female department, where she was found a corpse in about two hours after. Yesterday morning the Coroner held an inquest on the remains, and the jury rendered a verdict of "Death by an apoplectic fit."

We can assume that all the facts in this account—and in the thousands of other pathetic, humorous, exciting, incongruous, or sentimental tales found in the penny press—were accurate. But since they were not really news stories and thus had practical consequences for almost no readers of the *Times*, an inaccuracy here or a fictional invention there may not have seemed to make a great deal of difference. How widespread was the temptation to substitute fiction for fact? Oliver Gramling, in his history of the Associated Press, gives us a hint. Speaking of Daniel Craig, the second general agent of the New York Associated Press in the mid-nineteenth century, Gramling says:

> He was a stickler for correctness and insisted his men be likewise. He knew that it was a general practice for a reporter in one city to telegraph a few lines on the main facts of an event, leaving it to an imaginative editor on the receiving end to "blow up" the story into several hundred words with what "details" came to mind. Craig issued orders that if a story was important enough to warrant detail the details were worth the wire costs. The rule shocked an experienced "telegraph reporter," who protested that editors did not know the difference between real and imaginary news. (Gramling 1940, 30)

Thus, as American journalism developed during the nineteenth century, interlocking relationships among several factors developed simultaneously. Media income depended heavily on advertising revenue; advertising rates depended heavily on the size of the readership; the number of readers depended greatly on the interest level of the material being communicated. Popular newspapers, it was quickly discovered, could be profitable businesses. In 1833, Benjamin Day had founded the *New York Sun* as a sideline to his failing job-printing business; in 1849 (several years after the Great Moon Hoax), the paper was sold for $250,000. James Gordon Bennett had founded his *New York Herald* with $500 and some desks fashioned from packing boxes in 1835, and Henry Raymond had to raise $100,000 to start the *New York Times* in 1851. By the 1870s, such papers were worth one or two million dollars (Schiller 1981, 12, 184). A paper that catered to human interest became not only a business but also a big business. And the trend accelerated in the twentieth century and spread to the newly developed radio and television media.

The efforts to attract readers no matter what the costs in literal truthfulness and public usefulness were not universal. Many men and women recognized that the full meaning of journalism extended beyond satisfying the existing and most elementary interests of the public. They were willing to take risks to sacrifice titillation and even to go beyond the easy satisfaction of personal advantages. They sought ways of meeting the true demands of public affairs.

Journalism and Passion of Repeating Facts

Many editors and reporters, for example, became increasingly dedicated to a simple, accurate, dispassionate—even dull—presentation of facts, and only facts. Lawrence Augustus Gobright, the first Washington bureau chief of the New York Associated Press, put it this way in 1856:

> My business is to communicate facts: my instructions do not allow me to make any comment upon the facts which I communicate. My dispatches are sent to papers of all manner of politics, and the editors say they are able to make their own comments upon the facts which are sent them. I therefore confine myself to what I consider legitimate news. I do not act as a politician belonging to any school, but try to be truthful and impartial. My dispatches are merely dry matters of fact and detail. (Gramling 1940, 30)

Even during the Civil War, some northern newspapers made attempts to present information about the hostilities from the southern as well as the northern perspective. Horace Greeley *New York Tribune*, for example, regularly gave space to columns of material entitled *"FROM RECENT SOUTHERN PAPERS"* (January 1, 1862), *"Extracts from Rebel Sources"* (September 5, 1862), *"IMPORTANT FROM THE SOUTH"* (October 4, 1862), *"LATER FROM THEREBEL STATES"*REBEL STATES" (December 5, 1862), and *"LATE SOUTHERN NEWS"* (November 27, 1863). This was done even when the editor believed the southern reports were not to be trusted. An editorial comment in the April 19, 1862, edition, for example, said:

> Richmond papers of the 14th and 15th claim that 8,000 Union prisoners were captured at Pittsburg, part of whom have been sent to New-Orleans, and part to Memphis. They also claim to have taken 80 cannon. The extracts which we publish elsewhere contain other statements equally exaggerated and absurd.

In these ways, two different yet compatible approaches to the presentation of information were developing. One concerned the knowledge the reporters gained through their own observation of events and situations; the other, the manner in which that knowledge was presented to the readers. Journalistic knowledge, editors were insisting, had to be accurately obtained and truthfully, impersonally, and dispassionately reported. In describing the training he received on E. L. Godkin *Evening Post*, Lincoln Steffens said: "Reporters were to report the news as it happened, like machines, without prejudice, color, and without style; all alike" (Schudson 1978, 77, emphasis added).

The reporter was responsible not for the accuracy of what the source said, but only for the precision of the quotation or paraphrase. The task of pointing out a speaker's error belonged to the editor or to editorial writers, not to the reporter. As Colonel McClure, editor of the Philadelphia Times, said to Joseph Appel when the latter expressed some of his own views in a news story, "I want you to know and I don't want you ever to forget it, that when the *Times* expresses an editorial opinion I will express it and not you—go back to your work" (Ibid., 78).

Thus by the end of the nineteenth century journalists were developing, at least in the United States, the view that reporters should obtain their knowledge, especially their knowledge of observable phenomena, carefully, accurately, uninfluenced by passion or preference; and that newswriters should present this knowledge honestly, accurately, impersonally, and without expressions of feeling or opinion. In the twentieth century, this became known as objective reporting.

Because the bases for determining what information to include in a story or in what order to present that information were not well established, many reporters were unable to encompass all the characteristics in their work. This was especially true when the nature and qualities of affairs were in great dispute: when the reports dealt with political, social, and religious controversies, for example. Thus, even though it was possible to meet the desired norms in routine reports—in those in which the newswriter was little more than an honest machine—it was unsuitable for the coverage of more complex news events. But instead of permitting this "objectivity" to become an ideal and a basis upon which to build the other arts of journalism, many journalists, not seeing the realities underneath the word, rejected the whole concept.

Journalism and Public Interest

As the twentieth century proceeded, people generally seemed to become less and less interested in public affairs; a dwindling number were concerned about and willing to spend time and effort in the achievement of a common good. Instead, they were consumed by the search for personal goods and were devoted to a vast variety of entertainment. There were many exceptions, of course, but they were just that: exceptions. The bulk of the populace apparently "couldn't care less" about the common good.

At the same time, many of the media of mass communications both fed and fed off these attitudes. Recognizing what the public desired, most of the media catered to those interests—and profited from doing so. This area, also, of course, had many exceptions. But ironically, the mass media that were seriously endeavoring to feed and encourage the forum needed for the people's serious participation in public life were often handicapped by public distrust.

Some of the efforts to swim against the tide of indifference and to encourage public interest in public affairs seem to have been counterproductive. Taking advantage of the wide attention to entertainment, the media attempted to give birth to a new type of reporting, one that would please even while it informed. Unfortunately, those most extensively involved in these efforts failed to understand the true nature and environment of journalism. As a consequence, their efforts to meld the public delight in entertainment with the public need for knowledge of and participation in the issues affecting the good life of communities gave birth to a "new journalism," but one that resulted more in distrust than in a vibrant social consciousness.

The Facts behind "New Journalism"

For many who attempted to practice and describe the art of what they called the "new journalism," the explanation of what they were doing tended to focus more on a discussion of "new" than of "journalism." Tom Wolfe, chief guru of the "new journalism," said he preferred the term "para-journalism" (Wolfe 1972, 45), yet continued to use the former term and insisted that there is something new in this art form. Over the centuries, some writers used some of the "new journalism" devices of scene construction, dialogue, point of view, and status details, Wolfe admits, but it was not until the 1950s and 1960s that journalists began to employ and fully exploit all of them in their nonfiction writing. At least in degree and emphasis, therefore, something new burst forth during those decades. But was this new form of writing really "journalism"?

It was, Wolfe says, a new kind of reporting, and it was done by people who considered themselves to be journalists (Wolfe 1973, 49-51). But not all reporting, even when it is done by journalists, yields journalism, at least not journalism understood as the presentation of the practical knowledge that will help people make good decisions about personal or public affairs. Reporting presents information, facts. But history, for example, also does this. Some reporting presents information about the contemporary world. It may be information about the current batting average of a baseball player or data about the discovery of another dwarf star. But only when this new information is communicated to people who can use it as an aid to their current personal or public decision making does it deserve the name of "journalism." And very rarely do the stories described as "new journalism" have this immediate practical value.

Some of the reasons for this are inherent in the nature of the work. As Wolfe has indicated, the type of reporting that is required is much more thorough, more detailed than that which is necessary for day-by-day journalism. It is saturation reporting (Wolfe 1973, 50). Since such reporting requires a great stretch of time, the issue about which the new journalist is writing is one that must endure over a long period. The time at which the reader has to make a practical decision must be days, weeks, months in the future. A new journalism profile of a presidential candidate, begun months in advance and published before the election, would have journalistic value. But relatively few journalism topics suit the time frame that saturation reporting requires. In addition, even those who are willing to describe their works as pieces of new journalism don't seem to be much interested in the journalistic quality of the writing. Wolfe, for instance, is much more fascinated by its relation to the realistic novel. Likewise, Truman Capote described his *In Cold Blood*, considered a classic of the new journalism, as a nonfiction novel. Norman Mailer gave his *The Armies of the Night*, another work much praised by the new journalists, the subtitle *"History as a Novel, the Novel as History."*

Despite this jumble of nomenclature, much of the new journalism is really contemporary history, or biography, or autobiography. That is, the writer's intention is often to provide understanding simply for the sake of understanding (and entertainment), rather than understanding for the sake of assisting in the making of decisions about what should be done or avoided.

"New Journalism" and Real Journalism

Could we simply give the "new journalism" a more accurate name, such as "literary nonfiction," (Warnock

1989) and then dismiss it from any further consideration? By doing so, we would be ignoring a serious taint that seems closely related to the new journalism and that has stained the environment in which real journalism needs to work.

Although Tom Wolfe said he agrees that "the New Journalism should be as accurate as traditional journalism," some new journalists mislead their readers. Truman Capote *In Cold Blood*, for example, is justifiably admired as a great piece of literature based on true facts. But it also includes a great amount of invention, of fictionalizing. Although, as preparation for writing the book, Capote spent several hours a day for a year and a half training his memory so that he could transcribe long conversations "within 95 per cent of absolute accuracy" (Plimpton 1966, 2), the people whom he interviewed did not have this same training. Thus the conversations that the murderers Dick and Perry had in Mexico after they killed the Clutter family were passed on to Capote by Dick and Perry, whose memories lacked the quality of Capote's. But Capote sets those conversations forth, not as rough paraphrases but as direct quotations, as though Capote himself had been there to hear them and later record them "within 95 per cent of absolute accuracy."

If Capote's book had been called a novel based on fact, such aberrations would have done little harm. But Capote, Wolfe, and others have referred to *In Cold Blood* as a new type of journalism. One of the well-established conventions of journalism is this: whatever the writer places within quotation marks is exactly what that writer knows someone else has said. If the writer has any doubts about the precise accuracy of the statement, the writer omits the quotation marks and provides a paraphrase.

Tom Wolfe himself compounded the problem when he wrote what he considered to be a lighthearted spoof of the

New Yorker magazine. The title said the article was "The True Story." Unfortunately, some of the content was far from true. At one point, for instance, Wolfe pictures editor William Shawn (whom Wolfe had not been able to interview) at home, alone, listening to a Bix Beiderbecke recording of "I Can't Get Started." Of course, Wolfe was not there. He not only invented the scene but had Shawn listening to Bix Beiderbecke play a song that was not written until four years after Beiderbecke's death (Hersey 1980, 6-7).

It is not surprising, therefore, that although much praised in many quarters for the liveliness of its style, the new journalism was also acquiring a great number of critics. Most criticized was the blending of fact and fiction to the point that readers could not tell one from the other. John Hersey expressed it thus: "This has not been particularly good for fiction; it may be mortal to journalism," and then added, "The writer of fiction must invent. The journalist must not invent" (Ibid., 1, 25).

Secrecy of Contemporary Journalism

In sum, if one looks closely at public life today, it is not difficult to find areas for serious concern. The people are disinterested, even cynical. Vast numbers prefer and attend to, almost exclusively, their own personal affairs. Our educational systems ignore many of the attributes of citizenship, especially he means by which voters can make good choices among those offering themselves for public office. Many public officials castigate political opponents more than they propose and debate plans for solving community problems. How does journalism stand today among the flux of public affairs? What, if anything, can journalists themselves do at least to diminish the cynicism and distrust that hamper the public discourse?

— For one, journalists could be less secretive. One of the great anomalies of our times are the journalists who abhor secrecy in public affairs but accept it in their own work.

— Most of the media are insufficiently vigilant in alerting the public to the precise portions of their reports that are fiction rather than fact. Even the apologies and firings that followed the fabrications in the Janet Cooke, Patricia Smith, and Stephen Glass cases were insufficient to completely restore the trust of the readers in the reports they were receiving.

— Although reporters sometimes have good reasons for doing so, many are much too eager to keep from their readers, listeners, or viewers the identities of their news sources (Curley 1996, 3).

— Most of the major newspapers keep secret from their readers (but not from contest judges) the specific individuals who write the editorials in their papers.

— Journalists search diligently for the income of political leaders and privately held businesses, but are reluctant to publicize the income of public affairs journalists and the publications and organizations for which they work (Winternitz 1996, 61).

Dispelling unnecessary secrecy is one of the easiest things journalists can do as they work to gain the trust of the people.

Much more difficult is the careful reexamination of precisely who they are, what they are doing, why they are doing it, and what means are best for accomplishing the true goals of journalism.

Future Journalism

As long as large numbers of people live and work together and are unable to handle all their communication needs through interpersonal contact, there will be a need for journalism.

The works of journalism are as necessary to the making of good human choices as the products of the fields and waters are to the making of healthy bodies. When we are members of large communities, we depend upon others to alert us to the opportunities and to the dangers that we cannot perceive directly through our own senses or through interpersonal communications. And wise though we may be, we also need the explanations, evaluations, and exhortations of others in order to choose the best courses of action by which to avoid those dangers and take advantage of those opportunities as they rise up before us. Those "others" who provide large groups of people with the knowledge they need to live well, no matter what additional titles they may also bear, are journalists.

Thus those who forecast the end of newspaper print journalism and the beginning of portable electronic newspapers as the *New York Times* did on June 28, 1992, may be correct. But we must note carefully what it is they are predicting.

It is quite possible that some of the media of journalism, as we now know them, will cease to exist. Newspapers now suffering under the financial burden of enormous production and distribution costs may be supplanted by home computers, replacing the great rolls of paper, the enormous printing presses, the trucks and delivery persons scurrying from loading docks to distribution points to apartment buildings and private homes.

But even if this is achieved and people are willing to substitute for the habit of thumbing through sections of printed material the convenience of calling up on computer screens the information in which they are most interested and, with a click, printing out a copy for later study or filing, the need for journalists and for journalism will remain.

Knowledge does not develop by itself. It has to be gathered, often from reluctant sources. The sheer quantity of what is and can be known is so enormous that most people—necessarily involved with their own personal affairs—cannot attend to it all. Some persons, therefore, must make it their job to sift, winnow, select what will be most useful to this one and that one out of many publics. Much of what is chosen—if it is to be useful—must be checked for accuracy, revised for expression, organized, arranged, indexed. Knowledge of one type or from one source has to be blended with or distinguished from knowledge of other types and from other sources. All of this has to be set forth in words, pictures, or designs that designate, hierarchize, enhance, and draw appropriate attention to the parts and the relationships. Because the products of journalism are not self-generating, not only will journalism not disappear, but journalists themselves will also not disappear.

Bibliography

Abrams M.H., ed. 1958. *Literature and belief.* New York: Columbia University Press.

Adler Mortimer. 1958. *The idea of freedom*. Vol 1. Garden City, N..: Doubleday.

Adler Mortimer, and Charles Van Doren. 1972. *How to read a book.* New York: Simon and Schuster.

Aeppel Timothy. 1988. "Seabrook-driven bankruptcy: An omen for nuclear industry?" *Christian Science Monitor.* 1 February, 3.

Allison Graham, and Katie Smith. 1988. "A democracy with ever fewer voters?" *New York Times.* 11 March, 27.

Altschull Herbert. 1984. *Agents of power.* New York: Longman.

Anderson Jack, and Ronald W. May. 1952. *McCarthy, the man, the senator, the "ism."* Boston: Beacon Press.

Aristotle. *The rhetoric.* Trans. by W. Rhys Roberts. New York: The Modern Library, 1984.

Atkins Gary, and William Rivers. 1987. *Reporting with understanding.* Ames: Iowa State University Press.

Backman Jules. 1967. *Advertising and competition.* New York: New York University Press.

Bagdikian Ben H. 1969. "Right to access: A modest proposal". *Columbia journalism review.* Spring.

Barber James David. 1972. *The presidential character.* Englewood Cliffs, N.J.: Prentice-Hall.

——. 1980. *The pulse of politics*. New York: W.W. Norton.

Barnouw Eric. 1970. *The image empire*. Vol. 3. New York: Oxford University Press.

Barron Jerome A. 1973. *Freedom of the press for whom?* Bloomington: Indiana University Press.

Barry Dave. 1995. *Miami Herald*. 12 November.

Bartley Robert L. 1997. *Letter to author*. 15 August.

Benn S.I., and R.S. Peters. 1959. *The principles of political thought*. New York: Free Press.

Berkman David. 1992. *The rush to PR. Quill*. April, 32.

Bleyer Willard G. 1927. *Main currents in the history of American journalism*. Boston: Houghton Mifflin.

Bok Sissela. 1979. *Lying*. New York: Vintage Books.

Bostrom Bert N. 1984. *Talent, truth and energy*. Chicago: Society of Professional Journalists, Sigma Delta Chi.

Boutwell William D., ed. 1962. *Using mass media in the schools*. New York: AppletonCentury-Crofts.

Bovée Warren G. 1972. "The mythology of editorial anonymity". *The masthead*. Fall.

——. 1986. "Horace Greeley and social responsibility". *Journalism quarterly*. Summer.

——. 1991. "The end can justify the means—but rarely". *Journal of mass media ethics*. *6*:3, 135-45.

Bradley Barbara. 1988. "Ethics act bites down". *Christian Science Monitor*. 12 February, 1.

Brandsberg George. 1980. *The free papers*. Cited in Ernest C. Hynds, *American newspapers in the 1980s*. New York: Hastings House, 1980, 123.

Broad William J. 1988. "Secret advance in nuclear fusion spurs a dispute among scientists". *New York Times*. 21 March, 11.

Bryce James. 1899. *The American commonwealth*. 3rd ed., London: Macmillan.

Buchwald Art. 1981. *ASNE Bulletin*. July/August, 21.

——. 1983. *Milwaukee Sentinel*. 15 November.

Bulgatz Joseph. 1992. *Ponzi schemes, invaders from Mars, and more extraordinary popular delusions and the madness of crowds*. New York: Harmony Books.

Bunting Glen, and Paul Feldman. 1988. "Assessor threatens tax status of churches that provide asylum". *Los Angeles Times*. 5 February, 2, 3.

Burke Edmund. 1774. "Speech to the electors of Bristol". *Works of Edmund Burke*. Boston: Little and Brown, 1839. 2:12.

Cannon Lou. 1977. *Reporting: An inside view*. Sacramento: California Journal Press.

Cantril Hadley. 1951. *Public opinion 1935-1946*. Princeton, N.J.: Princeton University Press.

——. 1952. *The invasion from Mars*. Princeton, N.J.: Princeton University Press.

Carr Edward Hallett. 1961. *What is history?* New York: Vintage Books.

Carter Thomas Francis. 1955. *The invention of printing in China and its spread westward*. 2nd ed. Revised by L. Carrington Goodrich. New York: Ronald Press.

Cater Douglass. 1950. Cited in Lou Cannon, *Reporting: An inside view*. Sacramento: California Journal Press, 1977.

Chase Dennis J. 1971. *The aphilosophy of journalism*. *Quill*. September, 15.

Cherry Colin. 1966. *On human communication*. 2nd ed. Cambridge, Mass.: MIT Press.

Chesterton G.K. 1936. *The autobiography of G. K. Chesterton*. New York: Sheed & Ward.

Clark David G., and William B. Blankenburg. 1973. *You and media*. New York: Harper & Row.

Cohen Laurie. 1988. "Lowest jobless rate since '79". *Chicago Tribune. 2* April 1, 6.

Coleridge Samuel Taylor. 1817. *Biographia literaria*. London: Rest Fenner.

Collingwood R.G. 1956. *The idea of history*. Oxford: Oxford University Press.

Congressional Budget Office. 1988. *Reducing the deficit: Spending and revenue options*. Washington: GPO. March.

Connors Tracy Daniel, ed. 1982. *The Longman dictionary of mass media and communication*. New York: Longman.

Cultice Wendell W. 1992. *Youth's battle for the ballot*. Westport, Conn.: Greenwood Press.

Curley John. 1996. "Facts, fairness and the five w's". *Gannetteer*. January/February, 3.

Davis Charles N. 1998. "Access to prisons". *Quill*. May, 23.

Davis Elmer. 1969. *History of the New York Times*. New York: Greenwood Press.

Desmond Robert W. 1978. *The information process*. Iowa City: University of Iowa Press.

Dickinson Brian. 1986. "NCEW needs a sharper focus". *The masthead*. Fall.

Donaghue Peter. 1977. "Reconstruction of mandatory public access to the print media". *St. Louis University law journal. 21*:91.

Dressel Paul L. 1960. *Liberal education and journalism*. New York: Bureau of Publications, Columbia University.

Edel Abraham. 1967. *Aristotle*. New York: Dell Publishing.

Elsasser Glen. 1988. "Falwell denied damages in Hustler case". *Chicago Tribune. 25* February, 1, 14.

Emery Edwin, and Michael Emery. 1978. *The press and America*. 4th ed. Englewood Cliffs, N.J.: Prentice-Hall.

English Glenn. 1987. *Congressional record, April 22, H 2104*. Washington, D.C.: Government Printing Office.

Ernst Morris L. 1946. *The first freedom*. New York: Macmillan.

Fedler Fred. 1989. *Reporting for the print media*. 4th ed. New York: Harcourt Brace Jovanovich.

Feldmann Linda. 1988. "Americans are not so generous in latest famine". *Christian Science Monitor*. 4 February, 3-4.

Finke Nikki. 1988. "Does your computer have a virus?" *Los Angeles Times*. 31 January, 6, 1.

Franklin Marc A., and Robert Trager. 1981. *The first amendment and the fourth estate*. 2nd ed. Mineola, N.Y.: The Foundation Press.

Furnas J.C. 1935. —"And sudden death". *Reader's Digest*. August, 21-26.

Galbraith John K. 1968. *The new industrial state*. New York: New American Library.

Gartner Michael. 1997. *Letter to author*. 1 August.

Getlin Josh. 1988. *Los Angeles Times*. 5 February, 1.

Gibson Richard. 1988. "Cray unveils powerful supercomputer". *Wall Street Journal.* 10 February, 2.

Gifford C.A. 1975. "Ancient Rome's daily gazette". *Journalism History. 2* (Winter), 106.

Gissler Sig. 1988. "A lot goes into candidate recommendations". *Milwaukee Journal.* 3 April, J3.

Glasser Theodore L. 1984. "Objectivity precludes responsibility". *Quill.* February.

Gramling Oliver. 1940. *AP—the story of news.* New York: Farrar & Rinehart.

Grant Michael. 1970. *The Roman forum.* New York: Macmillan.

Green Bill. 1981. "The confession". *Washington Post.* 19 April.

Greider William. 1983. "News as event and news as code". In *Making sense of the news.* St. Petersburg, Fla.: Modern Media Institute.

Hannah Steve. 1986. *Milwaukee Journal.* 28 December, J7.

Hart James Allee. 1970. *Views on the news.* Carbondale: Southern Illinois University Press.

Hayslett R.T. 1968. *Statistics made simple.* Garden City, N.Y.: Doubleday.

Heinen Thomas. 1988. "Report to our readers". *Milwaukee Journal.* 6 March, 7J.

Hentoff Nat. 1973. Foreword to *Observations from the treadmill,* by my [pseud.]. New York: Viking Press.

Hersey John. 1980. "The legend on the license". *Yale review.* (October) 70:1.

Hiebert Ray E., Donald F. Ungurait, and Thomas W. Bohn. 1974. *Mass media.* New York: David McKay.

Himmelfarb Gertrude. 1995. *On looking into the abyss.* New York: Vintage Books.

Hodges Louis W., and others. 1981. "Pictures and privacy". *Quill.* April.

Host David R. 1973. *Education for Journalism.* Milwaukee, Wis.: Marquette University Press.

Hughes Helen MacGill. 1940. *News and the human interest story.* Chicago: University of Chicago Press.

Huston Margo. 1984. "Who will watch the watchdog?" *Newsweek.* 30 April, 16.

Hynds Ernest C. 1980. *American newspapers in the 1980s.* New York: Hastings House.

Jacobson Howard Boone. 1961. *A mass communications dictionary.* Westport, Conn.: Greenwood Press.

Jakande L.K. 1971. "A good editorial must not only offer opinions, but also argue a case". *The masthead.* Fall.

Kael Pauline. 1982. "Tootsie". *New Yorker.* 27 December, 68-72.

Kahler Erich. 1964. *The meaning of history.* Cleveland: World Publishing Co.

Kapoor Suraj, John Cragan, and Irene Cooper. 1990. "Publishers' and opinion-page editors' political perceptions". *The masthead.* Winter, 7-19.

Kennedy John F. 1957. *Profiles in courage.* New York: Pocket Books.

Klotzer Charles L. 1984. "Fallacious". *Quill.* April, 23.

Koelb Clayton. 1984. *The incredulous reader.* Ithaca, N.Y.: Cornell University Press.

Kozol Jonathan. 1985. *Illiterate America.* Garden City, N.Y.: Anchor Press.

Kurtz Howard. 1993. "Media experts say NBC credibility up in flames". *Milwaukee Journal*. 10 February, B7.

Lamke Kenneth R. 1991. "Military censorship may hurt in long run". *Milwaukee Sentinel*. 22 January, 2.

Landers Ann. 1988. *Washington Post*. 9 April.

LaRocque Paula. 1994. "Don't be afraid to write stories that read like fiction". *Quill*. June.

Leckey Andrew. 1988. *Chicago Tribune*. 11 April, 4, 3.

Lewis C.S. 1960. *The four loves*. New York: Harcourt Brace Jovanovich.

Liebling A. J. 1961. *The press*. New York: Ballantine Books.

Lippmann Walter. 1946. *Public opinion*. New York: Penguin Books.

——. 1955. *The public philosophy*. New York: New American Library.

Lowell A. Lawrence. 1913. *Public opinion and popular government*. New York: Longmans, Green and Co.

MacDougall Curtis D. 1940. *Hoaxes*. New York: Macmillan.

——. 1952. *Understanding public opinion*. New York: Macmillan.

——. 1982. *Interpretative reporting*. 8th ed. New York: Macmillan.

Marciano John. 1997. *Civic illiteracy and education*. New York: Peter Long Publishing.

Maritain Jacques. n.d. *An introduction to philosophy*. Translated by E.I. Watkin. New York: Sheed & Ward.

Matthews George T., ed. 1959. *News and rumor in Renaissance Europe: The Fugger newsletters*. New York: Capricorn Books.

McDonald Donald J. 1975. "Is objectivity possible?" In John C. Merrill and Ralph D. Barney , eds., *Ethics and the press.* New York: Hastings House.

McQuail Denis. 1984. *Mass communication theory.* London: Sage Publications.

Menand Louis. 1990. "A friend writes". *The new republic.* 26 February, 32.

Merrill John C., and Ralph D. Barney, eds. 1975. "Is objectivity possible?" *Ethics and the press.* New York: Hastings House.

Merrill John C., and S. Jack Odell. 1983. *Philosophy and journalism.* New York: Longman.

Merrill John C., and Ralph L. Lowenstein. 1971. *Media, messages, and men.* New York: David McKay.

Meyer Philip. 1979. *Precision journalism.* 2nd ed. Bloomington: Indiana University Press.

Middleton Kent R., and Bill F. Chamberlin. 1988. *The law of public communication.* New York: Longman.

Mill John Stuart. 1859. *On liberty.* Edited by Alburey Castell. New York: AppletonCentury-Crofts.

Mitchell Edward Page. 1928. "Introduction to the first edition, Frank M. O'Brien", *The story of the Sun.* New York: D. Appleton & Co.

Mooradian Karlen. 1972. *The dawn of printing.* Austin, Tex.: Journalism Monograph no. 23.

Mott Frank Luther. 1962. Cited in Jay Newman, *The journalist in Plato's cave.* Cranbury, N.J.: Associated University Press, 1989, 47.

Mott George Fox. 1950. *New survey of journalism.* New York: Barnes & Noble. my [pseud.]. 1973. *Observations from the treadmill.* New York: Viking Press.

Naisbitt John. 1984. *Megatrends*. New York: Warner Books.

Nash Vernon. 1938. *Educating for journalism*. New York: Teacher's College, Columbia University.

National Council for the Social Sciences. 1994. "Ten thematic strands in social studies". *Social education*. October: 365-68.

National News Council. 1979. "A report by the national news council, 1975-78". *In the public interest II*. 1979, 421-22.

Nelson Harold L., and Dwight L. Teeter Jr. 1982. *Law of mass communications*. 4th ed. Mineola, N.Y.: Foundation Press.

Neuman W. Russell. 1986. *The paradox of mass politics*. Cambridge, Mass.: Harvard University Press.

Neuman W. Russell, Marion R. Just, and Ann N. Crigler. 1992. *Common knowledge: News and the construction of political meaning*. Chicago: University of Chicago Press.

Newman Jay. 1989. *The journalist in Plato's cave*. Cranbury, N.J.: Associate University Press.

Newman John Henry. 1839. *Fifteen sermons preached before the University of Oxford between A.D. 1826 and 1843*. Westminster, Md.: Christian Classics, 1966.

——. 1941. *The idea of a university*, edited by Daniel M. O'Connell. New York: America Press.

Newsweek. 1988. How to survive April 15. 29 February, 43.

O'Brien Frank M. 1968. *The story of the Sun*. New York: Greenwood Press.

O'Dell DeForest. 1935. *The history of journalism education in the United States*. New York: Bureau of Publications, Columbia University.

Ogle Marbury B. 1950. *Public opinion and political dynamics*. Boston: Houghton Mifflin.

Padover Saul K., ed. 1953. *Thomas Jefferson on democracy*. New York: New American Library.

Park Robert E. 1940. "News as a form of knowledge: A chapter on the sociology of knowledge". *American journal of sociology 45*:669-86.

——. 1967. "News as a form of knowledge". In *On social control and collective behavior*, edited by R.H. Turner. Chicago: University of Chicago Press.

Patterson Eugene C. 1983. *Making sense of the news*. St. Petersburg, Fla.: Modern Media Institute.

Plimpton George. 1966. "The story behind a nonfiction novel". *New York Times Book Review*. 16 January, 2.

Porter W. James, Roger Cooper, and Michel Dupagne. 1993. "The three paradigms of mass media research in mainstream communication journals". *Communication theory, 3* (November): 317-35.

Pulitzer Joseph. 1904. *North American review*. May.

Raines Howell. 1997. *Letter to author*. 12 August.

Rogers Donald W. 1992. *Introduction to Voting and the spirit of American democracy*. Urbana: University of Illinois Press.

Rogers Michael. 1988. "The return of 3-D movies—on TV". *Newsweek*. 15 February, 60.

Rosenbaum David E. 1991. "Press and U.S. officials at odds on news curbs". *New York Times*. 22 January, 2.

Schell Jonathan. 1982. *The fate of the earth*. New York: Avon.

Schiller Dan. 1981. *Objectivity and the news: The public and the rise of commercial journalism*. Philadelphia: University of Pennsylvania Press.

Schlesinger Arthur. 1992. *The disuniting of America*. New York: W. W. Norton.

Schmidt Benno C. 1976. *Freedom of the press vs. public access*. New York: Praeger Publishers.

Schramm Wilbur. 1949. "The nature of news". *Journalism quarterly 26* (September) 3: 259.

——. 1957. *Responsibility in mass communication*. New York: Harper & Brothers.

Schudson Michael. 1978. *Discovering the news*. New York: Basic Books.

Schwartz Bernard. 1955. *American constitutional law*. Cambridge: Cambridge University Press.

Shaw David, and others. 1981. "Factual/fictional". *ASNE bulletin*. July/August, 3ff.

Sheppard Judith. 1995. "Climbing down from the ivory tower". *American Journalism Review*. May.

Simon Yves. 1951. *Philosophy of democratic government*. Chicago: University of Chicago Press.

Sims Norman. 1984. *The literary journalists*. New York: Ballantine.

Sloan W. David. 1980. *Pulitzer Prize editorials*. Ames: Iowa State University Press.

Steinberg S. H. 1961. *Five hundred years of printing*. Baltimore: Penguin Books.

Stonecipher Harry W. 1979. *Editorial and persuasive writing*. New York: Hastings House.

Stroud Joe Hinton. 1986. "Changing role demands activism". *The masthead*. Fall.

Task force report. ***1996***. *Journalism educator*. Winter.

Wedemeyer Gen. Albert C. 1958. *Wedemeyer reports!* New York: Henry Holt.

Wells Alan. 1972. *Mass media and society*. Palo Alto, Calif.: National Press Books.

Westerstahl Jorgen. 1983. *Objective news reporting. Communication research. July 10*:3.

Wilson Francis G. 1933. *Concepts of public opinion. American political science review*. 32:371-91.

Winternitz Felix. 1995. 990 and nonprofits. Quill. April.

——. 1996. *Muckraking or buckraking*. Quill. July/August.

Wolfe Tom. 1972. *The new journalism: A la recherche des whichy thickets*. New York. 21 February.

——. 1973. *The new journalism*: New York: Harper & Row.

Wortman Tunis. 1800. *A treatise concerning political enquiry, and the liberty of the press*. New York: George Forman.

Wright Charles R. 1959. *Mass communications*. New York: Random House.

Index